DESIGNING INFORMATION SYSTEMS SECURITY

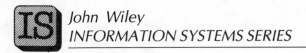

John Wiley
INFORMATION SYSTEMS SERIES

Editors

Richard Boland   **Rudy Hirschheim**
University of Illinois at Urbana-Champaign   **Oxford University**

Hirschheim: *Office Automation: A Social and Organizational Perspective*

Jarke: *Managers, Micros and Mainframes: Integrating Systems for End-Users*

Boland & Hirschheim: *Critical Issues in Information Systems Research*

Baskerville: *Designing Information Systems Security*

DESIGNING INFORMATION SYSTEMS SECURITY

Richard Baskerville

The University of Tennessee Chattanooga

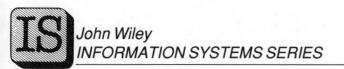 *John Wiley*
INFORMATION SYSTEMS SERIES

JOHN WILEY & SONS
Chichester · New York · Brisbane · Toronto · Singapore

Library of Congress Cataloging-in-Publication Data:

Baskerville, Richard
Designing information systems security/Richard Baskerville.
p. cm. — (John Wiley information systems series)
ISBN 0 471 91772 9:
1. Computers—Access control. 2. Data protection. I. Title.
II. Series.
QA76.9.A25B38 1988
005.8   dc19
87-31959
CIP

British Library Cataloguing in Publication Data:

Baskerville, Richard
Designing information systems security.
    — (John Wiley information systems series)
    1. Electronic data processing departments
    — security measures
    I. Title
005.8 HF5548.2
ISBN 0 471 91772 9:

Typeset by Cotswold Press Ltd, Eynsham, Oxford.
Printed and bound in Great Britain by Biddles of Guildford.

for bobbi

Series Foreword

In order for all types of organizations to succeed, they need to be able to process data and use information effectively. This has become especially true in today's rapidly changing environment. In conducting their day-to-day operations, organizations use information for functions such as planning, controlling, organizing, and decision making. Information, therefore, is unquestionably a critical resource in the operation of all organizations. Any means, mechanical or otherwise, which can help organizations process and manage information presents an opportunity they can ill afford to ignore.

The arrival of the computer and its use in data processing has been one of the most important organizational innovations in the past thirty years. The advent of computer-based data processing and information systems has led to organizations being able to cope with the vast quantities of information which they need to process and manage to survive. The field which has emerged to study this development is *information systems* (IS). It is a combination of two primary fields: computer science and management, with a host of supporting disciplines, e.g. psychology, sociology, statistics, political science, economics, philosophy, and mathematics. IS is concerned not only with the development of new information technologies but also with questions such as: how they can best be applied, how they should be managed, and what their wider implications are.

Partly because of the dynamic world in which we live (and the concomitant need to process more information), and partly because of the dramatic recent developments in information technology, e.g. personal computers, fourth-generation languages, relational databases, knowledge-based systems, and office automation, the relevance and importance of the field of information systems, and office automation, the relevance and importance of the field of information systems has become apparent. End users, who previously had little potential of becoming seriously involved and knowledgeable in information technology and systems, are now much more aware of and interested in the new technology. Individuals working in today's and tomorrow's organizations will be expected to have some understanding of and the ability to use the rapidly developing information technologies and systems. The dramatic increase in the availability and use of information technology, however, raises fundamental questions on the guiding of technological innovation, measuring organizational and managerial productivity, augmenting human intelligence, ensuring data integrity, and establishing strategic advantage. The expanded use of information systems also raises major challenges to the traditional forms of administration and authority, the right to privacy, the nature and form of work, and the limits of calculative rationality in modern organizations and society.

The Wiley Series on Information Systems has emerged to address these questions and challenges. It hopes to stimulate thought and discussion on the key role information systems play in the functioning of organizations and society, and how their role is likely to change in the future. This historical or evolutionary theme of the Series is important because considerable insight can be gained by attempting to understand the past. The Series will attempt to integrate both description — what has been done — with prescription — how best to develop and implement information systems.

The descriptive and historical aspect is considered vital because information systems of the past have not necessarily met with the success that was envisaged. Numerous writers postulate that a high proportion of systems are failures in one sense or another. Given their high cost of development and their importance to the day-to-day running of organizations, this situation must surely be unacceptable. Research into IS failure has concluded that the primary cause of failure is the lack of consideration given to the social and behavioural dimensions of IS. Far too much emphasis has been placed on their technical side. The result has been something of a shift in emphasis from a strictly technical conception of IS to one where it is recognized that information systems have behavioural consequences. But even this misses the mark. A growing number of researchers suggest that information systems are more appropriately conceived as social systems which rely, to a greater and greater extent, on new technology for their operation. It is this social orientation which is lacking in much of what is written about IS. Designing Information Systems Security presents an innovative and practical approach for going beyond computer security and assessing the control needs of the organization as they should be reflected in the design of an information system.

The Series seeks to provide a forum for the serious discussion of IS. Although the primary perspective is a more social and behavioural one, alternative perspectives will also be included. This is based on the belief that no one perspective can be totally complete; added insight is possible through the adoption of multiple views. Relevant areas to be addressed in the Series include (but are not limited to): the theoretical development of information systems, and IS innovation. Subjects such as systems design, systems analysis methodologies, information systems planning and management, office automation, project management, decision support systems, end-user computing, and information systems and society are key concerns of the Series.

March 1988   Rudy Hirschheim
                                                                            Richard Boland

Preface

I had the opportunity in 1979 to participate in one of the earliest efforts in designing a secure office information system. This unique system used television and computer-generated graphics as inputs to an automated television signal distribution system. The signals were routed (upon request) to the offices of several very senior Naval executives. The queries were directly entered by the officers using a menu and a numeric keypad interface.

The design incorporated the necessary controls to allow confidential information to be processed by the system. One of the most interesting fallacies which surfaced in the design was the unacceptably cumbersome security controls. In this situation, it was imperative that it be impossible to operationally bypass the controls. Even the most senior members in the office were not authorized to compromise the security of the system, and were constrained to observe all operational control constructs. The system fell into disuse after the novelty wore away, and it was removed after only two years' service. It was destroyed by its own security and its effects on office politics.

The controls which were designed into this system were both modern and conventional. These controls had provided verifiable and adequate service in the raised-floor environment of the operational computer system for a considerable period. Yet, these seemed out-of-place in the wood-panelled executive suites. Oddly, the security controls imposed on the manual information processing system of these offices seemed acceptable. It was the computer controls that were found oppressive.

Office automation, decision support systems, and the microcomputer revolution are now parading computer and communications technology into many commercial and industrial offices. I was particularly sensitive to recent literature proclaiming these systems to be "unprotected", "vulnerable" and "insecure". I began to realize that my earlier experience with the Naval offices was being played-out in the civilian arena with the opposite effect. The military office, unable to suppress the controls, suppressed the automated system. Civilian offices, in order to use the automation, seemed to be suppressing the controls.

What is there in computer security controls which should offend office designers and office workers? Manual controls have been in place in office information systems for years; what prevented the ready acceptance of the security with the technology? The research which followed found that the current perspectives on computer security may underlie the problems, and suggested that the time had come to promote security concerns from its narrow definition in computer science into the realm of information systems. This book introduces the topic as a legitimate element of the science of management, systems analysis, and of information systems design methodologists.

Because this topic has seen such little treatment in the literature of information systems, this book ranges over considerable theoretical territory. Its overt purpose began as a report of the effects of applying structured systems design techniques in solving an office security problem. Ultimately the work was forced to survey computer security technology, consider the unseen burdens of security, promote the methodology in its more general sense, and finally, unveil the critical social importance of the field which has seen such little consideration. The original project slowly migrated into the appendix.

The work that follows will offer some new ideas to practically all of those individuals who find themselves involved with information systems.

For the manager who is confronted with decisions concerning information systems, chapter 2 offers an introduction to computer security without descent into tortuous cryptographic calculi or the pith of operating system architecture. Chapter 3 suggests that management may presently be deluded in its current perception of the dramatic burden of poorly-designed security. Chapter 6 will introduce the manager to a new public role that the organizations' private information systems may soon acquire, and suggests preparations which can be made to minimize the future costs to the organization of fulfilling its new responsibilities.

For the systems analyst/designer who is confronted with demands for increased security in old and new systems, the second chapter can offer a review of the current work in the field and chapter 3 will suggest concerns which should inhabit future economic feasibility studies. Chapters 4 and 5 will provide a detailed explanation of how some familiar tools can be applied in the designer's new security tasks, and may suggest ways to enlist other current methods as an alternative to special security methodologies. Finally, the designer may gain insight from chapter 6 into a professional role which may be thrust upon designers in the future, a role in which professional and public responsibilities will supplant portions of the designer's organizational obligations.

For the computing professional charged with implementation of higher levels of computer security, the context provided by chapters 4 and 5 can prove invaluable. Invaluable, that is, from the viewpoint that unenlightened analysts may demand inappropriate technical solutions from computer science for security problems which are the intrinsic property of the logical system model. Chapters 3 and 6 will help to explain the deeply changing role of computer security in the context of its information system, its organization, and its society.

For the computer security practitioner, here is a new view of our field. Chapters 4 and 5 offer a methodology based on proven systems design practice, a methodology which seems wonderfully simple and straightforward compared to some of the very complex proprietary approaches. Checklists and probability arithmetic can be avoided while successfully specifying exhaustive and appropriate control sets. Chapter 3 will provide an understanding of problems which have haunted the operation of controls, and chapter 6 will describe the prospect of the leadership role that the security professional may have to assume in the immediate future of information systems.

For the student of management and information systems preparing to enter or advance a career, chapter 2 provides an excellent non-technical survey of the field of computer security, and chapters 3 and 6 offer insight into some of the issues confronting both management and the information systems profession as society progresses into an "information age". The concept of systems design generations in chapter 4, aside from providing an excellent context for the discussion of security design methods, will help the student to understand the foundations of systems practice. Finally, in chapter 7, the research student will find some of the fascinating, yet unanswered questions related to the text, offered as topics for further research.

Additional material. Three appendices are included to help support the reader in areas which may be unfamiliar. Appendix A is a case study which illustrates how the methodology can be applied. This appendix includes the source listing of a Prolog expert system. Unlike the examples in chapter 5, this listing is a complete and tested program, and details about its environment are included. The source and compiled programs, along with some additional software, are available on diskette as described in the flyleaf at the back of the text.

Appendix B is a brief review of the structured specification technique proposed by DeMarco and others. This will be useful if the reader is unfamiliar with this approach, and would like a more detailed context for the security version of the technique which is proposed in chapter 4.

Appendix C is a slightly more complete survey of two current security design methodologies reviewed in the text. These have important implications for the tools offered in this text, particularly as feasible alternative methods available to the analyst. These are also important in the perspective these provide on the current problems facing the security practitioner.

Acknowledgements

The original inspiration for this work can be traced to the Management Information Display System (MIDS) project conducted at the Headquarters, Commander-In-Chief, U.S. Naval Forces, Europe. Captain Cliff Freund was practically a technical visionary in his conception of this system, and I thank Mr. Ken Howerton of the Naval Electronics Command for the latitude he afforded me in implementing Cliff's system. The dramatic political capacity of the microcomputer has lived with me ever since that time. The "unsolvable" office automation security problems led directly to my formal research into the security implications of office automation, and subsequently to this book.

The systems "culture" of the London School of Economics was a partner in both the MIDS project and the formal office research. A critical social and political perspective of these ostensibly technical creatures was inspired by both the students and the faculty. This can also be said to have inevitably led to the work below.

Two individuals from those LSE days must be accorded significant influence in the work that follows. Frank Land (now with The London Business School), supervised both research projects mentioned above. His inspirations in the work below can be found in every chapter. Rudy Hirschheim (now with Templeton College, Oxford) was an obvious and intensive influence in the office research, and his contribution of criticism and encouragement in my efforts toward the completion of this book cannot be calculated.

Also, I must acknowledge the "others" that are in here with me. Echoes of conversations with Heinz Klein (SUNY–Binghamton) and Niels Bjorn-Andersen (Copenhagen Business School) are in chapter 6. Their comments on an IFIP TC 8 working group conference paper delivered in Atlanta had considerable influence on my thoughts about the social role of security. Comments from Victor Lane (St. George's Hospital Medical School, London) on an IFIP TC 11 working group presentation helped with the essential ideas concerning the unseen burdens of computer security.

Cudere always seems to be such quiet and insignificant gratitude for such thundering support, but how else can an author acknowledge the personal contributions which are so important to the book. Quintard Steele did the wonderful index. Many thanks to Clint Smullen for salvaging my Prolog and proof reading when it was beyond my power. Lastly, here is my unending gratitude to Roy and Anne Abel, who became my "family" during the many lonely London research trips and provided the encouragement, support and advice on the project.

Contents

Chapter 1

INFORMATION SYSTEMS SECURITY

The development of design techniques for information systems has progressed for a comparatively short span of time. It is difficult to trace the field back much further than a quarter of a century, a tiny speck in time considering the maturity of the civilization it serves. Security techniques for information systems may be younger, yet ... if indeed, extant at all. Understanding information security requires an understanding of its foundations in computer security.

Computer security is a technical topic surveyed in the following chapter. But it would be useful to consider computer security, momentarily, from its perspective as the discipline from which information security must spring. As a discipline, three aspects of the development of computer security can be identified: its technological progress, its participants, and its ethics.

THE PROGRESS OF COMPUTER SECURITY

If there is a field of information systems security, it has not yet clearly defined itself. The field is still not clearly delineated from computer security, risk management, management science or the sciences enveloping criminal justice. Consider the brief progression of information system developments which can lead to the topic of information systems security.

The development of data integrity. Control techniques were developed early in the history of computer-based systems to protect the data resource. These elements were installed in batch processing systems of the 1950's and 1960's to minimize the error content in the data. Check digits, radix-, range- and content-checks were among others which were heavily applied, particularly in an effort to prevent transcription errors from corrupting the data. During this era, elementary password controls became associated with computer account protection within the computer operating system [Waters, 1974].

The development of computer security. Multi-programming and real-time computing demanded sophisticated upgrades to the original data security concepts. Restart procedures had to develop into failure recovery techniques, account password control had to be extended to on-line files, and support for audits was demanded. During this phase, computer security became defined as a discipline, and developed along three major paths: operating system security,

1

hardware security, and database security. Computer security, in support of the centralized data processing of the 1960's and 1970's, enveloped such diverse subjects as encryption, system kernels, CPU state registers and field-level data protection [Martin, 1973 or Hsiao *et al*, 1979].

Network and communications security. Of course, computer security elements such as those above have continued to develop. However, overlapping the latter developments in this field is the science which began to materialize to protect data communications networks. In the 1970's and 1980's encryption matured into successes such as the Data Encryption Standard, public key encryption, authentication and digital signatures. Access control hardware, such as call-back devices and biometric authentication devices (e.g., retina scans or finger-print verification) became available [Davies and Prices, 1984]. The computer security discipline absorbed this massive new component.

Ethical demands. Computer security was confronted with a variety of intensi-fying ethical demands in the late 1970's and 1980's, and these became stock ma-terial for security management concern. Foremost is data privacy, a problem which has continued to grow with the automated systems which threaten it [Turn, 1982]. Public awareness of the threats of computer fraud was drawn by Donn Parker [1976] among others. Copyright infringement against computer software became a dramatic issue. Computer security broadened its boundaries again, adopting the societal problems and issues created by the technology it protected.

Microcomputer security. The 1980's, together with the continuing develop-ment of all other aspects of the field known as computer security, have intro-duced essential new components. Proliferating microcomputer technology confronts computer security with a major new hardware, software and data theft problem [Highland, 1985]; new organizational responsibilities in copyright protection; and the threat of microcomputer-based trespassers (computer "hackers").

PARTICIPANTS IN COMPUTER SECURITY

The original interests in computer security were motivated by a concern for accuracy, that is, for correctness in the data. This was true whether the computer was used for secret defense decoding or telephone directory publication. Very quickly, however, governments became interested in protecting the secrecy of their systems, data and communications, since these reflected sensitive diplo-matic and defense postures.

Governments. However, governments cannot be seen as dominating the technological development of the computer security field. Initially, government interests did lead the development and standardization of encryption techniques. (The amusing rumor still persists that the motivation for this leadership in the United States was to ensure that industrial encryption techniques were not permitted to exceed governmental cryptanalysis capabilities.) But direct government influence in commercial computer security developments is relatively rare. The US defense department has begun asserting some influence by publishing its computer security policies, such as the ubiquitous "orange book" (trusted system criteria); a partial list of these will be found in the references.

Financial Organizations. It is possible that financial organizations form the strongest block of influence in computer security. The application of communication security techniques in protecting electronic funds transfer, and the role of computer security in protecting the vast assets represented electronically in these organizations, from loss or fraud, is probably the major focus of computer security development. In this regard, the internal auditors could indeed be envisioned as the driving force in the field. Auditors, adhering to published standards in their profession, routinely command special access control software packages, communications access controls, encryption, and disaster recovery plans.

Software industry. The software industry has had minor influence in computer security developments. There has been a fruitless search for an effective technical method of securing the expensive development costs of microcomputer software. Various copy protection schemes have found their way into the marketplace, most finding defeat through special copying programs or incompatibility with the demands of the growing population of fixed disk systems. It is possible that developments from this market could someday lead to standardized microcomputer software copyright protection technologies deeply embedded in the hardware.

Technology industries. Aerospace, defense and computer technology industries, as well as being suppliers of computer security, are now numbered as major clients of the field. Trade secrets represented electronically demand maximized protection from loss to industrial espionage. Even marketing data is being recognized as a major corporate asset. There has been some discussion of new accounting techniques which measure and monitor the information asset [Merten *et al*, 1982]. Should this concept flower, computer security may find itself confronted with another major issue demanding its protection.

Thus, computer security finds itself the immediate concern of governments, and the financial, defense, aerospace, software and technology industries. These certainly represent participants that are also leading the industrialized nations of the world into the twenty-first century.

ETHICS IN COMPUTER SECURITY

Ethics deals with the investigation of morality, and the standards by which human conduct is guided and appraised [Bullock and Stallybrass, 1977]. This third aspect of the computer security discipline considers the implications of the technology from the perspective of the human values of the enveloping society.

Ethics and law. Generally, the discussion of the ethics of the field dwells on legal issues as a statement of the accepted deontology of the prevailing society. Appropriately, however, computer security thought has explored formal ethics and can be found to embrace the applicable philosophical principles (Pfleeger [1988] provides an excellent review of these issues).

Crime prevention. Computer security is often perceived as the "policeman" of computing technology, preventing or detecting computer crimes. From this respect the computer security field regularly concerns itself with the following social problems.

"*Fraud.* Computer security is charged with protecting computer-represented assets from diversion.

Treason and espionage. Computer security is charged with protecting national and industrial secrets from disclosure to unfriendly parties.

Theft. Computer security is expected to prevent the theft of computer equipment, or other assets (such as processor time or printer activity).

Invasion of privacy. Computer security has lately undertaken the role of defender of personal data against unwarranted distribution or publication.
Copyright violations. Computer security is applied in attempts to restrict illegal software transportation.

Trade secret theft and Patent infringement. Computer security is required to address problems with "reverse engineering" and illegal technology transfers through personnel migration.

Quality of work-life issues. Professionals, operators and other computer system users must confront the security features of the system as an intimate partner in their daily work life. In this respect, computer security should concern itself with its implications on the social quality of human work-life. Work in this area is sparse [Markus, 1984 or Baskerville, 1987], and may become one of the next major issues to be enveloped by the field.

The state as a participant. As computer security assumes its role as a social guardian in regard to crime and quality of life, it can be seen that government assumes a new role as a participant in computer security. This is becoming a governmental task as a regulator of information safety. Thus, particularly in Europe, omnibus data privacy laws have mandated certain minimum computer security efforts. Computer crime laws crystallize society's support of the philosophy of computer security. The influence of government in this respect may well continue to grow into prominence, projecting, for example, security standards onto commercial computer systems.

INFORMATION SYSTEMS SECURITY

The field of computer security has grown into a discipline of astonishing breadth. For example, consider the range of keywords from the preceding discussion:

> access control hardware, authentication, biometric authentication devices, callback devices, check digits, computer "hackers," content checks, copy protection schemes, copyright violations, cpu state registers, data encryption standard, data integrity, database security, digital signatures, disaster recovery plans, electronic funds transfer, encryption, failure recovery techniques, field-level data protection, fingerprint verification, fraud, hardware security, industrial espionage, invasion of privacy, operating system security, password controls, patent infringement, public key encryption, radix checks, range checks, restart procedures, retina scans, security standards, social quality of human work-life, system kernels, theft, trade secret theft, treason and espionage

It is a premise of this work that the field described above, while certainly originating from computer security, has long extended its reach into issues of management and societal concern beyond its original technology. While the semantics of the term "computer security" can be easily adjusted to reflect its real meaning, perhaps it would be useful to convey an awareness of its changing role by clearly defining the difference between "information systems security" and "computer security" (terms which currently find treatment as synonyms).

To continue the reference to this broadening discipline as computer security reflects the narrow influence of computer technology as the ultimate solution to all of the ills entailed by the discipline. As will be seen from the work that follows, such a provincial outlook may be inhibiting the field from moving ahead, and from keeping apace with continued progress in other arenas of the information systems field.

For these purposes, the term "computer security" will be applied as connoting threat concepts and the physical and logical techniques applied in protecting the electronic computer and communication systems; while "information systems security" is defined as the broader view, incorporating systems analysis and design methods, manual information systems, managerial issues, and both societal and ethical problems.

It is felt that such a redefinition of the terminology will promote an altered perspective in the practicing professional, and inject an appreciation for the breadth (and future broadening) to which the field is subject.

PREVIEW

Thus, the roots for this book are planted in different soil than earlier works in computer security. The work which follows recognizes computer security in its context as a component of information systems security. The full breadth of information systems thought will thus be applied in support of the "computer security" problem.

It would be unfitting to commence an exploration of information systems security from this perspective without first ensuring a foundation in elementary computer security thought. The second chapter, therefore, must survey the current topics in this discipline. The technology will be explored as a collection of targets, threats, and controls. Managerial issues are then surveyed from their traditional perspective of computer security.

Once an understanding of the existing field of computer security is conveyed, chapter three can explore the first important new perspective that information systems thought can offer to the security discipline: the hidden burdens of security. These burdens are discussed in terms of their cost in performance, flexibility and system lifespan.

The design of information systems security can then be considered from the perspective of modern systems analysis and design thought. Strangely enough, the design task may be actually simplified if, unfettered with existing security design approaches, it is simply conducted as a variation of normal information systems design.

Identification of *appropriate* controls has never been a simple task. The design techniques, while suggesting tools for specifying controls, do not solve this problem. Chapter five concentrates on this problem, suggesting a different model as a foundation for this difficult task. The practicality of this approach is demonstrable in the formal heuristics demanded by knowledge engineering.

In the last major chapter, the present role of information systems security is surveyed from the new perspective suggested above. The problems and demands of the various stake-holder groups are identified, and some unexpected prospects for future stake-holder orientation are unveiled. These prospects may suggest immediate actions available to organizations in anticipation of such positions.

The concluding chapter reviews the preceding work and suggests several immediate questions which demand further exploration in the future.

REFERENCES

Baskerville, R. "Logical controls specification," *Information Systems Development for Human Progress in Organizations*, IFIP TC WG 8.2 Conference, Atlanta, Georgia, May, 1987.

Bullock, A. and Stallybrass, O., editors, *The Fontana Dictionary of Modern Thought*. London: Fontana Collins, 1977.

Davies, D. and Price, W. *Security for Computer Networks*, Chichester: John Wiley, 1984.

Highland, H. "Microcomputer security: data protection techniques," *Computers and Security* 4 (June 1985) pp. 517–531.

Hsiao, D.; Kerr, D. and Madnick, S. *Computer Security*. New York: Academic Press, 1979.

Martin, J. *Security, Accuracy and Privacy in Computer Systems*. Englewood Cliffs: Prentice Hall, 1973.

Merten, A.; Delaney, P.; Pomerantz, B. and Kelly, P. "Putting information assets on the balance sheet," *Risk Management* (Jan, 1982).

Markus, L. *Systems In Organizations: Bugs + Features*. Boston: Pitman, 1984.

Parker, D. *Crime by Computer*. New York: Chas Scribners Sons, 1976.

Pfleeger, C. *Computer Security*. Englewood Cliffs.: Prentice-Hall, 1988 (cited from draft).

Turn, R. "Privacy protection in the '80s," *1982 IEEE Symposium on Security and Privacy*. Silver Springs, Md: AFIPS Press, 1982.

Waters, S. *Introduction to Computer Design (Planning Files and Programs)*. Manchester: National Computer Centre, 1974.

The following U.S. government documents are referenced occasionally in the text, these are given fully below with stock numbers and price (as of publication) below. These may be obtained by writing: Superintendent of Documents, U.S. Government Printing Office, Washington, DC 20402.

"DOD Trusted Computers System Evaluation Criteria (DoD 5200.28- STD)." GPO Stk # 008-000-00461-7 ($6.00).

"SCOMP Final Evaluation Report (CSC-EPL-85/001)." GPO Stk # 008-000-00438-2. ($3.00).

"PC Security Considerations (CSC-WA-002-85)." GPO Stk # 008-000- 00439-1. ($1.00)

"Dept. of Defense Password Management Guideline (CSC-STD-002- 85)." GPO Stk #008-000-00443-9 ($1.75)

"Guidance for Applying the DoD Trusted Computer System Evaluation Criteria in Specific Environments (CSC-STD-003-85)." GPO Stk # 008-000-00442-1. ($1.00)

"Technical Rationale Behind CSC-STD-003-85: Computer Security Requirements (CSC-STD-004-85)." GPO Stk # 008-000-00441-2. ($2.00).

Chapter 2

COMPUTER SECURITY

Anyone working in an environment where computers have assumed an important role should be intensely interested in computer security. Many computer systems are bristling with the opportunity for the individual to abuse (or to be abused by) the system. Computer security is also becoming a major concern of large segments of our society. This is not surprising as the computer is becoming as ubiquitous and fundamental to modern society as steam became to early industrial society. As these systems become essential, there should be a rising concern with their reliability, confidentiality, and availability. However, like any concept which spreads widely over society, computer security has developed many different connotations to different groups. It is becoming difficult to define the term satisfactorily in a single statement.

Consider the following descriptions of the nature of computer security:

"Computer security deals with the managerial procedures and technological safeguards applied to computer hardware, software, and data to assure against accidental or deliberate unauthorized access to and dissemination of computer system data."

— David Hsiao, Douglas Kerr and Stuart
Madnick in *Computer Security* [1979].

"The objective of computer security is to prevent unauthorized access to the use of (1) information being processed and produced and (2) the computer system resources; to ensure the continued availability of this information and the processing resources; and to comply with the legal protection requirements imposed upon management."

— Kenneth Kittelberger in *Computer Security
Management* [1983].

"EDP [Electronic Data Processing] security is defined as that state of mind reached when automated systems, data, and services are receiving appropriate protection from accidental and deliberate threats to confidentiality, integrity, or availability.

— Royal Canadian Mounted Police publication
Security in the EDP Environment [1981]

"The short term aim of such an exercise in [computer related] risk management is to help provide an efficient and effective computing service to the organisation, with the safeguarding of the organisation's ability to achieve its business objectives and the protection of its assets and viability, as the long term aim."

—Kenneth Wong in *Risk Analysis and Control*
[1977].

"The term *computer security* includes concepts, techniques, and measures that are used to protect computing systems and the information they maintain against deliberate or accidental threats."

— Rita Summers in the *IBM Systems Journal*,
[1984].

This last definition seems to capture the essentials of the various concepts: (1) computing systems and the information, (2) deliberate or accidental threats, and (3) protective concepts, techniques and measures. Such a definition allows the delineation of a boundary for the discussion below without excluding terminological connotations attached to computer security which are outside of the scope required here.

The following sections discuss the aspects of these concepts as follows. First, "computing systems and the information they maintain" are considered as *security targets*. Second, "deliberate or accidental threats" are discussed as *risks*. Third, concepts, techniques, and measures that are used in protecting these systems are treated as *controls*. This last section also covers the organizational factors enveloping these systems.

These concepts are brought into further focus by a consideration of the balance of controls and risks, and a discussion of the current status of computer security in our society.

SECURITY TARGETS

Most authorities agree that computer security must dwell within the overall scheme of protection for all of the organization's assets [Martin, 1973]. There does not seem to be a great deal of disagreement concerning the boundaries between the other elements of the overall organizational security program and that part of this program which can be justifiably referred to as computer security [Schmitt, 1982].

There are two general areas of computer security which can be easily identified in current thought: physical security and data security. Data security is the most heavily treated, and is usually considered as having aspects of data integrity, data accuracy and data privacy. The rapidly rising use of data communications is creating a strong group of new concepts in data security. Data communications should be carefully considered as a security target in any serious discussion of the field. This classification is useful in *inventorying* security targets. However, its use in *selecting* targets for protection can be questioned. Indeed, in later chapters, a more dynamic model will be developed for this purpose.

Physical Security

It would be an understandable misconception to believe that the physical protection of computing resources is the central focus of computer security. While it is the physical aspects of computer security which are the most readily apparent, these represent only one class of security elements. Still, physical security is often the "first line of defense" raised in the protection of computer systems.

Plant. The organization must be protected from perils arising from the loss or damage of its facilities. The structure which houses the system must be protected, whether this is an independent building, or integrated into another facility. Protection must extend to the necessary environmental conditioning machinery (heating, cooling, dehumidifying and ventilating, lighting, etc.). The furniture is a necessary part of the system: desks, chairs, bookshelves, equipment racks, etc. The features of the site must be considered, for the services extended to the facility by outside agencies are essential in the preservation of the operation: electrical, telephone, water and other utilities; fire brigades, police protection, etc.

Equipment. The organization must be protected from perils arising from the damage or loss of its equipment. The equipment must be protected. This obviously includes the computer and its peripherals. However, the subject must extend to other physical items related to the equipment. Media, for example, must be protected: disk packs, floppy disks, magnetic tape, and output forms (such as bank checks). Equipment manuals, guidebooks, and instructions are necessary for the continuation of proper systems operation.

Personnel. The organization must be protected from perils arising from loss or injury to its personnel. The tremendous degree of training and expertise required in the operators, technical engineers, programmers, analysts and administrators in computer information systems has increased the critical nature of protecting these individuals as an essential asset to the organization. Two major aspects in protecting personnel must be considered from the organization's viewpoint. Of course the primary concern is the safety of the staff: personnel must be protected from injury. However, loss of personnel due to dissatisfaction is also a threat. Heavy employee turnover can disrupt systems development projects and the routine operation or maintenance of existing systems.

Data Security

Data security is the central concern of much work in computer security. The information owned by the organization is becoming a recognized, vital element to both the survival and the success of the organization in meeting its goals. There are three qualities of data security which are usually considered in discussions of this topic: integrity, accuracy and privacy.

Integrity. The organization must be protected from perils arising from missing, incomplete or inconsistent data. The term data integrity is used here to mean preservation of the data from corruption or loss [Hsiao *et al*, 1979]. The data is conceptually distinct from its media; that is, its integrity is to be protected whether carried in magnetic, electrical, or inked form. Most authorities agree that maintenance of data integrity is an essential element of computer security [Hsiao *et al*, 1979].

Accuracy. The organization must be protected from perils arising from inaccurate data. Data accuracy connotes a slightly different attribute of data which is a candidate for protection. Accuracy refers to the maintenance of the data's legitimate relationship to that which it represents [Martin, 1973]. The accuracy of the data is essential in controlling the organization. For example, if a computer program incorrectly calculates the reorder point of an essential component of a manufactured product, insufficient quantity may be on hand to continue the smooth working of an assembly line. Planning effectiveness is dependent on data accuracy. For example, an error in correlating market-survey data could result in the production of an unmarketable product. Data accuracy is also essential in protecting the assets of the organization. For example, an inventory control program might miscalculate an ullage allowance, affording a dishonest warehouseman the opportunity to siphon off a portion of a product undetected.

Privacy. The organization must be protected from perils arising from the exposure of its data to unauthorized parties. Privacy has become of great concern as more and more confidential personal information is being kept about the general population in society's computer systems. However, in this context, the concept includes the privacy of all data from costly disclosure. For example, a trade secret, such as a geographic survey of a potential oil field, could cost the organization heavily if exposed to competitors or land owners during mineral rights purchase negotiations.

Data Communications Security

An important aspect of data security should be singled out for special attention. Increasing reliance on data communications and real-time processing has created new problems for computer security. Thus, data communications has become an identifiable asset deserving close protection [Nye, 1985]. While the devices connected to the communications link are considered as equipment to be protected, the communications link is subject to distinctly different threats and protective measures.

Input/Output. The organization must be protected from perils arising from damage or destruction of its communications with remote data capture or dissemination devices. Increasing reliance on point-of-action terminals is improving organizational effectiveness in many applications. However, the communications with these devices involves protection consideration on its own. For example, communications with electronic banking tills must be protected to avoid theft and customer dissatisfaction.

Network. The organization must be protected from perils arising from the damage or destruction of its computer-to-computer communications. The rising use of distributed data processing offers a new data threat to organizations. For example, an organization relying on a distributed database system has denoted the network communications link to be a vital element of its database management system. These communications links must be protected in order to preserve the integrity and accuracy of the database.

RISKS

Information security can be approached from the concept of *controls* and *risks*. A risk is the probability that an event will occur that will result in harm. The concept of risks, as usually applied in computer security, has encompassed more than just the probability factor — "risks" is used as an umbrella term which connotes the potential event itself, the probability of its occurrence, and the potential costs of its occurrence. Perry [1981] describes these risks as being rather like "holes" in the information system through which information can be lost or exposed. Controls are measures that reduce the risk (i.e., the size of the holes). Controls can rarely be economically applied in complete elimination of the risks. The controls are selected which economically reduce the risk to an acceptable level.

Risks are commonly categorized into three general areas: destruction, modification, disclosure.

Destruction

Each of the physical elements of the information system — plant, equipment, and personnel — is subject to destruction. The data is also independently subject to destruction (such as the bulk degaussing of a magnetic tape) which would result in an integrity loss.

Accidental Destruction

Integrity loss. Data which has been partially destroyed has been rendered incomplete, and is thus defined as having an integrity problem. Data is often incomplete when processing is interrupted and improperly resumed, or when data streams or files become lost or destroyed. For example, computer systems are subject to utility interruptions (loss of power or a communications switch failure in the PTT or PSTN system).

Catastrophes. The elements which comprise an information system can be functionally destroyed by any number of unintentional or uncontrollable catastrophes. **Environmental catastrophes** include fires, floods, windstorms and lightning. Additionally, electronic systems are subject to electromagnetic interference, dust and vibration. **Temporal catastrophes** would include losses due to an indefinite wait or a "deadly embrace"[1]. **Catastrophic errors** include accidentally overwriting an important file, dropping a delicate disk pack, or losing a message.

Intentional Destruction

It is difficult to discuss the intentional destruction of system elements without alluding to motives. Sabotage of the machinery or the processes may be the outlet of a disgruntled employee, or the objective of a ruthless competitor. Civil disruption could be involved — riots or terrorism.

Sabotage. Dissatisfied employees, computer vandals (sometimes known as "hackers"), or other individuals, whose target is specifically the organization itself, may present the most immediate threat of intentional destruction. Vandals have been known to break into systems and insert graffiti in a data base. This seemingly minor damage can cost thousands of dollars in labor and computer time to correct. Only recently have laws been passed to set penalties for such acts which are more severe than those for scrawling the graffiti on the walls of a public lavatory.

Terrorism. Perhaps the most blood-curdling threat to computer security is the vulnerability to terrorism found in most commercial information systems. Arguments by authorities such as Hoffman [1982], Menkus [1983] and Pollak [1983]

---

1   A "deadly embrace " refers to a situation where two processes simultaneously seize a subset of the specific resources that both require and each suspends processing until the other completes and releases its held resources. Temporal catastrophes are most frequently examined in the context of computer systems programs, however, these do occur in manual systems (particularly complex bureaucracies).

have generally failed to draw much attention to the problem. As a form of intentional destruction, terrorism would seem to be the most pervasive and unpredictable. Terrorism can seem pervasive by applying levels of force beyond normal vandalism, industrial sabotage or burglary. Further, the act can seem unpredictable because the attack may be motivated by the social role which is fulfilled by the system rather than any economic or industrial role. This problem is considered in further depth in chapter 6.

Modification

The elements of the computer system are all subject to modification. The computer can be rewired, communications misrouted, programs or files altered and personnel changed. Any of these changes can result in the rising of some harm to the system.

Accidental Modification

Integrity loss. Integrity problems arise when data is inaccurate or inconsistent. Inconsistencies arise when duplicate data is maintained in separate places, and is often due to temporal variations in processing (a regional file is updated more often than is the central file). Inaccuracies can result from improper data capture, transcription or processing. Most computer errors can be traced to faulty input; however, erroneous processing instructions can be a potential risk.

A confounding source of potential integrity problems is from the action of faulty controls. These problems are introduced into the system with the controls designed to eliminate other risks. For example, if check digits are added to account numbers in order to reduce transcription errors, there must necessarily be an increased opportunity for transcription errors by virtue of the additional digit's keystroke.

Intentional Modification

Any of the elements of the computer system is subject to intentional alteration, whether the intent is benign or pernicious. For example, a programmer may intentionally disregard documentation requirements in keeping with a personally constructed priorities scheme. This "modification" of the program development process may eventually present a major unforeseen cost to the organization in the form of excess program maintenance costs.

Fraud. These risks derive from some trusted member of the staff who violates this trust in order to steal something valuable from the organization. Much that is labeled "computer fraud" is, in fact, the mere manipulation of computer input or output, and does not particularly involve sophisticated computer technology or expertise. A survey by Wong [1983] of 95 British case histories revealed that over 60% of cases of computer fraud actually involved manipulating input data or source documents. Only 26% involved data processing staff.

Still, it is extremely difficult to protect the computer system from its programmers. For example, Atkins [1985] detailed how an experienced systems analyst surmounted every carefully placed control in a well-designed and thoroughly protected system. (The fraud was only discovered because the analyst was rude to another employee as he rushed to return a borrowed "supervisory" terminal used in violating the controls.) Such talented programmers obtain illegitimate access using methods which have now acquired exotic names:

1. *Trojan horse.* Access control can be violated by burying privileged instructions in a program likely to be executed by a privileged user. If the program is actually run by a privileged user (like the system manager), the privileged instructions would execute. This approach can be used to secretly transfer data from a protected file to a secret, unprotected file (known as a "back-pocket") [Boebert *et al*, 1985], or to illegally upgrade access rights of the perpetrator. Good trojan horses destroy all traces of their existence after successful execution. For example, a friendly user wrote a games program and welcomed the computer operator to use it. The operator executed the game from the system console at the highest privilege level. Unknown to the operator, a routine in the game copied the entire system password directory into the user's file ["How passwords are cracked", 1984].

2. *Virus program.* This is a similar approach to the trojan horse, except the illegal code embeds a copy of itself in other programs. A virus can regenerate itself wildly throughout a system, becoming massively expensive to eradicate. Cohen [1984] reports several experimental infections of a heavily loaded VAX 11/750 UNIX system. In each of five attacks, the attacker gained all system rights within an hour.

3. *Salami technique.* Small "slices" of the organization's financial assets can sometimes be transferred without notice. For example, "round-down" fractions of monetary units can be moved into the programmer's account.

4. *Superzapping.* Most computer systems have powerful utilities for use in data protection and management (the IBM SUPERZAP macro utility has become synonymous with its own misuse). These utilities can sometimes bypass operating system security. For example the IBM IEHLIST and IEHPROGM utilities can be used to spill the MVS file passwords from any volume ["How passwords are cracked", 1984].

5. *Terminal spoof.* An application program is written to simulate the log-in screens and dialogue. This program is left running at a specific terminal. The unknowing user attempts to log-in to the terminal, entering ID and pass-

word into the spoof. The spoofing application records the password in the perpetrator's file, issues a normal system log-in error message, and disappears. The victim will successfully log-in on the second attempt, never realizing that the first log-in was a fake.

6. *Back door.* During the development of large computer programs, the security features of the program under development greatly complicate and inhibit program debugging. Programmers commonly insert an access path that bypasses all the security features to permit ease of program development. This is known as a "back" or "trap" door. These are intended to be removed during implementation, but are sometimes accidentally or intentionally retained. Parker [1981] relates how a programmer who stumbled onto a back door left in a FORTRAN compiler used it to defraud a commercial computer time-sharing service. The compiler back door transferred control to instructions entered at run-time rather than compile-time.

The implementation of automated teller machines (ATM) introduces a new aspect to electronic fraud. Aside from the celebrated case of the Japanese kidnapper who attempted to extract his payoff unobservably from an ATM system [Whiteside, 1978], a more interesting problem arises from ATM networking. Any number of banking systems may be involved in "brokering" a transaction, and the transaction includes all security data: account number, card number and PIN number. It is impossible to protect the account from attack by another network member. The CIRRUS network, one of the largest in the U.S., depends on the discovery by the account holder of missing funds as the sole control against fraud through a "third-party" bank's computer [Gifford and Spector, 1985].

Theft of services. In addition, the equipment, supplies and facilities may be misdirected by the staff. Usually petty, but occasionally severe, this is a form of computer fraud which involves the misappropriation of computer services by staff. Truly rare is the corporate computer that is not happily prepared to engage a user in a round of chess, a brisk spree of zapping klingons, or to provide an individualized biorhythm chart. This problem becomes acute, however, when the services are appropriated for profit. This might involve programmer "moonlighting", or even the operation of an independent service bureau business using the company computers. In one of New York City's installations, an employee was running a business so large that the facility was overtaxed, and unwittingly expanded by the City to relieve the overload [Bloombecker, 1982].

Sabotage. The disgruntled employee seeking vengeance might choose to be more subtle in the attack. Rather than completely destroying some element of the system, it may only be modified; thus making detection of the occurrence of the attack unlikely. An example is the program *time bomb*: a malicious routine activates at a given time or under certain conditions. Examples include a programmer who added code into a payroll program which destroyed the entire payroll file when his record was altered to indicate termination [Parker, 1981]; and a graduate student in the 1970's who rigged a time-bomb in a major university computer system program. The university program regularly checked date and time, and long after the student's expected Ph.D. completion date, the program would have halted computer operation and printed a glorious signed confession on 100 interactive terminals [Parker, 1976].

Disclosure

The nature of the disclosure risk is rapidly changing. This fact could be considered one of the major driving forces of improved computer security. Robert Campbell [1983] comments, "The past three decades have seen the role of the computer grow from a technical curiosity to an administrative support tool, and finally to an integral part of important business systems." In years past, the information retained in computing systems was of little serious interest to those not directly using the information. This may be partially due to the expensive processing necessary to summarize the large volumes of data processed by the early, expensive computer systems. As the technology has progressed, however, the cost of producing such summaries has fallen. This increasing feasibility of one-time applications, in concert with the consolidation of organizational data within computer systems, renders the computer-based data potentially more valuable or interesting to parties other than those to whom the data reports were intended.

Thus individuals and organizations are demanding increased care and protection of their private information from the disclosure to those from whom harm would result from such a disclosure. (See the discussion below under "Privacy".)

Accidental Disclosure

Misrouting. Fisher [1984] mentions two similar examples of potential disclosures: misrouting of confidential data and improper disposition of waste media. A misrouted message is very likely to be examined by those for whom the information was not intended. Information on discarded or released media can be accidentally exposed. The easy example is the unshredded confidential printouts to be found in the organization's rubbish. Misrouting in the first instance can also be considered to be a form of integrity risk owing to its arising from a communication failure, and in the second instance is also a form of espionage risk (see below).

Browsing. Browsing is thought by some experts to be the most common computer security breach. This involves legitimate users who are experimenting with the computer system out of boredom or curiosity. Such users often accidentally stumble onto confidential files which can be examined and the information gained therefrom used as a token in advancement.

Other authors present browsing in a more sinister light. Donn Parker [1981] listed *scavenging* among the serious threats from technical users of the system. For example, few computer systems erase temporary storage areas after these areas are used. Internal memory and system disk packs may be temporarily used by one application, and freed after completion of the process. The data on the temporary media, however, will remain until overwritten. System programs can dump the bulk of this unprotected data for browsing.²

Such browsing or scavenging could be considered to be a less strongly motivated form of espionage (see below) as well as accidental disclosure.

Intentional Disclosure

Espionage. Unauthorized access to data maintained in an information system for the purpose of compromising sensitive proprietary or private information has long been the worry of government agencies. As a consequence, much work has been done in this area. The simplicity of industrial espionage and the growing concern over privacy are pressing the matter into the private sector. The protection of assets such as bids, designs, trade secrets or mailing lists, which could be of value to competitors, is increasingly required in computer systems bearing such information. Rein Turn [1982b] summarizes the growing needs of the private sector:

> "Failure to employ trusted systems could eventually be construed by insurance carriers, external auditors, regulatory agencies, customers, contract granters, and stockholders as management practice that is not prudent and reasonable."

Regulatory compliance with domestic and international laws concerning proper record-keeping, accountability and especially privacy is demanding more sophisticated techniques. There may be marketing incentives to increase protection against espionage. Clients of computer service bureaus and financial institutions may select the services to an increasing degree according to the security of their information systems.

---

2   As an example, this text was originally composed using expensive microcomputer word processing software. The program-loading process accidentally transfers portions of the text used by the developers to test the word processing program into memory. Although the word processing program does not permit access to the text, scavenging through the computer memory reveals several paragraphs of the test document (which discuss sensitive unsolved compatibility limitations of the program).

Consequences from unexpected disclosure can be profound. In late June of 1985, South African commandos raided an African National Congress headquarters in Botswana, killing fourteen people and stealing the ANC computer. When the system was restarted in Pretoria, the disgorged membership list precipitated dozens of arrests ["The computer that sang like a canary," 1985].

Computer system espionage refers to the unauthorized access to the data in an organization's computer system. This may be accomplished in two manners: intrusion and eavesdropping.

Intrusion. This is the access to the information system (whether electronic or manual), or some part of the information system by an unauthorized body or an agent of an unauthorized body. In its most sinister form, the agent is an authorized and trusted individual who has willingly or unwillingly agreed to compromise the information. The intrusion could also be electronic by actively defeating access security in a communications system.

Eavesdropping. The second manner in which espionage may be conducted in information systems is by eavesdropping. Eavesdropping is in its obvious connotation in manual systems. Electronically, eavesdropping may be either passive interception or wiretapping, and is presently the concern of much data communications research. Active wiretapping was for years considered to be effectively prevented by the complexity of its implementation, and has not been considerable in the past. With the falling cost of technology, such complex processing is growing feasible.

Wiretapping. This is the interception of data flowing over cables. Nye [1983] explains how simple and inexpensive (under $25) this process can be. The most difficult problem is gaining physical access to the cable closets, but even this is often simple.

Passive interception. This is done without any physical connection to cables or transmitting equipment, and does not require entry to private property. The probability of any U.S. toll call being carried completely by cable is now less than 30%, the carriers preferring microwave and satellite communications. While these can be monitored by expensive receiving equipment, high frequency channel switching limits this threat.

However, some industrial attention is now being focussed on detectable electromagnetic emanations.[3] All electronic systems radiate the information

---

3   This attention can be traced to a widely-reported paper presented by Van Eck in the 1985
     SECURICOM Conference [Van Eck, 1985] which was publicly explored by such media giants
     as The BBC and *The Wall Street Journal.*

being processed in a variety of ways. It is possible to detect these emanations and decode much of the original data. Reportedly, the electronic parts necessary to compromise a video display terminal (from about a mile away) are available through electronic hobby shops for about $35 [Menkus, 1986]. This problem has long been a common concern of sensitive governmental data processing agencies [Nye, 1985].

Statistical database compromise. Privacy in statistical databases is a particularly difficult risk. A statistical database is *compromised* whenever it is possible to obtain or deduce previously unknown information about an individual from one or more queries [Denning, 1978]. Practically every query path into a statistical database can be subverted for compromising queries, and numerical analysts are quick to discover loopholes in the protection schemes. As early as 1970, Hoffman and Miller illustrated the use of simple "count" queries in compromising a database. Schlorer [1975] has demonstrated a method of defeating protected-range count-query-sets by the use of a "tracker" to construct a legitimate sequence of compromising queries. In 1977, Hoffman discovered a subversion algorithm for databases which permit the addition of "dummy" entries. DeJong [1983], has even shown how databases can be compromised by simple queries into statistical means.

CONTROLS

Controls are emplaced to reduce the strength of the threats. Each control which provides this reduction in the threat will raise the level of implementation or operating costs: CPU time for an operating system security kernel, file space for audit trails, labor costs for auditors and so forth. Careful balance of controls' costs against the threats is desirable.

Commonly, a technique known as "risk analysis" is applied in cost-justifying controls. Risk analysis involves two factors: vulnerability of the information system as reflected by the estimated probability of the occurrence of the threat, and the estimated costs which would result in correcting the possible damage. For example, the vulnerability of a magnetic tape file to environmental risk is high: heat, magnetism, dust, even time. The cost of the damage could be the replacement cost of a large data file, perhaps thousands of dollars in manual labor. In weighing a highly valuable, highly vulnerable asset against the minor costs of a backup copy . . . the economy of such a control is justifiable.

At an opposite extreme, an example could be the compromise of a student programming assignment in a university computer system through insecure memory management. Here the vulnerability is lower, mainly because the effort required to obtain the appropriate memory dump would be greater than that of creating the data itself. Also, the cost of the controls is much higher. A trusted computer base which sanitizes reallocated memory space (with its incumbent development costs and CPU overhead) would be required. The economy of such a control is impossible to justify.

Risk analysis has some serious faults. First, it is heavily based on the guesswork entailed in estimating probabilities or future costs. Second, it can easily overlook many serious indirect consequences of the threat — such as the failure of a dependent supplier caused by an operating shutdown. Third, the concept of variable severity is subdued in the approach — such as the duration of a power outage. These problems will be treated in more detail in later chapters.

Traditional Control Classes

Controls are most often discussed within a framework of four classes: (1) deterrent controls, (2) preventative controls, (3) detective controls, and (4) corrective controls.

Deterrent controls. These controls provide an "atmosphere" conducive to compliance with control objectives by setting organizational policies which define the penalties for intentional harm or control disregard. An example would be a policy of immediate dismissal for computer "browsing" as a deterrent to support the controls [Gilhooley, 1980].

Deterrent controls are inexpensive, but the effects are difficult to measure. These can only serve to re-enforce the other controls below. It is possible that the major benefit of such policies is the focus of higher management's attention on the support of the security objectives. This attention is required to create these controls.

Preventative controls. Preventative controls are designed to reduce the risk of a threat's occurrence. Preventative controls represent a first line of defense for the computer system [Fisher, 1984]. When successful, threats to the system are suppressed prior to any effect on the elements of the system.

Detective controls. Detective controls are designed to identify the occurrence of some harm within the information system. These controls do very little in the way of insulating the system from perils, and offer little in solution of the problem. These controls simply raise an alarm that focuses attention on the problem.

Corrective controls. Corrective controls serve to reduce the effects of a threat after a loss has occurred. These do little to prevent the threat from damaging the system, but only aid in recovering from the damage, or reducing the extent of the damage.

Problems frequently develop in the practical use of the classification scheme described above. Recurrently, a particular control seems to fit nicely into two or more classes. In addition, the detective controls are often pointless without accompanying corrective controls. Clearly, a more practical taxonomy would be welcome.

Orthogonal Control Classes

Internal and external controls. Before discussing this new taxonomy, it is necessary to differentiate between *internal* and *external* controls. This distinction has not previously been clear in computer security work. External controls are viewed as operating *on* the information system, not *within* it. This viewpoint can create problems in classifying controls. For example, is a halon fire extinguishing system actually *part* of the information system? Most security literature seems to view such controls as external aspects of these systems — protecting the information system but not actually a component of the system (even though the halon system is protecting itself as well).

Surprisingly, the view assumed in this work is that controls designed as either logical or physical elements of information systems are indeed internal components of the information system. The halon system is an important component of the information system it is protecting. Similarly, a centralized access control system which controls personnel entry into all of the organization's rooms (including computer spaces) may be adopted as an internal component of an information system — even though the access control system predated the information system. The necessity for this precept will clarify as the following more practical control classification scheme unfolds.

Elements of threat. The literature commonly defines two major dimensions in considering threats: probability (risk) and cost (damage). However, a third dimension is required: severity. This third dimension allows for the variation in threat intensity. Power failure, for example, is a threat which exhibits attributes of frequency of occurrence (probability), and cost of the resulting interruption in information system service (damage). In addition, however, there is the attribute of severity: the duration of the failure, or the intensity of the failure (e.g., reduced voltage or "brown-out"), or the geographic extent of the failure. Short failures can be expected to occur with greater frequency than do long failures.

The following classification scheme uses the attributes *risk, damage,* and *severity* to more clearly classify controls.

Threat avoidance controls. These controls would chiefly attack the *risk* of the threat; that is, the probability of its occurrence. For example, the probability of a power failure can be reduced by providing power connections to two separate power grids. The result is a geometric reduction in the probability of complete power loss to the system. An alternative could be the provision of a 100% backup site on another power grid, operating continuously in parallel with the normal operational system (for example, the space shuttle's four backup computers which operate in parallel geometrically reduce the risk of computer failure to the fourth root). Such controls are commonly known as *fail-safe* controls.

Threat tolerance controls. These controls are directed toward the *severity* of the risk; that is, these increase the threat severity which can be absorbed without complete system failure. An example would be the provision of back-up power within the system; that is, an emergency power source such as a generator or battery bank. In this example, less severe threats will not result in system failure; very severe failures (e.g. long durations) could overtax the generator or batteries and ultimately damage the system's performance. Similarly, a geographically distributed computer system could tolerate an isolated power failure by shifting processing loads to other areas; however, a severely widespread failure could affect several of the distributed nodes and exceed the capacity of the remainder of the system. These controls sometimes provide "graceful degradation" of system performance as a measure of tolerance to less severe threat occurrences.

Notice the effect of the concept of *internal* controls in clarifying the distinction between avoidance and tolerance. Attaching two alternative sources of external power *avoids* the loss of power. Providing an internal power backup *endures* a loss of power.

Threat mitigation controls. These controls reduce the *cost* of the damage resulting from the occurrence of a threat. Such controls do not insulate the system from the frequency or extent of threat occurrences, but aid or implement *recovery* from the occurrence.

Detective controls are often found in this category, as these are designed to provide quick notice of a failure which leads to quick correction and minimized loss. These detective controls can vary in granularity of alarm indication; that is, their ability to identify the exact failure point. An example of this variance can be found in the difference between hash totals and check digits. Hash totals can provide an indication of data corruption of a certain data type within a batch. Check digits provide finer granularity by indicating data corruption of a certain data occurrence within a batch.

Recovery controls mitigate damage from a threat occurrence by enabling quick restoration of the system's performance to normal. Following the thread of the power failure example, a roll-back recovery procedure would reduce the restart time required following the power interruption. Note that recovery controls differ from the common corrective class of controls in that corrective controls span all of the proposed taxonomy. For example, "hot site" and "cold site" backup sites are commonly considered as different levels of corrective controls. Under the proposed classification, a "hot site" is an avoidance control (the probability of the loss of the system performance is geometrically reduced); a "cold site", however, is a recovery control (the cost of restoring system operation after its failure is reduced). Horizontal and vertical parity with automatic bit restoration is considered by many to be a corrective control. However, it would be viewed here as a tolerance control, since such a control does not prevent a degree of data corruption; but enables the system to endure the loss without failure.

Finally, mitigation controls provide a class broad enough to consider such organizational measures as the systems insurance policies now being developed to reduce the potential cost (to the organization) of many major threats, or the disaster recovery plans currently advocated as responsible management assets.

Physical Threat Avoidance Controls

Environmental controls. Siting has been found to be the critical control for many of these risks; i.e., placing the computer center in a low risk area: sheltered, away from flood plains or geological faults. Other common prescriptions are: avoid situating delicate gear near annoying machinery, the prohibition of smoking in computer equipment rooms and the use of static suppressive floor coverings.

Physical access controls. Control of access to the information system is the most effective means of protecting system components. Physical access can be controlled by limiting the number of entrances to any facility, and positioning these for ease of surveillance. Human access is limited by logging visitors, and controlling access by use of coded employee ID cards. "Camouflaging" the sensitive installation can be accomplished by removing directional or identifying signs to the facility or by not having outside glass in a threatened area. Designing a smooth building exterior at ground level is also recommended [BCS, 1972].

Segregation of duties. This organizational principle is advocated as preventative measure against fraud. Gilhooley [1980] points out that this area, long practiced in sensitive manual systems, is often overlooked in computer systems. Such segregation prevents a single individual from exercising control over a transaction from its initiation through its processing. Prause [1985] points out that an *individual* is thus prevented from committing a fraud, and that the forced collusion lowers the probability of fraud by increasing the perpetrator's risk. An example of such separation of duties in a computer system would be to deny programmers the authority to operate the computer, thus forcing the collusion be-

FIGURE 2.1 Eye Dentify information system

Hand-held biometric device for terminal security based on the vascular retina patterns. (Photograph courtesy of Eye Dentify Inc.)

tween both a programmer and an operator in executing a fraudulent program [Wade, 1983]. Indeed, it is possibe that the only sure protection which may be offered to a computer system against its programmers, is the exclusion of the programming activity from the operational system. Herschberg and Paans [1984] argue from evidence in five case studies, that such complete separation should be instituted (i.e., all programming is carried out in a separate facility).

Personnel. Pollak [1983] also suggests background investigations of personnel who are permitted into sensitive areas, and the protection of key victims (e.g., the database administrator).

Data Threat Avoidance Controls

Operating system controls. Practically all multi-programmed operating systems are provided with a minimum user-ID and password access control scheme. However, these are often poorly managed. Wood [1983] bemoans the sacrifice of security in system log-ins to a "user friendly" emphasis. He notes that passwords are the most common front-line privilege protection in most major computer security packages. Symons and Schweitzer [1984] proposed the Automated Logical Access Control Standard (ALACS) as a minimum business computer operating system security specification. The standard automates certain aspects of password management, such as minimum password length, frequency of change, and privilege violation algorithms. Such thorough password management is not often practiced in private sector organizations. Assignment of regularly updated and changed user ID's and passwords by a central authority, or the use of long passwords — for example, using a short phrase instead of a short word as a password mnemonic [Kurzban, 1984] — are rarely felt justifiable in commercial information systems.

Technology is providing alternative methods of improving log-in security through the use of biometric devices. These methods identify the individual by some physical feature. Examples include hand geometry measurement, retina scanning, dynamic signature evaluation, and fingerprint reading. These expensive technologies are currently finding use only as facility access authorization tools. However, the introduction of "smart" cards, used in conjunction with these biometric devices may reduce the implementation costs to a level acceptable for application in conjunction with log-in processes [Seidman, 1985].

Trusted Computer Base (TCB). Much work is ongoing for government agencies in the area of *trusted systems* or *TCB's*. Trusted systems are computer systems that have been subjected to formal verification of correctness of their access control mechanisms and that can provide multi-level security. They have sufficient integrity to allow simultaneous processing of multiple levels of classified sensitive information [Turn, 1982b]. Landwehr [1983] cites 11 projects completed and 16 projects underway which are developing trusted systems. Some of these involve upgrades of popular operating systems (e.g., UNIX, DEC VAX/VMS and IBM VM/370).

The U.S. Department of Defense, with contributions from the National Bureau of Standards, has developed a "Trusted Computer System Evaluation Criteria" [Schell, 1984]. This criteria is often referenced when specifying levels of computer system security. The evaluation classes under this criteria are found in table 2.1.

TCB's allow the implementation of the "lattice model" of non-discretionary access control [Landwehr, 1981]. This model basically classifies data into levels (e.g., TOP SECRET, SECRET, CONFIDENTIAL) and categories (e.g., NU-CLEAR, NATO). Access and transfer of information is carefully governed according to a set of security rules which enforce a security policy. Trusted systems fundamentally protect their categories of information from all but those users

---

**TABLE 2.1 TCB evaluation criteria classes.
(Ref: DOD 5200. 28-STD (The Orange Book))**

Division D: *Minimal*

    Class D: Minimal Protection. Meets no other criteria
below.

Division C: *Discretionary*

    Class C1:   Discretionary Security. Self-protection through user
authentication (e.g., user login password).
Example: most multi-user commercial systems, such as
HP's MPE operating system.

    Class C2:   Controlled Access. Encapsulation of important objects
in the system.
Example: most add-on security packages, such as
SKK's ACF2 package.

Division B: *Mandatory*

    Class B1:   Labeled Security. Explicit protection model, all objects
are protected.
Example: none.

    Class B2:   Structured. All security modules in the operating system are
identifiable.
Example: Honeywell Multics operating system.

    Class B3:   Security Domains. Security mechanism is the central kernel,
beneath, but isolated from all service modules.
Example: i.e. GEMSOS iAPX86 operating system.

Division A: *Verified*

    Class A1:   Verified Security. Verification tools support dynamic security analysis.
Example: i.e. Honeywell SCOMP military processor.

---

who are specifically allowed to use that information, and will also prohibit those users from disclosing the information that they are entitled to use. (At least, so far as it is in the system's power to prevent it. For example, a process reading a file which is classified TOP SECRET cannot write to a file classified only SECRET.) [Bell and LaPadula, 1976].

There are few installations which can justify the expense of overhead processing demanded by any system as secure as a TCB. However, Turn [1982b] argues there are certain operational economies (such as reduced insurance premiums) which could be derived from commercial implementation of such systems. As an alternative, a commercial security software package can be installed. Examples of mainframe products are ACF2, RACF, SECURE, GUARDIAN, GUARDFILE and TOP SECRET. These systems improve access control, often to data, catalogues, transactions, and system resources. ACF2, for example, can limit users to certain terminals. These systems do consume some system resources; e.g. ACF2 increases CPU time and device utilization by about one percent; and have substantial license fees [Johnston, 1981].

Database management systems. The database approach is also strongly advocated as a more secure repository scheme for organizational data. In listing the advantages that accrue from having centralized control of the data, Date [1981] cites the ability to apply security restrictions as one of the major considerations. The fine granularity of access control required for database management has been included in most multiprogramming-environment database systems. Some systems refer to this as "field-level" access control, and such controls are usually in addition to the controls provided by the operating system's file management programs. The data base administrator is able to define the types of access (READ, WRITE, UPDATE, APPEND, etc.) by user or application. In relational database systems, this control is provided by restricting the "view" of data relations allowed to different users or applications. Database systems also improve data integrity by reducing the redundancy of data occurrences in the data base, and insuring consistency during updating. However, data base systems must be managed properly, particularly with regard to backup and recovery, or failures can be particularly disastrous. As Date points out: "...without such procedures the security of the data may actually be *more* at risk in a database system than in a traditional (dispersed) filing system."

Statistical database privacy. Controls should be emplaced within the statistical sampling programs to prohibit the unintentional compromise of identifiable individual data described above. *Logging* can be used to monitor excessive activity into a database, or the database can be *inoculated* with random individual errors which maintain the statistical integrity of the data [Hoffman, 1977]. *Ad hoc* British census tabulations have been subjected to small random adjustments since

1971 ["Security of Census Population," 1973]. Query responses can be subjected to rounding to reduce the compromise threat of tracker or count queries. *Random subfiles* can be used to support statistical applications rather than a full data set. This last control is only useful in large databases, and is currently used for public-use data tapes supplied by the U.S. Census Bureau. The British Census Office has also endorsed such techniques, although such public-use tapes are not supplied ["1981 Census of Population," 1981].

Application controls. The individual applications can be designed with myriad preventative controls, the most common aimed at preventing errors from entering the systems. Forms design and field-checks on real-time systems can reduce incomplete or erroneous data capture, turnaround documents and point-of-action terminals can reduce manual transcription, and the use of multi-part covered output forms can prevent disclosure of personal or sensitive computer-generated documents.

In addition, proper system design and implementation techniques, including structured programming, proper documentation, and acceptance testing prevent the creation of error-prone computer applications. Carefully designed document control procedures can also eliminate some fraud opportunities.

Design audits. Some authorities argue the necessity for an audit of any proposed computer system design *prior* to implementation. The internal auditors would examine the design to attest to its alignment with the organizational objectives, and to attest to the integrity of the design [Weber, 1982].

Segregation of duties. Aside from the organizational aspects of segregation of duties (discussed under Physical Threat Tolerance), it should be mentioned that the access controls discussed above aid in enforcement of this physical control.

Communications Threat Avoidance Controls

Call-back. Computer systems can now be protected against unauthorized access from the public switched network by "call-back" devices. These devices prohibit dialed-in log-ins, but initiate a return telephone call to a user when activated by the user from the public switched network. The return call is placed to an authorized number from a list in the system. Thus, the sessions may only be initiated from previously authorized telephone sets [Smith, 1984].

Eavesdropping controls. Controls against eavesdropping have been classified by Nye [1983] as *tactical* and *strategic*. Tactical controls restrict the information from an eavesdropper for a limited period (minutes or days) while strategic con-

FIGURE 2.2 Model 3060 lineguard dial-up security

This interface between the public telephone network and the computer verifies the caller's access code and disconnects, then dials the caller back at the authorized number. (Photo courtesy of Western Datacom.)

trols prevent eavesdroppers from gaining the information until after much expense and elapsed time periods of months or years.

A certain security against passive eavesdropping is obtained by the use of the public switched communications network. Telephone companies load microwave and satellite links with as many simultaneous conversations or data streams as possible. An eavesdropper may have to sort through as many as 14,000 channels to find a target, which may then randomly change channels.

Methods have been developed to control electromagnetic emanations for governmental data processing. Known as TEMPEST, various techniques are applied to the equipment to reduce these compromising emanations to acceptable levels. However, the added expense to the hardware is not currently justifiable for normal industrial practice [Nye, 1985 and Fialka, 1985].

The best known control for prevention of eavesdropping is encryption. Cryptography, the art of secret writing, involves processing data through some encipherment process which hampers the eavesdropper from recovering the data from the cipher. The process involves a *key* which is required to encrypt or decrypt the data. Cryptanalysis is the breaking of the process above. It is generally accepted that any encryption scheme can be broken by cryptanalysis — the

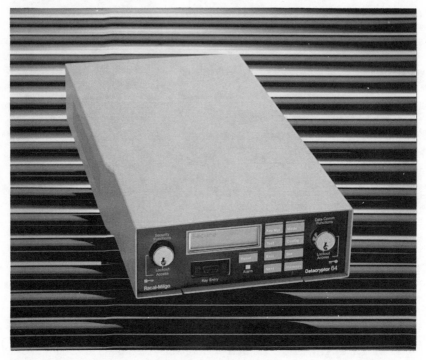

FIGURE 2.3 Racal-Milgo Datacryptor 64

Data Encryption Standard (DES) communications encryption device with key management; remote control and self-testing diagnostics. (Photo courtesy of Racal-Milgo.)

validity of encryption lies in extending the time required to successfully complete cryptanalysis [Bamford, 1982].

Physical Threat Tolerance Controls

Power Line Remedies. Electrical problems can be endured through the use of power line conditioners, uninterruptable power sources, and backup generators. Several degrees of protection can be established, with rising costs involved in each. See table 2.2.

Distributed systems. Pollak [1983] points out that a distributed system design geographically disperses its physical assets, and is naturally less vulnerable to physical threats. However, such designs potentially introduce other data vulnerabilities; e.g., inconsistency in the data resources.

TABLE 2.2 Degrees of power line protection

Protection	Cost
None	
Surge Protection	$
Filtered Line	$$
Conditioned Line	$$$
Backup Generator	$$$$
Uninterruptable Power Source (UPS)	$$$$$

Media precautions. A number of techniques can be used to permit media to endure moderate threats. The use of higher quality magnetic media usually inhibits age, heat, humidity and other physical damage. Additionally fire-retardant and environmentally conditioned storage can improve the robustness of media.

Data Threat Tolerance Controls

Very few controls have been developed in this area. This is undoubtedly due to the essential nature of data accuracy and integrity. Usually the slightest inaccuracy or integrity loss is intolerable, hence data threat tolerance and mitigation controls dominate.

Cross parity checks. To a certain degree, the use of horizontal and vertical parity by some systems programs will restore damaged data. The double parity check allows the system to map and reconstruct missing or erroneous bits.

Database complexity. In protecting data privacy, there may be room for development of new data threat tolerance controls. Consider how database systems provide access control security. In addition, the physical data elements are often "normalized" into segregated pointer-driven files. In these systems, certain degrees of browsing can be endured without compromising private information. For example, the database system may store salary figures with chains of physical record locations as links to employee name. Access to the data without access to the database system can be tolerated to a certain degree. Both individual elements (employee names and employee salaries) could be compromised without disclosing the relationships between the individual records.

Communications Threat Tolerance Controls

Backup. Alternate communications links can be provided. For example, a dial-up link might provide a degraded back-up for a leased-line link or a packet-switched link. In critical applications, alternates to utility links may be desired. For example, a 1975 fire in a New York switching center cut off 100,000 subscribers (including several data centers) for nearly a month [Menkus, 1983]. Backup communications via short-wave or other privately-owned links might be considered as corrective controls for such risks.

Robust configurations. Certain communications configurations provide degraded performance following a loss rather than catastrophic failure. *Front-end processing* provides limited capabilities in a main computer failure by shifting essential processes to the front-end; while a front-end failure can be endured by shifting essential communications functions onto the main computer [Hicks, 1984]. *Network topology* can affect communications reliability; for example, a failure of the central node in a *star* network results in the catastrophic failure of the entire network. Any single node could fail in a *ring* network without interrupting communications between any other two nodes [Weber, 1982].

Physical Threat Mitigation Controls

Siting. Although of most importance in avoidance, siting can also substantially mitigate certain physical threats. For example, situating near good fire and police protection can diminish the effects of certain physical hazards.

Alarms. Aside from the fire detection alarms mentioned above, burglar alarms, water alarms, recording hygrometers and power line recorders are available to draw attention to environmental problems.

Hardware diagnostics. Computer circuitry is often designed with self-checking circuitry, for example, parity bits in the memory, and both horizontal and vertical parity in tape and disk storage. System degradation or failure is automatically logged, usually with an audible alarm to alert the operator to the problem. In addition, technicians can be provided with special diagnostic programs which test system components for degraded performance or failure.

Performance monitors. Hardware or software monitors can be installed to detect the occurrence and causes of system performance degradation such as bottlenecks or response time increases. Data provided by these monitors can be used to avoid degraded or overloaded systems without unnecessary system expansion. However, software monitors can consume considerable overhead processing and hardware monitors are costly. Deitel [1983] points out that such monitoring is providing limited benefits as the cost of hardware is falling, and generally justifiable only in large-scale data processing environments.

Backup. Costs arising from threats to physical elements of the system subject to risk can be reduced by arranging alternative elements to substitute for the damaged item during repair or recovery from the loss. Almost every element in the system can be backed up:

1. PLANT — "cold" backup site contracts or mutual backup agreements. Backup power supplies, backup cooling and heating, backup water supplies.

2. EQUIPMENT — "hot" backup site, standby equipment, backup communications links, backup files, backup documentation.

3. PERSONNEL — backup for key personnel like the Database Administrator or Chief Programmer, and retaining on-call consultants.

Insurance. Thompkins [1985] points out only a small fraction of major corporate information assets are insured, noting, for example, that 57% of U.S. banks do not carry specific data processing insurance. Several types of insurance can offer relief from physical losses in computer systems. Standard business *property insurance* will cover equipment and plant losses. Lost income due to a computer failure can be recovered with *business interruption insurance*. The cost of restoring a damaged system, i.e., consultants or service bureau costs, is covered by *extra expense insurance*. *Small system insurance* is available which provides combinations of the types of insurance above for small business computer systems [Mayo, 1985]. Presently, about 70 companies offer information insurance, but the high premium costs (1% to 4% of total company revenue) may be restricting growth [Korzeniowski, 1985].

Data Threat Mitigation Controls

Operating systems. The data security systems mentioned earlier can also provide some detective functions as well as avoidance. For example, ACF2 includes migration facilities which permit the data administrator to identify current data access paths prior to defining permissible data access paths. When enabled in a pre-engagement mode, the system provides a warning to users violating the forthcoming access scheme [Johnston, 1981].

Another common operating system control is the automatic expiration of passwords. For example, the IBM MVS JES2 batch entry can be installed with a defined validity period for any password. At the expiration of the validity period the user is warned and the password must be changed within a specified period. Old passwords are retained to insure the new passwords are original.

Application controls. There are numerous controls which can be implemented within computer application programs. An example is the very common check digit, a technique in which one digit within a large numeric field (e.g., an account number) is mathematically derived from the remaining digits. When properly implemented, check-digits can detect most errors, including transposition. Other data capture examples include format checks, radix checks, range checks, hash-totals, and existent code checks [Waters, 1979]. Applications can also use cross-footing, audit trails, time and date stamps, independent reconciliations, and digital labels on storage volumes to permit application detection of mounting errors.

Seals. A relatively new concept developing out of cryptographic techniques is the ability to "seal" computer files or data streams. While providing no protection or discrete access limitations, seals reveal when data streams or files have been altered. Such seals (functionally, forms of encrypted hash totals) have been effectively applied by the banking industry in Sweden [Linden, *et al*, 1982].

Auditing. In Wong's 1983 survey, it was found that the largest group of fraud cases (20%) were uncovered by auditors or system controls. The accounting profession is slowly achieving the capacity to effectively audit data processing installations. This is aided by the recognition of this area as a specialization within the auditing field. Both internal and external audits are designed to detect failures in the computer system's ability to support the organizational objectives or the system's ability to protect the assets of the organization. Audit testing of applications, and the examination of computer data through audit software are two examples of detective controls applied in system audits.

Recovery. There must be provisions for restoring the computer data to the condition which existed immediately prior to a failure, with particular care that transactions being processed at the time of a failure are not lost. Batch processing systems are easily restored using retained copies of former master files and sorted transaction files. Real-time and database systems are more difficult, as transaction logs, checkpoints, file dumps, or record images must be maintained [Waters, 1974].

Audit Trails. Errors can be corrected by using the implosive or explosive nature of audit trails. Proper audit trails will allow the tracing of an erroneous data element back to the transaction which caused the error; or allow the tracing of an erroneous transaction to all data elements affected by the transaction. Audit trails thus permit extensive correction of errors in data processing systems.

Insurance. In addition to the insurance coverage for physical losses, several types of insurance will provide coverage for data-related losses. Lloyds of London introduced *computer crime coverage* in 1982, and this is now available from other insurers. Losses to third parties from programming errors or other unintentional acts can be insured against by *errors and omissions coverage*. *Fidelity* insurance can provide protection against intentional losses caused by employees [Mayo, 1985].

Communications Threat Mitigation Controls

Checksums. Most computer communications hardware provides the transmission of checksums or block check characters with each data transmission "unit". These characters are conditioned by the bit values of the other data in the unit, providing a parity check of each message unit. Degradation or failure in the communication link would likely be detected by checksum errors [Martin, 1967].

Signatures. An interesting benefit of some Public Key Encryption (PKE) techniques is the ability to generate an encrypted signature. PKE techniques such as the scheme described by Rivest, Shamir and Adleman [1978] (commonly known as the RSA scheme) use two keys — a *public key* for encryption and a *private key* for decryption. The encryption algorithm uses a "one-way" or "trap-door" function which renders the derivation of the private key from the public key into a prohibitively lengthy computation process (e.g., seventy years).[4] The RSA scheme is invertible; i.e., data encrypted with the private decryption key may only be decrypted with the public encryption key. Thus a message may be "signed" by encryption of a signature with the private key. The receiver of the message can verify its authenticity by decrypting the signature. Fake messages can be detected by this technique, as it is a prohibitively long process to discover the encrypted signature, even knowing the decrypted value and the public key.

Authentication. The cryptographic seal technique described earlier can also be used to seal messages without encryption. This is a much older application of the technique, and has long been in use in telexed financial messages. In data communications terminology, the seal is known as an *authenticator* and accompanies the message. The authenticator is verified using a previously exchanged secret key [Davies, 1984]. Authentication has been particularly important to the financial industry because of the introduction of undetectable encipherment

---

4   The general principle of a reliable PKE scheme is hotly debated by numerical analysts. Several such schemes (such as the Merkle–Hellman knapsack) have been demonstrably broken in the past. Desmond [1984], reports the recent defeat of a widely used knapsack code by the Sandia National Laboratory. As of this writing, the RSA scheme remains under "heavy assault," but unbroken.

errors in numeric messages. Such errors could cause unrecoverable transactions in erroneous monetary amounts, or to erroneous institutional account numbers.

Organizational Factors

Many authorities contend that computer security is primarily a management issue, and many argue that security programs should be soundly based on an organizational commitment. Schmitt [1982] identified the following basic problems of data security:

1. The development of an effective data security program requires the involvement of all levels of management to insure that the program is properly implemented.
2. Recent legislation places on management the the responsibility to insure the accuracy and integrity of corporate data.
3. If a failure does occur, management will ultimately be held responsible.

A number of organizational factors are related to this management involvement. These include the awareness of the members of the organization of security responsibilities, the environment in which the organization operates, the computer security program, and the audit functions.

Organizational Awareness

Most authorities argue that top management must create an atmosphere of support for computer security; that without this atmosphere, any program will be ineffective. It is thought that the organization should develop a succinct corporate security policy. Here, for example is an excerpt of the IBM Corporate Policy on "Privacy and Data Security":

> "Although the customer has overall responsibility for the protection of data, IBM has a responsibility to assist our customers in achieving the data security they require. In this regard, IBM will offer systems, products, services and counsel that clearly contribute to the solution of data security problems."
> — IBM Corporate Policy Letter Number 130, 15 November, 1973.

Environment

Many aspects of the environment in which the organization operates can affect the nature of the organizational commitment to computer security, and the necessity for that commitment.

Legal. Legislation concerning computers and their data is developing at a profound rate. Several areas which affect different organizations include:

Privacy legislation. Many privacy issues are becoming more prominent. The public is becoming acutely conscious of the dramatic capabilities of computer analysis of large databases. When those databases contain personal information, the implications are very disturbing. Chapter six will examine these implications in the context of the roles of computer security.

Rein Turn [1982a] offers the following definition of privacy: "Privacy is a term with multiple meanings. However, in the context of automated record-keeping systems which contain personal data about individuals, 'privacy' refers to the rights of individuals regarding the collection, storage, processing, circulation, and use of personal information about themselves."

Westermeier [1983] asserts: "Privacy laws may profoundly affect policies, practices, and procedures covering the collection, maintenance, use, and disclosure of personal information." But the exact constellation of privacy legislation affecting the organization must be identified, a task which can grow to dizzying proportions. Consider the following sources of privacy statements:

1. *Provincial regulations.* In the U.S.A., dozens of state laws regulate privacy practices of banking records, credit-bureaus, insurance companies, educational records, etc. [Smith, 1981]. In addition, all but two states have enacted computer crime laws, some of which can have privacy implications [Shaw, 1985]. Organizations which deal with regulated data must consider such laws when operating in those states.

2. *National regulations.* Great Britain, the United States, West Germany, France, etc. have enacted national privacy laws which protect the rights of citizens, residents, or "legal persons". The organization must consider its responsibilities under the national laws, which can differ from country to country. For example, corporations are entitled to privacy under Danish law, but not under German law. The scope of such laws varies; for example, at least five different national laws determine privacy rights in the United States. These regulate credit data, financial data, EFT data, federal data, and educational data separately. Minor regulations affecting private organizations abound: Defense Department, General Accounting Office, General Services Administration, etc. [Browne and Bigman, 1983]. European laws tend to be "omnibus" by nature, in that one law regulates in both the private and the public sector. The nature of such laws can also vary; for example, the U.S. laws provide legal remedies for abuse, while European laws tend to be preventative (regulated by a licensing apparatus) [Turn, 1982a]. The British Data Protection Act of 1984 represents such a licensing scheme, and during its implementation, the newly created Data Protection Registrar was inundated by an estimated 500,000 registration applications [Pounder, 1985].

3. *International guidelines.* The rush to protect the privacy rights of citizens by national legislative bodies is not always done at the sacrifice of business interests. Sir Norman Lindop, who headed the British *Committee on Data Protection*, believes international "commerce, not liberty" is the driving force behind these laws [Lindop, 1984].[5] The two major conventions were developed by the Council of Europe and the Organization of Economic Co-Operation and Development (OECD) (the U.S. is a party to the latter). These two documents are rather general in nature, but acknowledge the privacy mandate of continued free flow of information between countries [Turn, 1982c].

Clearly, there is a strong privacy concern evidenced by the legislative activity illustrated above. However, there is clear evidence that organizations may not be responding appropriately [Schmitt 1982]. Indeed, privacy laws and right-of-access interests are becoming convoluted issues in many instances: for example, a new service is being offered to California physicians which searches a public-domain courts information database to alert the physician to patients with malpractice suit histories ["Row brews over database", 1985].

Crime legislation. Prosecutions under criminal codes developed for non-computer crimes have proven unsuccessful in many courts [Finn and Finn, 1985]. The laws surrounding computer crimes are even less uniform than the privacy laws [Bloombecker, 1985]. In the U.S.A., for example, there is a history of criminal prosecution of computer crime under no fewer than 29 different federal laws [Ingram, 1986], and organizations must contend with 48 different state statutes [Shaw, 1985].

Copyright decisions. Increasing losses to software manufacturers have led to a number of successful prosecutions under a wide variety of legal methods. Software has been found under different circumstances to be protected under patents laws, copyright laws, trade secrets laws, unfair competition laws and contractual protection. Recently, software copyright owners have successfully prosecuted organizations whose employees violated the author's rights.

Social. The organization should consider its social environment in evaluating both responsibilities and threats. Terrorism, as discussed above, is becoming a stronger threat to data centers. An organization existing in a less stable social environment should consider stronger measures in protecting its data centers against a societal breakdown.

---

5 Sir Norman noted that undercurrents carrying forward British privacy legislation included problems such as the impending exodus of major European data processing centers from Britain owing to the lack of privacy legislation. American Express, for example, would have been forced by German law to relocate its London data processing operation if British privacy legislation did not protect the privacy of German residents' financial data.

Market. The market in which the organization is operating dictates the strength of aspects of its data security program. For example, a firm manufacturing defense materials would face stronger industrial espionage threats than a firm manufacturing cosmetics. Further, the defense firm has a deeper responsibility to its society to protect its information from threats, as such threats may constitute both a social and organizational risk.

Computer Security Program

John O'Mara [1985], director of the Computer Security Institute, referred to computer security as a "management blindspot," and attributes this to an unfamiliarity of senior management with the nature and significance of the technologies' vulnerabilities. He believes that the creation of a formal computer security program would solve this problem.

Security administrator. O'Mara [1985] cites the beginning point of a computer security program as the assignment of responsibility. The EDP security officer's role should be clearly defined as to (1) area of responsibility (computer, data or information), (2) scope of responsibility (security or risk), and (3) level of responsibility (officer, manager, administrator or analyst).

Program elements. Authors disagree as to the exact general composition of a good security program. O'Mara [1985] mentions risk analysis, cost/benefit analysis, insurance requirements, disaster recovery plan, and monitoring. Schmitt [1982] mentions physical security, contingency plan, data access controls, network security, data classification and security policy. Hammer [1982] mentions programming, operations, data base administration, facility security, auditor, staff support, functional users, and computer security group. The product of this program, however organized should be an adequately protected computing resource. Most authorities mention contingency plans, operating policies, and auditing.

Disaster recovery plan. The organization can formalize a statement of contingency steps in the event of a major computer disruption. Kull [1982] lists some of the wide ranges of issues encompassed by such a plan: identification of critical applications, damage assessment, evacuation procedures, emergency processing, salvage operations, permanent-site restoration, and methods of keeping clients and the public informed about developments. There are strong indications that present disaster recovery plans are given low-priority treatment, and as such, are inadequate. Boyer [1982] cites six surveys from Britain and America between 1975 and 1978 which indicated that, at best, fewer than half of the surveyed installations had adequate recovery plans. More recent data from

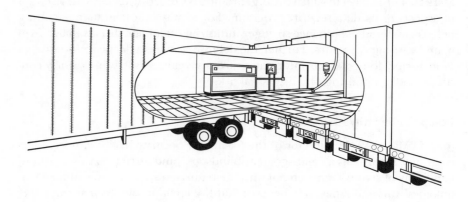

FIGURE 2.4 Compugard mobile backup computer sites

security industry research indicates little, if any, improvement in such planning [Gardner, 1985].

Operational policies and procedures. The security concerns of the organization should be expressed at the line level by monitoring the secure design, implementation and operation of the computer system. Such policies and procedures should define the necessary aspects of computer system development projects, program development methods, and operating guidelines. For example, Newton [1985] recommends the inclusion of Service Level Agreements (SLA) in all system specifications to provide management with specific indications of the expected system availability levels. In addition, a data classification scheme should be defined. For example, IBM's data classification and control policy defines classification levels (IBM Internal Use Only, IBM Confidential, IBM Confidential-Restricted, Registered IBM Confidential), and classifying guidelines (e.g., "Classifications must be displayed on each page of classified reports and printouts.") [IBM, 1980]. Such policies and procedures should be enforced by a monitoring apparatus which would detect dangerous variations in the operations.

Audit Function

The overall audit function exists to establish the reliability of the organization's information. Auditing has a management goal (internal auditing) which seeks to assure the information system is effectively and efficiently supporting the goals of the organization, and an attesting goal (external auditing) which seeks to verify the protection of the organization's assets by management [Weber, 1982].

EDP auditing. The need for a specific branch of auditing to deal with computer systems is continuing to develop. This branch requires familiarity with the technology of computer systems as well as audit principles and techniques. The EDP auditor must be able to understand the system, requiring familiarity with system documents. The auditor must be able to verify processing, requiring test data generation, and transaction tracing. The auditor must be able to verify the data, requiring the use of audit software to select, access and verify data samples [Summers et al, 1981]. EDP auditing is maturing from its early focus on the processing (audit-around-the-computer) to a balanced, more technologically sophisticated focus on both processing and data (audit-through-the-computer).

External EDP auditing. The external auditors must use these techniques in order to attest that the system integrity is preserved. For example, the auditors will usually trace assets represented in the data to the actual physical asset. This would involve using audit software to randomly sample the data files for complete records of an asset, and then physically locating the asset.

Internal EDP auditing. In addition to the attest goal, the internal auditor must assure management that the organization's resources are being used effectively. This may include a statement concerning the efficiency of the computing resource or the EDP department. In addition, many authors now advocate an audit of major system development plans [Weber, 1982]. Thus an auditor may participate in the design process, or be asked to attest to the efficiency or effectiveness of a proposed system. In addition, the organization may choose to emplace "active auditing" which routes audit-oriented exception reports to the internal auditors for routine evaluation [Bonyun, 1981].

CURRENT STATE

It is safe to say that data security in large-scale EDP systems has become an established and well-explored field. This is an area which perhaps engenders the most concern within an EDP system.

Guynes, Laney and Zant [1983] conducted a survey of 43 EDP departments of large corporate headquarters in the Dallas–Fort Worth area. Every one had provisions for file re-creation in the event of loss, 89% controlled access to the computer room, all maintained control logs of computer operations and 84% assigned and controlled user IDs. The study continues, however, to establish that many accepted controls were not properly effected in the surveyed firms. Consider the implications of this survey in its darker light: over one-tenth of these Texas firms have completely uncontrolled access to their computer systems. A similar study in Ohio also found a considerable fraction of complete security apathy: 15% of 204 surveyed firms could identify no responsible individual for data security [Bloombecker, 1984].

There are indications that the scope of computer security problems is broadening dramatically, enveloping, for example, public rights in security of information systems. In chapter 6, it will be shown that these rights are materializing at present in privacy matters. However, public rights in accuracy and performance may soon follow.

There has been a great deal of popular attention in the public media about recent computer abuse. Particularly a practice in which individuals steal computer time, or abuse a "victim" computer through public communications networks (sometimes known as "hacking"). These violations, however, do not result from any innate lack of protection in computer systems, but rather from incompetent or inadequate implementation of established security procedures.

A 1984 BBC television program provided interviews with hackers who related how easy it was to break into systems. Passwords could be guessed or even obtained over the telephone by easy ruse ["Spies," 1984]. *The Hacker's Handbook* [Cornwall, 1985] lists twenty-five most common passwords and suggests easy techniques for successful illegal entry into systems. Proper password management, such as those suggested by Wood [1983], would not only be likely to defeat such amateurs, but would also deter most proven experts. The U.S. military form "tiger teams" who attempt to break into sensitive military computers. Successes usually derive from poor password management.

Computer security technology appears to be available to meet most of the current threats; however, the application of this technology seems persistently inadequate. Despite a decade of study, many federal computer systems were still found to exhibit inadequate password controls in a 1986 General Accounting Office Audit [Betts, 1986]. Martin Hellman [1984], writing of the implications of the Beyond War movement to computer security, compared efforts in obtaining computer controls to the efforts in securing nuclear weapons treaties. The principals seem unwilling to work to obtain the desired result on *reasonable* terms. In the case of computer security, this commodity is only desired strongly enough to warrant acquisition when it is available at virtually no cost. Hellman singles out the security of many electronic funds transfer systems as examples. These, he finds, seem to discover the implementation of adequate controls to be fraught with impossible costs and barriers. Hellman contends that the organization needs to reorient its values to account for the inevitable importance of security. This is no doubt true in many instances. However, there may be other problems which impede the proper implementation of computer security: the techniques used to identify risks and design controls could be inadequate.

Thomas Whiteside's extensive survey of computer crime case studies arrived at this very conclusion: "In every case we reviewed in detail, the incidents were directly traceable to weaknesses in system controls. *The weaknesses were the result of deficient systems designs, improper implementation of controls by operating personnel, or a combination of both.*" [Whiteside, 1978, emphasis added.]

This is a book about adequate controls design and proper controls implementation.

REFERENCES

Atkins, W. "Jesse James at the terminal," *Harvard Business Review* (July/August, 1985).

Bamford, J. *The Puzzle Palace*. Boston: Houghton Mifflin, 1982.

BCS, *The British Computer Society Code of Good Practice*. Todmorden, Lancs: NCC Publications, 1972.

Bell, D. and LaPadula, L. "Secure computer systems, unified exposition and multics interpretation." MITRE Corp,Bedford, Maine, March, 1976.

Betts, M. "GAO audit uncovers security lapses in Treasury's network," *Computerworld* **20** (24 Feb, 1986): p. 10.

Bloombecker, J. "Computer crime victims have recourse to novel legal remedies," *Computerworld* **19** (25 Nov 1985): pp. 57, 65.

Bloombecker, J. "Employee computer abuse: what to do?", Computers and Society **12** (Winter 1982): pp 12–15.

Bloombecker, J. "Introduction to computer crime," in *Computer Security: A Global Challenge* edited by J. Finch and E. Dougall. Amsterdam: North-Holland, 1984, pp. 423–430.

Boebert, E.; Kain, R. and Young, B. "Trojan horse rolls up to the DP gate," *Computerworld* **19** (2 Dec 1985): pp. 65–69.

Bonyun, D. "The role of a well-defined auditing process in the enforcement of data security." *Proceedings of the 1981 Symposium on Security and Privacy*, Silver Springs, Md: IEEE Press, 1981, pp. 19–25.

Boyer, T. "Contingency planning: an opportunity for DP management," *Computer Security Journal* (Winter, 1982).

Browne, P. and Bigman, Y. "Federal legislation and impact on security management," in *Advances in Computer Security Management II,* edited by M. Wofsey. Chichester: J. Wiley, 1983, pp. 53–72.

Campbell, R. "Computer security as a management issue," in *Advances in Computer Security Management II*, edited by M. Wofsey. Chichester: J. Wiley, 1983, pp. 25–38.

Cohen, F. "Computer viruses: theory and experiments," in *Computer Security: A Global Challenge* edited by J. Finch and E. Dougall. Amsterdam: North-Holland, 1984, pp. 143–157.

Cornwall, H. *The Hacker's Handbook*. London: Century Communications, 1985.

Date, C. *An Introduction To Database Systems*. Reading, Mass: Addison Wesley, 1981.

Davies, D. "The use of digital signatures in banking," in *Computer Security: A Global Challenge* edited by J. Finch and E. Dougall. Amsterdam: North-Holland, 1984, pp. 13–21.

Davies, D. and Price, W. *Security for Computer Networks*. Chichester: John Wiley, 1984.

DeJong, W. "Compromising statistical databases responding to queries about means," *ACM Transactions on Data Base Systems* **8** (Mar 1983): pp. 60–80.

Deitel, H. *An Introduction To Operating Systems*. Reading, Mass: Addison Wesley, 1983

Denning, D. "Are statistical data bases secure?" *Proceedings of The National Computer Conference 1978*. Arlington, Va: AFIPS Press, 1978, pp. 525–530.

Desmond, J. "Scientist cracks knapsack public key code," *Computerworld* (3 Dec 1984).

Fialka, J. "Study sheds light on vulnerability of computers to electronic spying," *The Wall Street Journal* (18 Oct 1985): p. 31.

Finn, N. and Finn, P. "Don't rely on the law to stop computer crime". *Computerworld* 18 (17 Dec 1984): pp. ID11–15.

Fisher, R. *Information Systems Security.* Englewood Cliffs, NJ: Prentice-Hall, 1984.

Gardner, J. "How to assemble a comprehensive disaster recovery plan," *Computerworld* 19 (25 Nov 1985): pp. 70-71.

Gifford, D. and Spector, A. "The CIRRUS banking network," *Communications of the ACM* 28 (Aug, 1985): pp. 798–808.

Gilhooley, I. "Data security," in *Advances in Computer Security Management I,* edited by T. Rullo. Philadelphia: Heyden, 1980, pp. 33–57.

Guynes, S.; Laney, M. and Zant, R. "Computer security practice," *Journal of System Management* 34 (Jun 1983): pp. 22–26.

Hammer, C. "Managing computer security," *Computer Security Journal* (Winter, 1982).

Hellman, M. "Beyond war: implications for computer security and encryption," in *Computer Security: A Global Challenge* edited by J. Finch and E. Dougall. Amsterdam: North-Holland, 1984, pp. 41–47.

Herschberg, I. and Paans, R. "The programmer's threat: cases and causes," in *Computer Security: A Global Challenge* edited by J. Finch and E. Dougall. Amsterdam: North-Holland, 1984, pp. 409–422.

Hicks, J. *Management Information Systems: A User Perspective.* St. Paul, Minn: West, 1984.

Hoffman, L. "Impacts of information system vulnerabilities on society," *1982 NCC Conference Proceedings.* Arlington, Va: AFIPS Press, 1982.

Hoffman, L. *Modern Methods for Computer Security and Privacy.* Englewood Cliffs, NJ: Prentice-Hall, 1977.

Hoffman, L. and Miller, W. "Getting a personal dossier from a statistical data bank," *Datamation* 16 (May, 1970): pp. 74–75.

"How passwords are cracked," *Computer Fraud and Security Bulletin* (Nov 1984), pp. 1–10.

Hsiao, D.; Kerr, D. and Madnick, S. *Computer Security.* New York: Academic Press, 1979.

IBM, *Privacy and Data Security.* IBM Corporate Policy Letter Number 130 (November, 1973).

IBM. *Data Processing Asset Protection Within IBM.* IBM Information & Administrative Systems Corporate Instruction No. 104 (31 Jan 1980).

Ingram, D. "Investigating and Prosecuting Computer Crime and Network Abuse," *13th Annual Computer Security Conference,* Atlanta, Georgia, November, 1986.

Johnston, R. "Security software packages," *Computer Security Journal* (Spring, 1981).

Kittelberger, K. "Scope of computer security problems," in *Advances in Computer Security Management 2* edited by M. Wofsey. Chichester: J. Wiley, 1983.

Korzeniowski, P. "Firms run into obstacles to insure MIS data," *Computerworld* 19 (23 Dec, 1985): p. 4.

Kull, D. "Disaster recovery — just in case," *Computer Decisions,* (Sept, 1982): pp. 180–209.

Kurzban, S. "Easily remembered passphrases — a better approach," *SIGSAC Review* 3 (Fall–Winter, 1984): pp. 10–21.

Land, F. "The integrity of statistical data bases," London School of Economics working paper, 1975.

Landwehr, C. "The best available technologies for computer security", *Computer* 16 (Jul

1983): pp. 86–95.

Landwehr, C. "Formal models for computer security", *ACM Computer Surveys* **13** (Sep 1981): pp. 247-278.

Linden, C. and Block, H. "Sealing electronic money in Sweden," *Computers and Security* **1** (Nov 1982): pp. 226–230.

Lindop, N. "Seminar on Data Privacy," given at London School of Economics, 29 February, 1984.

Martin, J. *Security, Accuracy and Privacy in Computer Systems.* Englewood Cliffs, NJ: Prentice Hall, 1973.

Martin, J. *The Design of Real-Time Computer Systems.* Englewood Cliffs, NJ: Prentice-Hall, 1967.

Mayo, K. "Safeguarding business computers," *Business Computer Systems* **4**, (Jun 1985): pp. 62–67.

Menkus, B. "A major new computer security vulnerability revealed," *Administrative Management* **47** (Feb, 1986): pp. 62–63.

Menkus, B. "Notes on terrorism and data processing", *Computers and Security* **2** (Jan 1983), pp. 11–15.

Newton, J. *"Strategies for problem prevention,"* *IBM Systems Journal* **24** (Nos 3/4, 1985): pp. 248–263.

Nye, J. "Network security and vulnerability," *1983 National Computer Conference Proceedings.* Arlington Va: AFIPS Press, 1983, pp. 647–653.

Nye, J. "Who, what, & where in communications security," in *Computer Security Handbook: The Practitioner's "Bible",* Northborough, Mass: Computer Security Institute, 1985, pp. 6A1– 6A37.

O'Mara, J. "Computer security: a management blindspot," *Computer Security Handbook: The Practitioner's "Bible".* Northborough, Mass: Computer Security Institute, 1985.

Parker, D. *Computer Security Management.* Reston, Va: Reston Publ. Co., 1981.

Parker, D. *Crime By Computer.* New York: Chas Scribner, 1976.

Perry, W. *Computer Control and Security: A Guide for Managers and Systems Analysts.* New York: John Wiley & Sons, 1981.

Pollak, R. "Implications of international terrorism on security of information systems", *Proceedings of IEEE INFOCOM 83.* New York: IEEE, 1983, pp 270–276.

Pounder, C. "Following the form of the act," *Computing* (10 Oct 1985), pp. 29–32.

Prause, P. "EDP fraud prevention: a 'separation of duties' checklist," in *Computer Security Handbook: The Practitioner's "Bible",* Northborough, Mass: Computer Security Institute, 1985, pp. 9A13–9A14.

Rivest R.L.; Shamir, A. and Adleman, L. "A method for obtaining digital signatures and public-key cryptosystems," *Communications of the ACM* **21** (Feb, 1978): pp. 120–126.

"Row brews in US over database of medical lawsuits," *Computing* (28 Nov 1985): p. 30.

Royal Canadian Mounted Police, *Security in the EDP Environment* 2nd edition. Security Information Publications 1, RCMP-GRC 'P' Directorate, Security Systems Branch: October, 1981.

Schell, R. "The future of trusted computer systems," in *Computer Security: A Global Challenge* edited by J. Finch and E. Dougall. Amsterdam: North-Holland, 1984, pp. 55–67.

Schlorer, J. "Identification and retrieval of personal records from a statistical data bank," *Methods of Information in Medicine* **14** (Jan 1975): pp. 7–13.

Schmitt, W. "Data security program development: an overview," *Computer Security Journal* (Winter, 1982).

"Security of Census Population," CMND. 5365, London: HMSO, July, 1973.

Seidman, S. "Futuristic authentication schemes overcome passwords' limitations," *Computerworld* **19** (25 Nov 1985), pp. 58, 67.

Shaw, S. "Computer crime bills debated on Capitol Hill," *Mini–Micro Systems* **18** (Aug 1985): p. 48.

Smith, J. "Callback security system prevents unauthorized computer access," *Mini–Micro Systems* **17** (Jul, 1984): pp. 257–262.

Smith, R. *Compilation of State and Federal Privacy Laws*. Washington: Privacy Journal Press, 1981.

"Spies in the Wires," *Horizon*, BBC2 Television (30 Jan 84).

Summers, R. "An overview of computer security," *IBM Systems* Journal **23** (No 4, 1984): pp. 309–325.

Summers, R.; Fernandez, E. and Wood, C. "Auditing controls in a database environment," *Computer Security Journal* (Spring, 1981).

Symons, C. and Schweitzer, J. "A proposal for an Automated Logical Access Control Standard (ALACS): a standard for computer logical access security," in *Computer Security: A Global Challenge* edited by J. Finch and E. Dougall. Amsterdam: North-Holland, 1984, pp. 115–127.

"The computer that sang like a canary," *Newsweek* (8 July 1985): p. 48.

Thompkins, J. "Living in a dream world of uninsured computers," *Management Technology* (May, 1985): pp. 30–35.

Turn, R. (a) "Privacy protection in the '80s," *Proceedings of the 1982 IEEE Symposium on Security and Privacy*. Silver Springs Md: IEEE Press, 1982, pp 86–89.

Turn, R. (b) "Private sector needs for trusted/secure computer systems," *1982 NCC Conference Proceedings*. Arlington, Va: AFIPS Press, 1982.

Turn, R. (c) "Security issues in transborder data flows," *Computer Security Journal* (Winter, 1982).

Van Eck, W. "Electromagnetic radiation of information by video display units," paper presented to SECURICOM 85, Cannes, March, 1985.

Wade, J. "Physical and personnel security considerations for data processing systems," in *Advances in Computer Security Management II*, edited by M. Wofsey. Chichester: J. Wiley, 1983, pp. 117–142.

Waters, S. *Introduction to Computer Design (Planning Files and Programs)*. Manchester: NCC, 1974.

Waters, S. *Systems Specification*. Manchester: NCC, 1979.

Weber, R. *EDP Auditing: Conceptual Foundations and* Practice. New York: McGraw-Hill, 1982.

Westermeier, J. "Legal implications of computer security," in *Advances in Computer Security II*, edited by M. Wofsey. Chichester: J. Wiley, 1983, pp. 39–51.

Whiteside, T. *Computer Capers: Tales of Electronic Thievery, Embezzlement and Fraud*. Toronto: Fitzhenry and Whiteside, 1978.

Wong, K., "DP fraud: a revealing look at criminal minds," *Computing* **11** (19 May 1983), p. 24.

Wong, K., *Risk Analysis and Control: A Guide For DP Managers*. Manchester: NCC, 1977.

Wood, C.C., "Effective information security with password controls", *Computers and*

Security **2** (Jan 1983), pp. 5–10.

"1981 Census of Population: Confidentiality and Computing," CMND. 8201, London: HMSO, March, 1981.

Chapter 3

THE BURDEN OF COMPUTER SECURITY

Computer security, like any technological commodity, is obtained at some cost to the consumer. At first glance, the nature of this cost seems obvious, such as the price of encryption devices when a financial data network desires increased protection. However, such obvious expenses are superficial. The true costs of security in information systems can be concealed, immeasurable and immense.

PERFORMANCE

The first easily overlooked expense of computer security can be found in the effects of increased security on system performance. Network encryption, for example, is likely to increase transmission processing time, volume of transmitted data, and increase retransmission demands. The management of encryption keys will increase communications overhead. Other forms of increased computer security can introduce other performance burdens.

Processing Overhead

Security operation. When the real burdens of computer security come under scrutiny, the operational costs are the first to gain recognition. These costs include additional computer or communications processing, manual operations, human supervision and management, and system maintenance. Often the costs of system operation "upon violation" are still overlooked. For example, in addition to normal "inviolated" operational costs of a communications security system, there will be a swell in security operating costs with each encroachment. Specifically, there is the operational labor involved in changing account names, passwords or dial-back numbers upon discovery of assaults by intruders ("hackers"). Further, there would be management costs in prosecuting an intruder captured by a "hacker trap" in the access software. However, even these costs are still superficial when contrasted with the deeper burdens which follow.

Controls information storage. In addition to operational processing costs, there is usually an increase in normal data storage upon the introduction of increased security. Personnel files may bulge with background information, access privileges and employee contracts. Within computing systems, password lists, encryption keys, data seals and access rules must be stored. Some storage overhead is more obscure: for example, encryption systems must deal with two copies of each data element: one plaintext and one cyphertext.

Controls errors. The increased processing and storage overhead of security techniques reflexively introduce additional failure points. Cryptosystem errors may result in otherwise unnecessary retransmission, a common occurrence in banking authentication systems. For example, the most common such error is that of the mistyping of a password, a form of "retransmission" of an improperly encoded control.

Interference

When control errors become severe or commonplace, the performance degradation rises to a degree of "interference." In such cases, the controls actually defeat the system's ability to perform.

Defeated legitimate access. As access controls become stronger, the frequency with which legitimate access attempts are defeated will rise. For example, in extremely sensitive military password systems, passwords are changed frequently, randomly, and without notice to the user. The user "discovers" the invalidation of his password upon access denial. The user must then personally appear before the security officer in order to obtain his new valid password. Less extreme forms of this overhead exist in any computer access system, for example, when passwords transparently expire for less-frequently-used accounts. Occurrences of defeated legitimate access are quite common in almost every implementation of operating system access control software or data access control software.

Desktop computers and professional workstations are presenting management with a severely different "theft of services" problems (see chapter 2). A survey by a California software publishing company exposed serious abuse of these systems by executives. Fully 80% of the 750 respondents reported misuse by personal diversion (most frequently for personal correspondence), 60% used their employer's equipment for games, and more than 25% reported personal finance or job searches as common uses. Software publishers are including "hot key" features in some games, which switch instantly to spreadsheet displays in case "the boss" strolls by ["Personal use takes over...," 1987].

Technological control for this abuse can be effected by controlling the capability of loading software into the machine from transportable media.[1] This solution, however, then prevents all legitimate software loading and updates by the end-user. Some common desktop computer functions become impossible on

---

1   Products such as Fischer Innis' "Watchdog," or Master Control Systems' "Master Security" can perform this function.

the controlled desktop system (without involving busy data processing or information center staff). Examples include such tasks as temporary reconfiguration for displays and demonstrations, legitimate loading of software for evaluation, and the temporary rearrangement of facilities in cases of equipment failure.

Destruction of objects. Less frequently, controls can actually destroy system objects. Microcomputer-based encryption software permits strong levels of data privacy in personal computers. However, poor key management practices can leave the operator without access (or recourse) to the data after key loss. Software copyright protection schemes sometimes defeat proper software operation when transferred to fixed disk drives.

Security Staff

A terrible conflict is directly reflected in the nature of staff appointments in information systems security. On one side of this conflict, it must be recognized that proper security controls should be nested deeply within the information system "primitives." Because of this nesting, controls performance can affect the performance of almost every elementary process within an automated or manual component of an information system. In direct conflict with this premise, however, management has traditionally found information systems security difficult to justify (this tradition is more thoroughly explored in chapter six). This, unfortunately can confound security staff appointments in a number of ways.

Original recruitment. Technical staff in information systems have become an expensive commodity. Too frequently, cost consciousness leads to the definition of security staffing requirements in terms of lower salaries and lower technical qualifications than those which might be set for other managers, analysts or programmers [Finch, 1985].

DP transfers. In certain organizations, it is the data processing manager who must face the task of populating the security team. Since this manager's primary interest is the functional performance of the systems, there is a strong (but short-sighted) motivation to transfer staff who have historically performed poorly in the overloaded system maintenance and development tasks. In addition, when well-qualified staff are transferred into a demoralized security sphere, the low professional esprit can encourage an immediate flight from either the department or the firm altogether.

"Policeman" mentality. Exacerbating the staff performance problem, computer security is sometimes organizationally defined under "corporate security," "building security" or the "security officer." Even though the staff may be competent analysts, programmers or engineers, they begin perceiving themselves as the computer "policemen." Obsessions with fraud can obscure the important issues of data integrity or privacy.

Actions such as these not only infect the security staff with unqualified colleagues, but have historically discouraged excellence in performance by those competent computer security staff who find themselves cast among the mediocre. It can be seen that management's low economic loyalty to information systems security is sometimes reflected in the constitution of the technical staff. This, in turn, can lead to poor performance of the designers, and the controls that are specified. In such circumstances, there should be no surprise that some control implementations result in dramatically reduced system performance, user rejection, or even a functional failure in the controls' intent.

FLEXIBILITY

The most critical burden of computer security has historically been the loss of system flexibility. Initially, this claim would probably surprise most systems analysts (and even a few computer security professionals). However, a detailed examination of the effects of computer security on the essential nature of the computer system design can provide a remarkable new perception of security system issues.

Security "rigidification"

Computer security almost invariably imposes restrictions and confinements on the target information system's behavior. Most computer security design approaches have operated from the foundation of defining allowable system operations, and then implementing controls which prevent variation. Thus, security controls impose an otherwise unnecessary rigidity in the information system.

Processing. Access restrictions will impose essential constraints on processing behavior. For example, a call-back system may only permit certain types of access from certain "authorized" telephones or at certain times, and in the process impose venue rigidity. Consider a sales executive working on an important client scheme from overseas, who discovers that 9:00 a.m. in London is 3:00 a.m. in New York, and that telephone access to the sensitive corporate simulation software is restricted to the hours of 6:00 a.m. to midnight. Another example would be the one-time modification of a billing program to include cost-plus billing for unusual items, such as employee insurance — which would run afoul of the data access rights afforded by the security software to the billing application.

Data structures. Security imposes further rigidity on the structures of data found in information systems. For example, the modification of an existing employee record's structure by dividing the TELEPHONE-NUMBER field into separate DIALING-CODE and TELEPHONE-NUMBER fields could "crash" a hash total control in an seemingly unrelated application. In another example, the inclusion of additional data in a financial transaction communication could inadvertently destroy the authenticator calculations at the receiving end.

Acceptance of Rigidity

It can be argued that the rigidity imposed by security does not present an unjustified price for the return. Historically, problems which developed out of the rigidity dictated by the controls were solved operationally. However, to some extent, the acceptance of such rigidity may have been due to the essentially rigid nature of the computer-based systems themselves. It is possible that the invasion of heretofore human processing by computer-based applications may present security with computer systems which are more fluid in nature. An examination of the current range of computer applications in terms of rigidity will highlight this evolution.

Transaction processing systems. This was the earliest arena of management information to undergo computerization. The types of, and processing of, fundamental business events were easily predicted and charted. Because of this, traditional computer systems analysis and design flourished. System requirements could be clearly defined, implemented and operated. Changes in such systems were difficult, and accordingly, these were made as infrequently as possible. Thus, the rigidity of these systems was already extant even without proper security. Two classes of transaction processing systems exist: data processing and process control.

Traditional data processing. These systems record or trigger each business event within the organization. This high volume application is traditionally a domain of large computer systems, significant technical staff, and grand development projects.

Process control systems. More recently, businesses have begun to adopt computers as controllers effecting certain events. These systems may actually conduct as well as record a transaction. Instances include automatic warehousing systems and environmental control systems which, for example, automatically shut down unnecessary lighting. These systems usually possess the rigidity exhibited by purely data-oriented transaction systems.

Reporting systems. Reporting systems are usually perceived as extensions of transaction processing systems — summarizing, analyzing, and formatting the data captured during transactions. Reporting systems are seen to be maturing, however; and while these were very rigid in their original forms, they have progressed into newer, less rigid roles. Accordingly, early forms of reporting systems are less affected by the effects of security than certain newer forms. Reporting systems can be classed as cyclical, exception, triggered or demand.

Cyclical reporting. Cyclical reports are produced on a regular basis according to some specified interval: e.g., monthly, quarterly, or annual reports. Probably the earliest form of reporting, such systems are cast as creatures of transaction processing systems, and share the rigid nature of their breed.

Triggered reporting. These reports are also creatures of transaction processing systems, unlike cyclical reports only in their less predefined recurrence. A triggered report is generated when some transaction (or combination of transactions) occurs. Still, the rules pertaining to the composition and incitement are usually as rigid as cyclical reports.

Exception reporting. The advent of the exception report represents the first appearance of rudimentary flexibility in computer-based information systems. Reports are only generated when the combination of transactions invites management attention. While the triggering routine and the rules which describe the composition of the report are rigid, the basis on which the rules operate can be easily changed (such as the range of "acceptable" budget adherence).

Demand reporting. Demand reporting introduces a new attitude of unpredictability in reporting systems. While the composition of the report can be defined, the rules for its requirement are totally arbitrary. The report is produced on request. Still, like exception reports, the process of constructing the report, and the data structures required in its construction can be firmly predicted, thus lending most forms of reporting systems easily acceptable to most forms of security controls.

Decision support systems. Decision support systems represent a clear departure from the rigid nature of the transaction processing and reporting systems. The data structures and processing requirements are completely unpredictable, and thus present computer security with serious conflicts. Many traditional control approaches founder on these conflicts. Decision support systems are often discussed using the Simon model of "staged" decision making: the intelligence stage, the design stage, and the choice stage.

The intelligence stage. This stage requires the use of data gathering and analysis tools in the identification and clarification of problems and opportunities requiring resolution. During this stage, decision support systems are vulnerable to one of the most basic, and most severe error sources: transcription errors. Typographical errors, outdated downloaded files, or misconstructed queries can undetectably destroy the integrity of the essential definition of the problem. In addition, an executive may require broad access to the organizational database, making read access rules virtually impossible to define.

Design stage. This stage uses the tools above and simulation or modeling tools to formulate alternative solutions to the problem or opportunity. Such models are rarely subjected to rigorous testing or internal audits. This is because these are often constructed for a single situation. Yet the individuals constructing the models are very frequently "self-taught" in the use of these systems. Such training does not include reliability and testability concepts.

Choice stage. This stage is only recently coming under automation with the use of expert systems in actually suggesting the optimum resolution to programmed decisions. Even though these systems presently require information professionals in their construction, there is rarely opportunity for routine performance audits.

Office information systems. The progress away from rigid information systems culminates in office automation. These systems have been characterized for their variety, informality and irregularity, often subjecting unstructured data to unpredictable processing algorithms. For example, a word processor may be used to create a letter. Such a data object has a structure which is mostly unpredictable ("maybe it will contain a table, and maybe it won't" or "send Fred a copy with the table, but send George a copy without the table"). In addition the processing is unpredictable ("go ahead and send this to George, but have Jack sign the copy for Fred").

Accordingly, the progress into areas where traditional computer security techniques falter also culminates in office information systems. Attempts to impose security in office automation almost invariably result in circumvention (usually by reversion to previous manual methods). Most successes in office system security have resulted from application of traditional physical security techniques used in paper-based systems. For example, military security sometimes forbids fixed disk systems in favor of floppy disk systems — providing a media (the floppy) which can be secured in a vault with other paper-based documents.

LIFESPAN

It almost seems implicit that security should be dedicated to the extension of the system's lifespan. Wong [1977], for example, charts the dangers to hardware survival through several regions: "infant mortality," "kinks" during system maturity, and the decline in reliability due to "ageing." "Mean time between failures" (MTBF) is the common measure of this reliability. It is to be expected that well-placed controls will ease the infant mortality and ageing unreliability, and extend the general MTBF. In this way, the system's survival would be aided, and the lifespan extended.

However, it could also be argued that the effects of rigidity alone, whether imposed by traditional systems analysis or by superimposition of security, can reduce the lifespan of an information system. If this precept is accepted, then it follows that the additional rigidity imposed by security systems will probably reduce the serviceable life of the information system. This is a dramatic reversal of the commonly held view that security features can extend the lifespan of an information system. If this is possible, then reduction of system usage by only a few months could usurp all other costs as the greatest penalty imposed by computer security.

Stability of environment

Stable environments, those which impose few external changes on an information system, are said to promote the longest lifespans for that information system. Organizations operating in marketplaces which exhibit little growth, technical innovations or changes in competition usually possess enduring information systems. For example, retail vendors of coal and ice have seen little change in their markets since the 1960's. Changes in these information systems have only been precipitated by computer technological improvements. Unstable environments, however, can quickly destroy the viability of relatively young information systems.

Demands on adaptability. Changes in the organization's environment often require changes in the organization's information system. This is sometimes called adaptation. The ability of an information system to adapt is closely akin to its flexibility. A more flexible system adapts more readily than a more rigid system. We have seen that security can increase rigidity, thus lowering system adaptability. Thus, in unstable environments, a concealed cost of security may be a sharp curtailment in system adaptability and consequent lifespan.

Demands on robustness. Robustness refers to that quality of an information system which enables it to endure increases in information volume or system loading. The connotation of robustness is narrower than adaptation, referring mainly to expansion inhibitors such as storage and channel capacity. However, even in this narrower view, the inflexibility imposed by security can have adverse effects. For example, the processing overhead exacted by access control software contributes to performance degradation during increased data accesses; encryption hardware can ultimately limit channel capacities.

Tests of designer predictions. Flexibility, and the adaptability and robustness consequent to it, can be designed into any information system. This flexibility usually represents additional implementation costs, and is often only incorporated when justified in the designers' forecasts of system demands. Security controls further complicate the designers' task, increasing the costs of flexibility, and further confining system adaptability to the exact limits specified by the designer.

Severity of Security

It may be subsequently seen that an increase in security requirements may further diminish the projected lifespan of an information system. The effects can be illustrated both in increases of system rigidity, and decreases in system performance.

Increased rigidity. If computer security depends itself upon system rigidity, and rigidity contributes to limitations on the lifespan of an information system, then it would seem evident that increased security requirements are likely to further curtail lifespan. For example, consider the lifespan implications of the decision to raise data access security granularity from "data set level" to "field level".[2] At first glance, it may be perceived that the system flexibility has increased by virtue of the ability to grant access to part of a file. In fact, the rigidity has simply been fragmented. Under the increased security, applications lose their former default access to their own "classes" of data (e.g., payroll program access to all employee data). A requirement that, for example, income taxes be withheld against company car privileges, would not only require payroll program modifications, but with the "improved" field level security, access right modifications are additionally required. Thus, the modification process has been further complicated, increasing maintenance costs, raising operating overhead, and diminishing the returns (and consequently the lifespan) of the system.

Decreased performance. The effects of the performance issues discussed above would necessarily limit the period of economic feasibility of most computer-based information systems. For example, financial institutions in some developing countries operate on the brink of exceeding their system capacities. These systems frequently require multiple transaction retransmissions in order to pro-

---

2   "Granularity" refers to the lowest level within the data hierarchy at which discrete elements can be protected. Data set level means access must be granted to entire files or data sets. Field level means access may be granted to certain fields (or data types) within data sets.

vide a valid authenticator. An international decision to implement full message encryption, rather than the simple encrypted seal would probably signal the end of those struggling systems' economic viability.

Technological obsolescence. The system performance lifespan issue is further complicated when obsolescence of the security equipment or techniques are themselves considered. Computer security techniques, under the influence of two circles, are among the most furious of technological development spheres. These two circles are international espionage, where the largest of governments invest millions in the discovery of sophisticated technological assaults and defenses; and hobbyist experimentation, where inexperience, youth, penury and persistence quickly unearth any simple, overlooked exposures in the protection schemes. Under such pressures, high security systems currently face shortened lifespans from the technological obsolescence of the control techniques alone.

Type of System

Recent design methodological work has suggested that the adaptability, flexibility and lifespan of an information system may indeed be related to the system model which underlies the design. The concept, sometimes called "Information Engineering" (IE), pointed to data modeling as the basis for an enduring system design. The IE methodologies disdained the process-based orientation of traditional systems analysis and design, not because of structural design questions, but because the processes are more likely to change over time than the data structures. IE methodologists claim that the data model underlying an organization's information system changes with far less frequency than the processing algorithms. A system design based on data models is thus claimed to be far more adaptable than a design which focuses on the processes ["Information engineering," 1982].

Acceptance of this argument further compounds the stratification of security burdens according to the system flexibility taxonomy developed above. It can be argued that the more intrinsically rigid information systems are process model based, and the intrinsically flexible information systems are data model based.

Process model based. The traditional data processing environment is easily conceived to be process model based. Transaction processing and reporting systems must be carefully founded on rigid, clearly defined processing elements. The effect of this removal from data model dependence may be to lessen the system flexibility, and consequently, the system lifespan. Confinements imposed by security rigidity may exacerbate the effects, but indeed may be less noticeable in the context of existing system structure.

Data model based. However, some of the newer applications of computer technology can be seen to depart from process dependent models. Decision support systems access the organizational data in an unpredictable fashion. Office automation sometimes seems whimsical in its processing algorithms. According to the precept that such models are more stable than process oriented alternatives, these systems (when properly designed) are expected to endure. Yet security would appear to be difficult in such systems, since the flexibility can be defeated by superimposition of rigid process modeled security structures.

COSTS

Thus far, the burden of computer security has been discussed in more abstract terms of sacrifices in performance, flexibility and lifespan. However, it may be useful to summarize these burdens in the less abstract terms of the financial costs associated with an information system life cycle.

Analysis

Correct analysis and specification of system security requirements will directly affect what is probably the most important financial feature of the system, its lifespan. The correct delineation of the minimum controls level would definitely enhance the flexibility and adaptability of the system. However, the essence of the analysis problem is much more complex.

Analysis: a confrontation with the office. Consider the analysis of an office information system. Suddenly, techniques successful for decades of designing formal, large-scale data processing systems staggered and failed when applied to office systems [Hirschheim, 1985]. New approaches to office design came under intense study and development. The literature became permeated with references to widely disparate methodologies and models. Unlike research in software analysis, which has finally tended to adopt the structured techniques proposed by Yourdon and Constantine [1979]; and unlike research in large scale information systems analysis, which seems to be closing on participative methodologies (such as Mumford and Weir's ETHICS [1979] or Checkland's Soft Systems Methodology [1981]) and structured specification [DeMarco, 1979]; the work in office automation design is both myriad and contentious. There is no evidence of widespread adoption of any particular methodological theme. Office models and design methodologies appear to remain in an immature state, and the industry awaits research which leads to an acceptable, practical methodology.[3]

---

3   A brief review of these office models and methodologies is found in the following chapter.

The debate over office systems analysis is not peripheral to information systems security analysis and design; it represents the essence of the problems confronting this sphere. Security must be designed for all of the newer applications of information technology: office automation, decision support systems, expert systems, etc. Cacophonies of new analysis and design models and methodologies are being both demanded and pronounced.

Cost effective analysis. Which of these generally new approaches would be most effective from the security perspective? The lifespan issues discussed above would suggest that a data model oriented approach is likely to provide the most enduring system, while simultaneously providing a rigid framework conducive to security controls. The cost of a process oriented approach may be in the production of a system which has its rigidity imposed purely by controls considerations, and its lifespan considerably shortened relative to the data model based system. The difference in the potential effective returns of the two alternative systems could be immense.

Design

Similar arguments extend into the design phase of an information system. The benefits of flexibility and robustness can dwarf their implementation costs. Security and controls designs which minimize rigidity are paramount. Yet many security design approaches use techniques discarded decades ago by the general information systems design community. The effect is sometimes to superimpose security restrictions on an information system which was conscientiously designed to avoid similar operational constraints.

Security designers are forced by management to justify controls using difficult probability arithmetic (risk analysis). Here, the effect is to focus security design attention purely upon controls costs — and the imposition of the least expensive controls mechanisms. As is shown above, consideration of controls performance without the context of system behavior and adaptability, can presage the eventual early demise of the system effectiveness. Such a demise can be a massive cost relative to a tiny savings in controls operation.

Additionally, design of ineffective controls (i.e., a poorly protected system) can also inflict massive losses upon the organization in terms of data integrity, fraud or other such losses described in chapter two.

In chapter 4, this design issue will be explored in depth, and alternative design approaches are offered which can greatly diminish controls rigidity.

Implementation

Effective implementation of security controls will add to the cost of system creation. These costs may be a significant or an insignificant portion of the overall system implementation costs. However, these costs will probably be insignificant when compared with the cost of an ineffective implementation. Auditors have complained bitterly of instances in which an audit report required acquisition of data access control software, and follow-up inspections then revealed that the software was acquired — and shelved! Again, the potential for losses such as those described in chapter two is a far greater burden than the cost of proper controls implementation.

Operation

Here again, the costs of effective controls operation will probably not represent the greatest security burden to the organization. Such costs are minuscule compared to the costs of a significant loss due to poor design, or serious lifespan reduction due to poor analysis. However, the latter costs can be misconceived as operating costs, as in instances of heavy communications costs stemming from retransmitting cyphertext.

Further, the costs resulting from ineffective controls operation can be far more burdensome that the costs of proper controls operation. For example, consistent disregard for authentication failure will eventually cost the financial institution more in erroneous transaction expenses than the retransmission costs entailed in proper authentication.

Maintenance

As in operating costs, essential problems in the analysis and design stages can be misconceived as a high maintenance burden. In the example cited earlier, an unnecessary imposition of field-level access control can increase software maintenance complexity. Rising maintenance costs are often cited as indicators that the system has matured beyond its adaptability range, and that a new design is required. Thus when security in a young information system creates a significant maintenance burden for the organization, it is probably the penalty of ineffective analysis and design.

Restricted Lifespan

The major burden of computer security can be summarized as one regarding the early death of an information system. The costs of designing, implementing and operating controls can be microscopic compared with the penalty of say, a five year loss in system lifetime. Yet essential problems of rigidity and flexibility are overlooked in the narrow-sighted search for "cost-effective" security. Even the preponderance of performance costs (such as defeated legitimate access) is unnoticed in favor of minutiae (such as processor utilization overhead).

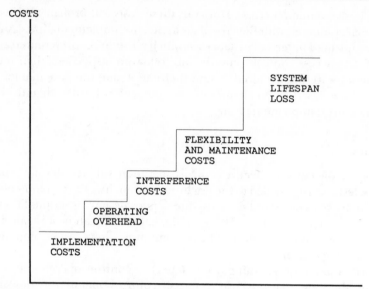

FIGURE 3.1 The true burdens of computer security

ORDEAL OF DESIGNERS

Designers confronted with system security issues face perhaps the ultimate computer-related human ordeal. Security can only add to the obvious costs of an information system. Security is likely to seriously disfigure system performance,
afflict system adaptability and extinguish system effectiveness far earlier than
predicted. Yet ineffective security can lead to costs so dramatic that the viability
of the organization itself can be threatened. Adding to the paradox, management will demand careful justification of any controls costs. This entails probability arithmetic on only the most superficial of security costs and benefits. The
result is likely to be computer security which is ultimately shoddy, ineffective,
and intrinsically poisonous.

REFERENCES

Checkland, P. *Systems Thinking, Systems Practice.* Chichester: J. Wiley, 1981.

DeMarco, T. *Structured Analysis and Systems Specification.* New York: Yourdon, 1979.

Finch, J. "Security of office systems," paper presented to IFIPS WG8.2 working
conference on office systems, Helsinki, 2nd October, 1985.

Hirschheim, R. *Office Automation: A Social and Organizational Perspective.* Chichester: J.
Wiley, 1985.

"Information engineering", *Computerworld In Depth: An Overall Plan,* 1982.

Ladd, I. and Tsichritzis, D. "An office form flow model," *Proceedings of the 1980 National
Computer Conference.* Reston, Va: AFIPS Press, 1980.

Montini, S. and Sirovich, M. "Office access control objects," in *Computer Security: A Global Challenge* edited by J. Finch and E. Dougall. Amsterdam: North-Holland, 1984.

Mumford, E. and Weir, M. *Computer Systems in Work Design — The ETHICS Method.* London: Associated Business Press, 1979.

"Personal use takes over office machines," *Computing* (25 June, 1987).

Yourdon, E. and Constantine, L. *Structured Design.* Englewood Cliffs, NJ: Prentice-Hall, 1979.

Wong, K. *Risk Analysis and Control: A Guide for DP Managers.* Southampton: National Computing Centre, 1977.

Chapter 4

INFORMATION CONTROLS DESIGN

If the precept developed in chapter one is accepted (viz., that computer security is achieved in the context of information systems security), then the same arguments support the view that *design* of computer security is achieved in the context of *design* of information systems. It is necessary to cast this context in order to provide a good foundation for the discussion of controls design. Many issues, however, within the field of systems analysis and design are contentious; and there are many volumes available which address these issues. The task at hand is not the defense of any one particular view of these issues. However, the ordeal of describing security in myriad design methodologies would be too encyclopedic to undertake in a single text. Rather, it is suggested here that the concepts of information system controls design will benefit most views of information system design when cast within those contexts. Advocates of these views are encouraged to consider these concepts within their respective approaches.

GENERATIONS OF INFORMATION SYSTEMS DESIGN

Methodologies for analysis and design of information systems have developed ordinally through several distinct "generations" in much the same manner as their chief technological component, the electronic computer. However, it is possible to attach chronological dates to computer generations, while this is not so easy with systems analysis and design methodologies. A computer generation becomes obsolete, and slowly dies out. This may, in fact, also be true in systems analysis and design. However, as shown below, analysis and design methodologies seem to be migrating across technological scales.

First Generation Design: Checklist Methods

The earliest form of analysis and design of computer-based information systems was a result of complete dependence on vendors for technical expertise. An organization would pose their information problem to vendor analysts, and the analysts would propose possible computer-based solutions. In this fashion the roles of the technical and sales representatives of these vendors overlapped heavily.

Since the underlying motive of the designer was (directly or indirectly) a system sale, the process of system design commenced with the possible system configurations from the specific vendor's product lines. Thus, analysis began with the possible solutions and worked backwards toward the problem. Lucas [1976] named this approach the "checklist approach to systems analysis."

In the early days of mainframe computer systems, this approach was common. It also resulted in the implementation of technically or economically infeasible large-scale computer systems. Quickly, the larger organizations developed expertise to analyze and design their own information system.

However, the development of minicomputers brought computer-based information systems within the grasp of smaller organizations. In this arena, the checklist method again pioneered early system acquisitions. Again, the reaction was the development of independent expertise (although the economy of scale created the "consulting" marketplace that heavily supports such medium-scale computer systems).

More recently, checklist methods have dominated microcomputer system design. Forces in the developing market, including economies of scale and scarce expertise, led to complete dependence on vendor (this time, the retail sales shop) analysts. However, this can be seen to be changing. In larger organizations, Information Centers have taken on the role of analysis and design by the use of "soft" and "hard" controls on such system acquisitions [Couger, 1986].

Checklist migration. Unlike computer generations, design generations appear to have migrated across computer scales. It is unlikely that this approach will soon "fade away," as have electron valve (vacuum tube) computers. The dependence of home computer users on vendor expertise ensures the survival of this approach for the foreseeable future. Further, the introduction of an altogether new technological base (e.g., neurocomputer architecture) could "regenerate" checklist designs completely.

Second Generation Design: Systems Engineering.

The elimination of the product catalog as the primary starting point for system design resulted immediately from the use of vendor independent systems analysts and designers. Elementary tools were borrowed from the engineering field (e.g., flowcharts, block diagrams, ASME document flow diagrams) and from the checklist approach (e.g., record layout forms, printer layout diagrams). However, while some tools were borrowed from the preceding approach, the starting point was quite different. The new starting focus was on the problem rather than the potential solutions.

The development of "system life cycle" concepts to describe the process of system development highlights this generation of design (see figure 4.1). Over time, the emphasis crept further away from implementation and closer to analysis. Careful technical and economic feasibility studies were required to predict the system's success.

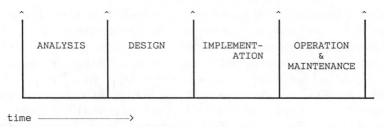

FIGURE 4.1 Elementary system life cycle model

However, the second generation designers were perceived to be genuine "engineers." Profitability, technical performance and system functionality dominated the concerns of the methodologists. Whole approaches were "borrowed" from the engineering field, such as top-down design and general systems theory. These engineers often operated with poor understanding of the organizational "context" in which the system was to function, including, sadly enough, those who would use the information products of the system. For example, their view of "human interaction" was couched in terms of ergonomics, that is, the technical design of human interfaces (switch positions, keyboard height, etc.)

Third Generation Design: Systems Modeling

One essential problem recognized early in the application of system engineering in information systems design was the variation in "style." The "style" of the analyst or the organization dictated the approach and level of detail required. The division of work between the analyst, designer and programmer was often decided within the context of each project. Early work in "structured" approaches to systems analysis attempts to provide a uniform system specification. Prescriptions for the division of work and level of detail are fixed by the rigorous nature of new tools.

Structured approaches It is difficult to identify a single individual to whom credit can be attributed for the structured approach to systems analysis. The approach seems to have grown from the relatively unconcerted work in structured program design. Larry Constantine wrote an interesting historic note in his preface to *Structured Design* [Yourdon and Constantine, 1979]. Constantine credits the development of structured design to work by various students (Glenford Meyers is especially mentioned) from IBM's Systems Research Institute who built upon Constantine's ideas of "transform analysis."

Regardless of its genesis, the literature of structured analysis is dominated by the approach of one authority: Tom DeMarco [1979]. Chris Gane and Trish Sarson [1979] present a study of the tools and techniques of the structured approach and Yourdon [1979] presents this approach in the context of software engineering. These works present similar techniques and benefits.

The product of structured systems analysis is a system specification or target document. This document should delineate the optimal target system, and provide a vehicle for later evaluation of the success of the project. The specification should provide enough details to accurately predict the economic feasibility (cost-benefit), the project schedules and the performance characteristics of the proposed system. Thus, the specification must provide an effective *model* of the system being designed.

Structured specifications carefully remove physical elements from the target document. Logical specifications detail *what* must be accomplished, and physical specifications deta *how* this must be done. By eliminating the physical aspects from the model, the model may be logically manipulated for performance predictions *without* physically creating the target system. It is this emphasis on the logical modeling concept which identifies this generation of design approaches.

The goals of structured analysis include the provision of a "maintainable" specification. This means that the document can be corrected without extensive re-analysis or re-design of the specification. The specification should also maximize the effective use of graphics in providing system details ("one picture is worth a thousand words"). The logical model of the system must be complete before the system implementation begins.

Structured analysts employ a new set of tools to achieve this modeling. These tools include data flow diagrams, a data dictionary, and transform descriptions (composed of structured English, decision tables, hierarchy charts, etc.).

Structured specifications are removed from the managerial issues: e.g., cost-benefit, project management, politics, equipment selection, personnel considerations, and performance analysis. These problems are left to be resolved in the organizational climate of which the analysis is a part.

The structured approach resolves many problems which have plagued the engineering approaches. Last-minute changes wrecked those specifications on which system implementation had begun, thus changes were not permitted after this point (known as "freezing" the specification). Such changes can be easily incorporated in the "maintainable" structured specification. Redundancy is avoided and wordy descriptions eliminated by the reliance on graphics to convey the details of the design. Removal of the physical elements eliminated implementation dependencies from the design. The specification ceased to be "tedious", both to its creator and its user.

The use of the rigorous structured design approach has the effect of moving a considerable amount of the "codification" work out of the program-design stage, and into the analysis stage of system development. The improved use of graphics causes both narrative and redundancy to be reduced dramatically. The physical nature of the system is also carefully removed from the specification.

Variants of the model approach. The popularity of structured approaches offered by DeMarco, Gane and Sarson and Warnier-Orr have eclipsed a vast amount of other methodological research into modeling as a tool for systems development. For example, ISAC, similar in vein to DeMarco in its desire for a reduced model of an information system, uses a completely different set of tools (e.g., activity graphs and component analysis graphs) [Lundeberg *et al*, 1981]. In addition, office automation projects presented designers with formidable new challenges, and some impressive modeling techniques were developed. Bracchi and Pernici [1985] recognize an evolution in office models from early *conceptual* models to the newer *logical* models.

Conceptual office models. Bracchi and Pernici identify three categories of conceptual models. (1) *Data models* take the interaction with data as their basis. These models underlie some of the research directed at creating a monolithic office system; e.g., Office By Example (OBE) [Zloof, 1982] which extended the Query By Example relational system into a generalized office support system. Bracchi and Pernici also categorize early OMEGA work, OFFICETALK-ZERO, and OFFIS as data models. It might also be appropriate to include the Form Flow Model [Ladd and Tsichritzis, 1980] in this category. (2) *Process models* organize the office attributes around the procedures; e.g. SCOOP [Zisman, 1978] which uses Augmented Petri Nets to describe office procedures. The information control nets model proposed by Ellis [1979] can be considered a process model. (3) *Mixed models* offer a combination of both data and process models; e.g. OPAL [Ahlsen *et al*, 1984] in which applications are based on object management. OPAL objects can be "packets" of both data and actions.

Logical models. These models allow fundamentally different office tools to be combined within the same system by translating the physical nature of each tool into an abstract description. In other words, each tool (e.g., a word processor) is represented by its own individual model. The individual models can then be used as building blocks in composing an overall "architectural" model. Bracchi and Pernici point out that these are equivalent to the logical models used in database or information systems design. They consider this an evolutionary direction of office models.

Several models seem to approach logical modeling by providing the ability to create individual models; e.g. POISE [Croft and Lefkowitz, 1984] which permits a logical description of the interface between the user and the system tools. Bracchi and Pernici note that full architectural models for office systems have yet to be developed.

Office methodologies. Hirschheim [1985] provides an excellent summary of the prominent methodologies available for office use. Design methodologies specifically directed toward office systems include:

1. Hammer and Zisman's Methodology, which focuses on the office functions in the context of the overall organization [Hammer and Zisman, 1979].
2. Office Analysis Methodology, which analyzes office "objects" moving through a series of state-changes by "procedures" toward a goal-state. The objects are subjected to three "stages:" initiation, managerial, and termination [Sirbu *et al*, 1982]. A refined and extended revision of this methodology, Office Analysis and Diagnosis Methodology, is described by Sutherland [1983].
3. Information Manufacturing. This methodology approaches office systems design in a manner similar to manufacturing process design – with office information as the "factory" product [Aklilu, 1981].
4. Tapscott's User-Driven Methodology uses pilot studies to examine features and effects of office system design [Tapscott, 1982].
5. MOBILE-Burotique is a methodology developed as part of the French KAYAK Project. A strong set of data-collection tools is applied in thoroughly studying the office information flow [Dumas *et al*, 1982].

Fourth Generation Design: Sociotechnical Design

Third generation design corrected one major flaw of its engineering predecessor, viz., the preoccupation with the functional hardware. However, it could be argued that the preoccupation had merely "shifted" from the hardware structures onto the data structures. The ergonomics of the systems engineers began to soften into genuine interest in the "harmony" of the automated and manual components of the system. The humans involved ceased to be viewed entirely as "users", and took on the more appropriate role as component parts of the system.

Researchers are well into a new generation, perhaps with a new "preoccupation." Fourth generation design picks the human element as its focal point. In its earliest forms, such approaches were known as "user-driven" design: involving those who would operate the system heavily in its design and positioning the analysts and designers in "advisory" or "support" roles. (It should be remarked that some early attempts were farcical, and users' contributions to such efforts were discarded by the technologists.)

Several methodologies have been developed which pivot on a deep understanding of the social impacts of any proposed computer system. Interest in these approaches is growing as evidence mounts that indicates such concerns decrease the risk of catastrophic system rejections by users. This work is now gaining a practical following, particularly in Europe. Two well-known approaches are:

1. Checkland's Soft System Methodology, which avoids focussing toward component parts of a system. Reduction of the system problems defeats understanding of the synergistic social aspects of information systems [Checkland, 1981]. This methodology also emphasizes conceptual modeling, and thus straddles both the third and fourth generations.
2. Mumford's ETHICS (Effective Technical and Human Implementation of Computer Systems) is a strong participatory methodology intended to produce effective, socially compatible information systems. Mumford [1983] has shown how the ETHICS methodology can be applied successfully in designing office systems.

SECURITY DESIGN ACROSS THE GENERATIONS

The preceding ordering of system design approaches provides an excellent context for understanding the role of security in today's information system design projects.

Few authorities would argue that security should not be included in an information system design. Indeed, the developing EDP auditing practices dictate that new information system designs are candidates for internal audit review *prior* to implementation stages [Weber, 1982].

While this premise is intuitively attractive, there seems to be little evidence that it has found formal practice. Security considerations in most overall design methodologies appear almost as afterthoughts. Frequently, the analyst is encouraged to consider security and controls at certain junctures in the design process; however, no tools or methods are specifically provided for this purpose. An analyst truly concerned about security must turn to independent security methodologies. To fill this role, several such independent security design approaches have been developed. Those reviewed below are offered by their proponents in an independent frame of reference. That is, these are "stand-alone" computer security analysis and design methodologies. All of these methods approach a wholly designed system. Indeed, there is an assumption in most of these methodologies that a fully extant and operating system is to be examined, evaluated and modified for security.

First Generation Security Design

The "checklist" approach to security design is still widely practiced today, even on some of the largest of computer systems. While this does not necessarily involve "vendor" experts, it does spring from a lack of expertise on the part of otherwise competent analysts.

Checklist approaches generally do not begin with a view of the risks involved. Checklist approaches begin their design with an examination of known controls. A list is provided of every conceivable control which can be implemented in a computer-based system. The analyst first checks to see if the control is already in place, determines its necessity if not found, and implements the control when required.

Some very impressive checklist approaches are available. IBM offers customers an 88 point "Security Assessment Questionnaire" as a first step toward computer security. This document provides references to other IBM material which describes the considered controls in detail [Fisher, 1984].

This encyclopedic approach underlies most of the early work in computer security, and much of it persists in the literature. Good examples are found in the Hemphills' [1973] *Security Procedures for Computer Systems,* the SAFE Checklist [Krauss, 1972], *Checklist for Computer Center Self-Audits* [AFIPS, 1979], and Kenneth Wong's *Risk Analysis and Control* [1977].

The AFIPS work is perhaps the least pretentious of the checklists, and is offered as an example. Nine separate checklists comprise the work:

1. Planning and Risk Analysis
2. Physical Security
3. Backup and Recovery
4. Administrative Controls
5. Systems Hardware and Software
6. Communications
7. Distributed Risk
8. Applications
9. The Security Audit

An extract of one of these lists may serve to illustrate their exhaustive appeal. Table 4.1 presents a small portion of the "Distributed Risk Checklist" (102 items in the original AFIPS work).

Checklist approaches to both systems design and security design share one delineating attribute: both approaches start with the possible solutions. The checklist approach to information systems design starts with the known hardware configurations. The checklist approach to security systems design starts with the known controls which could be implemented. The analyst selects the best match to the information problem under examination.

Perhaps in both early systems analysis and early security analysis, the limited range of solutions (controls) allowed designs to be approached from the basis of "what can be done", rather than "what needs to be done". Computer security analysis may only just be departing from this era. Most texts on computer security still offer a pedagogical organization based on control typology.

Risk Analysis: Why?

The effectiveness of checklist techniques for designing computer security is open to challenge. The temptation is to squeeze the security problems onto the

---

TABLE 4.1 AFIPS distributed risk checklist (extract).
(Reproduced by permission of AFIPS)

A. Stand-Alone Small Systems

Imperatives

This section is oriented to those installations which have small systems with some pro-gramming capability. Minicomputers, process control systems, intelligent terminals, and remote batch terminals all belong to this category. However, the questions in this section are oriented to the above systems when they operate as isolated or stand-alone de-vices. Questions relating to their interaction with other systems are in succeeding sec-tions.

Primary Issue

Is the use of the system resources understood, properly authorized and adequately audited?

Low Risk (Minimum Security Requirements)

1   Are there operating procedures for each location? Are they in place? Are they simple, are they customized for each type of equipment, and do they contain security instructions?
5   Is the site always attended during normal working hours and locked when not in use?
12 Can all transactions be traced to their source?

Medium Risk

14 Is there a specific individual responsible for security at the site?
18 Has each user undergone security awareness training?
24 Are terminals physically and logically disabled when not in use?

High Risk

31 Is the operating system and data management software designed with security and control features? Are these features understood and used in a positive manner?
32 Are program changes controlled?

[Extracted from AFIPS, 1979]

---

available solutions. Checklists tend to specify ALL controls for every system, not merely those which would be both effective and necessary for the particular sys-tem in question. The result may be that, without tempering, checklist security design may encumber information systems with unnecessary, expensive modifi-cations.

"Tempering" is provided by risk analysis. Risk analysis attempts to estimate the cost–benefit of the controls suggested by checklists.

Risk Analysis: How

Risk analysis defines two major elements of risk (R): P, the probability of an exposure's occurring a given number of times per year, and C, the cost or loss attributed to such an exposure. Risk is calculated as

$$R = P \times C$$

TABLE 4.2. Probability range table
(See Note 1 below table 4.3)
Reproduced by permission of AFIPS

Subjective Frequency Time	Value (P)	Annualized per year	Loss Multiplier
Once in 300 years	1	1/300	.00333
Once in 30 years	2	1/30	.03333
Once in 3 years	3	1/3	.33333
Once in 100 days	4	365/100	3.6500
Once in 10 days	5	365/10	36.500
Once per day	6	365/1	365.00
10 times per day	7	365/.1	3650.0
100 times per day	8	365/.01	36500.

TABLE 4.3 Cost/loss range table

(See Note 1 Below.)

Subjective Cost ($)	Constant Value (C)
0–10	1
10– 100	2
100 – 1K	3
1K – 10K	4
10K – 100K	5
100K – 1M	6
1M – 10M	7
10M – 100M	8

Note 1. The risk formula for use with P and C from the tables above is expressed as follows:

$$R = \frac{10^{(P-3)}}{3} \times 10^{C}$$

The probability P is determined by using a Probability Range Table (see table 4.2), which provides various subjective frequency times, and an equivalent annualized "loss multiplier." For example, a subjective estimate of frequency of loss due to the risk exposure of an information system element might be "once in three years." This yields an annualized loss multiplier of .3333 (one-third of a loss per year).

The cost/loss value C is estimated with the aid of a Cost/Loss Range Table (see table 4.3), which provides the subjective cost of a single loss in decimal exponential steps; i.e., $10, $100, $1000, $10,000 and so forth. For example, an estimated loss of $20,000 would yield a cost/loss value of 100,000 (the next highest exponential increment of 10).

The risk resulting from the examples of P and C above would be calculated to be $33,333. This figure could then be used in assigning implementation priorities for new controls, and cost justifying any control changes in the system.

The brief description above approximates the original risk analysis methodology proposed by Courtney [1977] and promulgated as a Federal Information Processing Standard [NBS, 1979]. This technique has seen wide acceptance. FitzGerald [1978] offers an alternative version of the technique which offers the analyst a finer granularity in estimating P and C.[1]

The NCC Approach

This last collection of tools was devised by Kenneth Wong in his 1977 *Risk Analysis and Control* and represents an intellectual pinnacle of the first generation techniques. The program commences with a series of carefully orchestrated checklists (the 'onion skin' approach), and culminates with a considerably more sophisticated version of risk analysis. The NCC approach is applaudable in the thoroughness of its measurement of the real consequences of a loss. Risks are organized around "loss units" and a range of consequential losses are projected across direct, indirect, and intangible loss categories. The probability of a risk must be applied to the sum of the consequential losses (see figure 4.2).

Second Generation Security Design

More recent developments in security design for information systems have adopted the top-down approach of the systems engineer. These approaches abandon the exhaustive checklists as a starting point for design, and concentrate on functional descriptions of systems. Several approaches can be found in

---

1   The need for such improved granularity can be seen in the preceding example, which managed to arrive at an annualized risk of $33,000 from an estimated $20,000 loss once every three years.

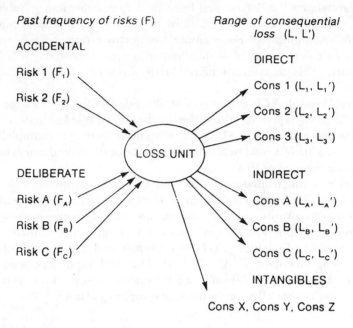

Past frequency of risks (F)

ACCIDENTAL

Risk 1 (F_1)

Risk 2 (F_2)

DELIBERATE

Risk A (F_A)

Risk B (F_B)

Risk C (F_C)

LOSS UNIT

Range of consequential loss (L, L')

DIRECT

Cons 1 (L_1, L_1')

Cons 2 (L_2, L_2')

Cons 3 (L_3, L_3')

INDIRECT

Cons A (L_A, L_A')

Cons B (L_B, L_B')

Cons C (L_C, L_C')

INTANGIBLES

Cons X, Cons Y, Cons Z

FIGURE 4.2 Risk analysis loss unit concept

(From Wong, 1977. Reproduced by permission of the National Computing Centre Ltd.)

the literature, and a large number of similar proprietary methodologies have been developed by management consultants, but there is little evidence of wide-spread practice of any particular method.

For purposes of comparison with the methodology presented later in this chapter, two of the published second generation approaches are briefly de-scribed here. These methodologies are well defined, excellent examples of their genre. Since they provide a basis for departure for a third generation, more complete summaries are provided in the appendix.

Fisher's Program

Royal Fisher, in his *Information Systems Security* [1984], presents his practical and comprehensive approach to the design problem. He draws generally on the powerful IBM base of experience, and offers an excellent, formulated security program without descending into the technical implementation details that consume computer security works.

Figure 4.3 depicts the organization of Fisher's approach. Fisher stresses the need for management to set a comprehensive security/asset protection organiz-

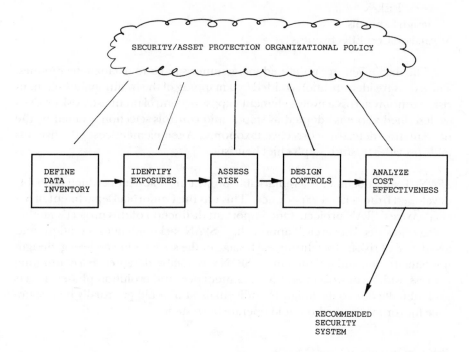

FIGURE 4.3 Fisher's information systems security methodology

ational policy. A data security plan constitutes part of an asset protection program which should be related to a disaster/recovery plan. Fisher suggests that a comprehensive data security plan would be comprised of the following individual plans:

Vital Records Plan
Access Control Plan
Emergency Response Plan
Interim Processing Plan
Restoration Plan
Data Classification Program

The above elements constitute the necessary organizational "climate" for implementation of a healthy security program. After this climate is effected, the following steps comprise Fisher's methodology:

1. Define The Data Inventory
2. Identify Exposures

3. Assess Risk
4. Design Controls
5. Analyze Cost Effectiveness

The data inventory is defined in a manner similar to database techniques. The exposure identification is aided by a mapping of the traditional six element risk taxonomy across a twelve element exposure control point list. Risk analysis as described above is adopted as step 3, and controls selection is aided by the preventative–detective–corrective taxonomy. A ten element cost effectiveness table provides the fifth step's chief heuristic.

SPAN. Fisher documents a remarkable project in an appendix which probably developed from related experience. This was the California Department of Social Services' SPAN project. One important distinction of this project's methodology was its "life-cycle" approach. SPAN acknowledges creation and avoidance of risk-factors during each stage of the system's life cycle; e.g. design, implementation and maintenance. SPAN was notably designed as a continuing process, with a controls operation, maintenance, and evolution phase. This is undoubtedly due to its design by individuals who would eventually be responsible for (or to) those who would operate the system.

Parker's Computer Security Program

Donn Parker developed this methodology after receiving an assignment to write a security handbook for the Computer Security Institute. The methods were actually tested at SRI International, but Parker notes there has not been wide testing outside of this experience.

The methodology is divided into six phases:

1. Identify the assets to be protected.
2. Determine the threats to the assets.
3. Perform risk assessment.
4. Identify and select safeguards.
5. Present recommendations to management.
6. Implement and advance the program.

The identification of assets is aided by a model which maps assets onto a grid defined by type, form, location and accountability. Threat identification is aided by another model which identifies threats by source, motive, act, result, and loss. As an alternative to risk analysis, Parker explains a less costly technique: exposure analysis. This analysis categorizes exposure according to the capabilities attributed to individuals with system access. Safeguards are identified with the aid of a twenty element set of selection principles, and selection of the safeguards is founded on a four element matrix of cost and urgency levels.

Fisher's and Parker's work is extremely important in the development of information system security. Each represents a pioneering effort in publishing a comprehensive second-generation methodology to the general management community. Additional details are provided in the appendix as a basis for the critique below; however, the two original works cited in the references are strongly suggested as worthy background reading for anyone considering the use of structured techniques in security design.

Automated Tools and Methodologies

References in the literature are found which list automated approaches in computer security design. Most of the referenced systems are too elementary in function to serve as complete information systems security design methods. The referenced systems (such as IBM's RACF, SPG's TOP SECRET, and the Cambridge Systems Group ACF2 product) are operating systems or database information system. In addition, the research in trusted computer bases is resulting in another class of automated tool: computer security verification. These tools are produced as component parts of specific Division A TCB product developments (see table 2.1). From the overall view of information system design, TCB verification, operating system modules, and database access tools must be considered to be oriented more toward the implementation of certain controls than toward the design and selection of controls in general.

There are also a number of automated "decision support" tools on the market (RISKCALC, IST/RAMP) which support the routine calculations in risk analysis. These tools are too narrowly directed at risk calculation to be able to model security effectiveness.

SECURATE

SECURATE [Hoffman *et al*, 1978] is one approach which does stand out as more of a design or selection process. The SECURATE approach represents a relatively impressive attempt to automate the security analysis process by providing detailed ratings of a system security profile.

SECURATE is intended as a computer installation security evaluation and analysis system. SECURATE models the installation as three sets of entities: a set of objects, a set of threats and a set of security features. SECURATE accepts and calculates security rating functions based on fuzzy set theory to identify strong and weak points in the system design. This can also be used to compare alternative security system designs.

The object–threat–feature triplets will be familiar as a concept applied in some database and operating system security software designs. OBJECTS are the resources within a computer system. The damage or loss of an object would represent a cost to the owner. THREATS are defined as activities which intruders might employ to gain unauthorized access to an object; or as chance events which might jeopardize an object. FEATURES are measures which protect the system from threats to some degree.

Figure 4.4 represents the basic computer security system as the sets T (threats), F (features), and O (objects). The relations in a "protected" system can be expressed as edges in the form T_iF_j and F_jO_k. An unprotected object will be expressed in an edge of the form T_iO_k.

The basic premise of the evaluation of this model by SECURATE is that each triplet (T_i, F_j, O_k) contributes to the overall security rating in $T \times F \times O$.

The problem of imprecision in measurement of risk, value and loss is attenuated by the use of Clements' "linguistic variables." Linguistic variables are assigned values in the form of words rather than numbers (e.g., *high, low* or *medium*). Linguistic values can be modified to improve granularity (e.g., *somewhat high, slightly lower than pretty high*).

The manipulation of these sets of linguistic values and modifiers offers an interesting example of fuzzy set theory. A *compatibility function* converts the linguistic values to a base scale (e.g., a non-fuzzy probability curve) and modifiers are implemented as functions which receive the values and return a geometric or linear modification of the values. A simplified example might be the functional conversion of *high* to a probability curve which ranges from .6 to 1. Modification of *high* by *very* might be represented by the square root of the argument

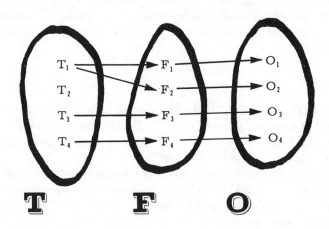

FIGURE 4.4 SECURATE triplets
(Reproduced by permission of AFIPS.)

(in this case the curve of *high*). The curve would be sharpened and shifted to the right, yielding a probability curve for *very high* which ranges from .8 to 1.

Considerable attention is paid to the user interface in order to provide acceptable data entry means, and useful evaluation displays. The displays provide evaluations by both system section (overall system, certain subsections, or individual subsection) and "outlooks" (weakest link, selected weakest link, etc.).

Ratings are provided using the fuzzy metric means in terms of the linguistic values and modifiers of the input language. For example, the operating system subsection might be rated "(MOREORLESS MEDIUM) TO (SORTOF HIGH);" the software subsection (which includes the operating system subsection) might be rated only "SORTOF MEDIUM."

The displays can be used to identify poorly protected objects which have seriously reduced the overall system security. Also, these displays can be applied in experimenting with the addition or elimination of features by studying the SECURATE model of the effects on overall or sectional security.

SECURATE was implemented in the APL programming language and has been tested at a number of installations including a large bank and a utility company. User reactions are reported to include a clearer understanding of installation security; although to a great degree this was thought to be the result of creation of the input data for SECURATE. The use of fuzzy variables is highlighted as one of the successes of the project, with users reporting an appreciation of the technique in estimating system parameters after initial skepticism. However, critics argue such fuzzy metrics are statistical nonsense [Saltmarsh and Browne, 1983].

Smith–Lim Approach

The Los Alamos Safeguards Systems Group developed an automated assessment tool similar to SECURATE, but it is based on a different model [Smith and Lim, 1984]. This model contrasts three generic *Threats* and four generic *Targets* as dimensions creating nine threat–target pairs (see figure 4.5). The missing three pairs result from the assumption that environmental threats do not distinguish between specific targets. Each threat–target pair is evaluated using a hierarchy of event trees. Like SECURATE, linguistic variables are used for data capture and output.

Risk is assessed by plotting the evaluated vulnerability (absence of safeguards) and impact (severity of outcome) on a linguistic algebra matrix map (see figure 4.6). The symmetry of this map is adjusted to the preference of the organization.

This system was developed more recently than SECURATE. Interestingly, this approach takes advantage of the advancing power of microcomputer hardware and software. It was written in BASIC using DBASE II database structures, and runs on a portable IBM PC-compatible computer.

```
                  ------------------TARGETS----------------------
                  Facility    Hardware    Software    Documents

T      Natural    ┌──────────────────────────────────────────────┐
H      Hazards    │                                                │
R                 └──────────────────────────────────────────────┘
E      Direct
A      Human       ☐          ☐           ☐            ☐
T
S      Indirect
       Human       ☐          ☐           ☐            ☐
```

FIGURE 4.5 Smith–Lim threat–target pairs
(Reproduced by permission of AFIPS.)

```
                              -----------------  IMPACT-------------
              V               VH      H       M       L       VL
              U
              L      VH        VH     VH      H       L       L
              N
              E      H         VH     H       M       L       L
              R
              A      M         H      H       M       L       VL
              B
              I      L         H      M       M       L       VL
              L
              I      VL        M      M       L       VL      VL
              T
              Y
```

FIGURE 4.6 Smith–Lim linguistic algebra matrix map
(Reproduced by permission of AFIPS.)

Expert Systems

Carroll and MacIver [1984] report early experimental success with the development of an expert system for the security certification of a computer facility. This system is also based on a two dimensional model contrasting *Components* against *Attributes*. The components are personnel, hardware, processes, and information. The attributes are reliability, integrity, identification, access control, authorization, isolation, accountability and detection. The system is being developed in Prolog, a language popular in artificial intelligence research. The initial goal is to develop the knowledge base to a level adequate to permit risk analysis of individual controls. The acquisition of a knowledge base adequate to use the system for security control design is considered to be a long–term prospect.

Problems with Early Security Methods

Aside from the fundamental philosophical problems in applying distinct security analysis and design methodologies, there are certain deficiencies in each of the security methods discussed above which may trigger reconsideration of their suitability as professional practices.

First, some of the methodologies above are incomplete in their consideration of the system at hand. Risk analysis and the automated approaches fall into this category. It is doubtful that the original proponents of these approaches ever intended that these be given consideration as complete methodologies; but some of the literature on the subject has found it expedient to categorize these as such [Parker, 1981]. These approaches more properly belong in the category of systems analysis tools. These tools are available to the security analyst for application within the context of an overall methodology. Such treatment is offered by both Parker and Fisher to portions of Courtney's work in risk analysis.

Risk analysis, although extremely important to security analysts, is finding a growing number of detractors. The pros and cons of this argument are detailed in chapter 6. Risk arithmetic can become unrealistic with low probabilities modifying enormous losses. The monetary basis of risk analysis is unable to legitimately address the social importance of safety, privacy and accuracy. The challengers also target probability estimates for their questionable relation to reality.

Checklist methods are presently winning discredit in the literature for their incomplete consideration of the overall computer security environment [Carroll and MacIver, 1984]. As was emphasized earlier, similar motivations led to the general rejection of vendor-oriented checklist methods as respectable systems analysis practices.

There are many similarities among the known formulated methods. Each generally organizes its approach into phases similar to the following:

1. Identify entities to be protected.
2. Identify risks to those entities.
3. Identify controls which reduce risk.

4. Cost-evaluate the controls.
5. Implement appropriate controls.

The differences between the methodologies lay mainly in the detailed approach and tools applied in each phase.

Parker differs from both the Fisher and SPAN methodologies by his emphasis on personnel. This may be a result of the developer's particular interest in computer crime and abuse (Parker is a renowned authority in this area). For instance, tools offered by Parker's method are organized by occupation. This may not be appropriate for all information systems, particularly where environmental threats predominate (e.g., process control systems).

Fisher's approach may indeed be the most generalized and structured technique. However, the tools proposed by Fisher often lack maintainability. Maintenance or modification of a system possessing proper controls may require complete re-examination or re-analysis of the security, as there is no allowance in the methodology for design updating (as was suggested in the SPAN experience).

The more formulated methodologies also require a process to discover the interdependencies of the control set. To a great degree, this complex step is due to the physical and functional basis of the control identification process, rather than a data model basis. These interdependencies develop as the same data structure flows through various processes, thus requiring the functional model to be "mapped" back onto the data model.

All of these approaches acknowledge risk analysis as an appropriate tool of control selection. Such analyses have inherent difficulties. First, the problem is divided into "risk" and "cost." Evaluating the risk depends on an estimate of the frequency of occurrences, while the duration of such occurrences remains to be averaged into the cost estimate. Such duration factors can affect cost geometrically rather than linearly; e.g. doubling the duration of a communications failure in an airline reservation system could square the loss factor. Evaluating the potential loss due to risk-factor occurrence could also reflect an unacceptably narrow perspective. Indirect consequences from such occurrences can be easily ignored. For example, loss of goodwill due to the airline reservation system failure above could direct frequent passengers to a competitor permanently. Such indirect consequences could, over time, be more damaging than the direct losses.

Finally, two central oversights detract from all of the methodologies. First, all examine an *existing* system. No provision is made to incorporate these methodologies into any of the existing information system analysis, design and management methodologies. The security analysis project and its documentation are considered a separate, isolated process in relation to other system design projects (with the possible exception of the data dictionaries). This attribute of these methodologies is felt to lead to poorly integrated and unmanageable controls, and the application of philosophically disparate approaches assures two disparate perceptions of the target system. Ontologically, it can be argued that the system designer and the system security designer are operating on two different systems, thus assuring a conflict between the controls and the original system performance.

The second major oversight of these approaches is the poor consideration of manual or non-computer functions. Even Parker's preoccupation with personnel is essentially a view of the threats that such people direct toward the computer-based information (see table C.1). Although it is believed that most of the methods can be adapted for design of manual systems security, there is no experience or fundamental consideration of such usage in the literature.

THIRD GENERATION SECURITY DESIGN

It is strongly felt that current security methodologies, still locked in the second generation, are too narrow in scope to permit the best integration of security into an information system. The use of the term "information" system is an essential element of the meaning of this statement. An information system *may* or *may not* contain a computerized element. The methodologies above are intended to integrate security into "computer" systems.

The computer security methodologies, by approaching an existing operational system, operate on the final physical model of the system. The result is an emphatically physical control set. This has been moderately successful when these systems are formal, regular and predictable; i.e., large-scale data processing systems. However, the economics of information systems technology are bringing such systems into new environments, e.g., office systems. Office systems have been characterized as informal, irregular, and dependent on unformatted data. Indeed, where these systems are automated, the boundaries between man and machine may shift unpredictably. Attempts to impose physical controls on such a fluid, irregular system could prevent continued successful operation of the system.

Office Security Models

Appropriately, the few developments in third generation security design have been in the arena of office information systems. Several studies have focussed on the problems surrounding the application of operating system access control models to office information systems. Fugini and Martella [1984] propose the access controls necessary in an early office model developed by Bracchi and Pernici called the Semantic Office System (SOS). This model included static, dynamic and evolutionary sub-models. Fugini and Martella added an authorization system to this model which included "authorization rules" in the dynamic sub-model and "rights propagation rules" in the evolutionary sub-model.

Montini and Sirovich [1984] developed an alluring independent office access control model which observes the concept of office workers as individual objects assuming roles within the office. The roles are described in terms of objects known as _hats_; the individual's access rights are defined by the current set of capabilities assigned to the user; i.e., the _hats_ he is "wearing". The user may "put on" or "take off" _hats_ as required by his duties. Authorization for _hat_ configuration is governed by a supervisor function called the _hatter_. The model falls short of defining _hatter_ constraints.

However, these approaches are narrowly focused on office systems, and may be inappropriate for other types of systems. In addition, there is little experience with these proposed approaches. On consideration, it may be foolish to reject all security tools which have been proposed in the methodologies surveyed above since these have resulted from generations of practical experience. Risk analysis, control-point identification and other tools may well prove useful in any effective methodology. However, the overall approach in which these tools were invented may prove inadequate for the purposes considered here.

Toward a Comprehensive Third Generation Approach

It is probably necessary to reject the frameworks of these first and second generation security approaches as inadequate methodologies for use in any modern information system. Isolation of the security analysis and design from the overall approach to information systems design would seem to be a violation of the "top-down" premise of structured analysis and design theory. Overlaying the security requirements after the remainder of the system reaches complete specification amounts to "bottom-up" design. Such physical changes can be considered to be unholy violations by some methodologies.

It is possible that the best approach to development of a security analysis and design methodology, both for office use and for field practice in general, would essentially be to nest it as a component part of an existing, established, successful overall information systems analysis and design methodology. This will not only solve the functional conflicts which develop from a separate security methodology, but should alleviate the philosophical conflicts as well. In addition, the availability of an integrated design methodology would encourage the increased use of such a methodology as a system design tool, with important implications for the security and integrity of the set of information systems found in our society as a whole.

The question may then arise as to which of the myriad design methodologies is the best candidate for merging with the security methods. An attempt to surmount this problem would invite the imbroglio of comparative analysis of all design methodologies. This would not be productive, as at the end of such a study, only the original proponents of the identified methodology are likely to have been won as subscribers to the derived security methodology. Instead, it is contended here that security tools can and should be integrated into all design methodologies. This work can be conducted as part of the original methodological development, or as an evolutionary improvement to the original methodology.

For the purpose of third generation systems design, however, any selected methodology must provide an abstract logical modeling stage to permit logical, rather than physical controls design. It has been suggested above that physical controls inhibit the flexibility required in any well-integrated information systems. By imposing controls in a logical model of the system, such controls may be expected to conquer the shifting physical boundaries without defeating the system's functionality.

The structured analysis methodology is selected here to exemplify the implantation of such an "evolutionary improvement." Any justification for its selection as the best method is recognized as arbitrary. It is offered as only as an *example* of such work, and to illustrate the potential success of further studies.

Structured Systems Analysis Approach To Security

It may be possible to establish a new approach to information systems security analysis and design which benefits from the extensive experience with structured analysis and design. The following discussion assumes the reader is familiar with the principles of this approach. (It may be wise to review the synopsis of DeMarco's view of this technique, which is provided in Appendix B, before continuing with this material.)

Desideration in the structured analysis approach to security design includes:

Systems analysis technique compatibility. If the approach is compatible with existing analysis and design methods and tools, this will ease incorporation of the methodology into the overall process of information systems analysis and design. Such incorporation would promote acceptance of the methods by analysts who are not security specialists. The information systems security expert will certainly be of continued benefit as a specialist. However, the broad adoption of a working methodology for security analysis by the general population of information systems analysts and designers can be expected to improve the security posture of society's entire information system set. Hoffman [1982] presented an alarming paper to the 1982 National Computer Conference, pointing out the rising vulnerability of society to profound disruption by the damaging of its increasingly delicate information systems technology. In this context, improvement in the overall information systems security posture is perhaps the single most important tendency of the approach which follows.

The importance of this compatibility is expected to grow as organizations increasingly depend on complex integrated information systems. Newton [1985] recognizes this in proposing that organizations "develop a significantly greater emphasis on the prevention of problems as opposed to the 'reactive' mode of problem resolution." The adoption by systems designers of a design approach which specifically addresses security features of the target information system harmonizes with this emphasis.

Security analysis compatibility. The approach should be compatible with existing security analysis and design techniques. These approaches have found acceptance in the present field practice. Consideration of these would maximize the benefit from previous security analysis and design methodological experience, and encourage uniform adoption of the new technique by both systems designers and security designers. This uniformity would alleviate any ontological problems created by the application of two essentially different methodologies.

Flexibility of application. The approach should not narrow its scope to emphasize any particular sector of information system applications (e.g., banking). The approach should also enable the integration of security design into either the initial design of new information systems or the analysis and design of security features for existing information systems.

Universal effectiveness. The approach should permit equally effective design of either manual or automated systems security, thereby permitting its application in systems rich in man–machine boundaries.

Maintainability of design. The product of the analysis and design should aid the evolution of the system in adapting to changing requirements. The control design vehicle should provide an enduring tool for performance evaluation, design maintenance and modification, and the manageable evolution of the information system. This is essential in modern information systems which must readily adapt to the flexible environment in which many such systems must survive.

Additionally, we may achieve a methodology which may be used not merely for security controls design, but as a secured information systems analysis and design approach. The development of such a methodology would be an essential precondition for the reorientation of organizational values toward security. Such a reorientation is deemed inevitable by Martin Hellman [1984] as security-consciousness rises in many organizations. Hellman sees an identity-shift in systems designers from, for example, "developing a system to transfer funds," to "developing a system to transfer funds securely." The availability of a secured systems design methodology is prerequisite to such an identity shift.

The approach offered here accepts the premise that structured analysis is suitable for modern systems design (such as office automation [Wallenius, 1985]), and closely approximates achievement of its stated goals. These goals include:

1. Graphical orientation.
2. Clear partitioning.
3. Rigorous in nature.
4. Maintainable specification.
5. Iterative design process.
6. Logical in analysis, not physical.

Most of the stated desiderata for information systems security analysis and design are achieved by *starting* with structured analysis and design:

1. As we are applying a widely accepted and practiced analysis and design technique, we achieve compatibility with a large sector of current field practice. Where this is not practiced, it is at least well-known and familiar to a very large number of practitioners.
2. The rigorous and iterative attributes of structured analysis have been shown effective in analyzing widely dissimilar requirements for either initial design or redesign of systems.
3. The logical modeling required in structured analysis allows its effective usage regardless of physical system basis (e.g., manual or automated).
4. Maintainability is achieved by the graphic, partitioned and logical nature of structured specification.

The methodological approach proposed here will apply structured analysis to information systems in its original form, and adhere to the goals and qualities that are the stated characteristics of such analyses. Although the structured analysis approach will be applied as presently practiced, it will be extended slightly to embrace careful security consideration. The tools of structured analysis must be improved to identify risks and controls.

The structured analysis technique is sometimes thought of as a "toolbox" approach. A limited number of compatible "tools" are permitted to be applied in generating a structured specification. The question of expanding this toolbox collection to include current security analysis and design tools as practiced should be considered.

Some of the most important security tools in current use were described earlier. These were:

1. Exposure checklists.
2. Controls checklists.
3. Risk analysis.
4. Security principle checklists.
5. Data exposure control point model.
6. Exposure analysis.
7. Scenario analysis.
8. SECURATE-type tools.

In considering this list, it should be recalled that structured systems analysis specifically and purposefully ignored the following:

1. Cost–benefit and feasibility analysis.
2. Project management.
3. Performance analysis.
4. Synthesis of solutions.
5. Organizational politics.
6. Equipment selection.
7. Personnel considerations.

Interestingly, most of the security systems analysis tools above properly find their chief application the areas not considered by structured analysis:

1. Checklists apply chiefly to synthesis of ideas.
2. Risk analysis applies to feasibility.
3. Exposure analysis applies to feasibility and personnel.
4. Scenario analysis applies to feasibility.
5. SECURATE applies to performance analysis.

To a certain extent, therefore, these security tools can be "inserted" into the structured methodology as those missing elements purposely overstepped by the approach. Thus, checklists can become an aid to idea synthesis, risk analysis helps in feasibility consideration, and so forth. In this manner, security designers may find themselves able to continue the use of some familiar tools (as a matter of style) within the context of an appropriate third generation approach.

However, the data exposure control point model must be rejected for two reasons. First, it is physically-oriented in that it clearly operates on a physical model of the information system. Second, it presents a redundant version of design data from another design tool: the data flow diagram. Structured analysis regards such redundancy as anathema.

Since the existing security tools generally fit "in between" the structured phases, it is still necessary that certain "improvements" to the existing structured tools be considered in order to completely integrate security into the methodology. In keeping with the desiderata above, these improvements will avoid, so far as possible, the invention of wholly new features by adapting the existing structured methodology tool set wherever possible.

STRUCTURED SECURITY ANALYSIS AND DESIGN FOR INFORMATION SYSTEMS

As preface to the discussion of a general methodology in systems security analysis and design, it would be appropriate to recall Ockham's Razor: *pluralitas non est ponenda sine necessitate* (plurality is not to be posited without necessity) [Ockham in Boettner, 1964]. Thus, the fewest necessary changes to "secure" structured analysis and design will be presented.

Systems security analysis and design can be carried out in the same manner as structured systems analysis. That is, it is necessary to create a physical model of the existing system, translate this physical model into a logical model, and then introduce controls into the logical model. Should such an approach have been used in the design of the system under consideration, it would only be necessary to submit the design to additional iterative logical analyses as required to introduce controls.

Two improvements are necessary to add explicit security consideration. These two improvements would implement two of the basic phases found among our existing security analysis and design approaches. The five security design phases were: identify entities, identify risks, identify controls, evaluate and implement. The first phase, identify entities, can be considered to be a natural product of the normal structured specification (the identification of processes and data structures). The last two phases, evaluate and implement, are not structured design considerations since these phases involve feasibility and physical implementation.

The remaining two phases, identify risks and identify controls must be integrated into our analysis and design process. If possible, it would be important to use existing security analysis tool constructs; that is, terminology, models, and techniques.

The identification of threats (risk exposures) involved six classes of risks commonly identified in the existing methodologies: these are intentional modification, accidental modification, intentional destruction, accidental destruction, intentional disclosure and accidental disclosure. If the data dictionary entries for both dataflows and files are extended to include consideration for each of these risks, it is likely that all data elements will be deeply considered for security throughout the system under investigation. Importantly, this consideration occurs in the logical modeling phase, not in the physical design phase.

Before the mechanics of such entries are introduced, however, it should be determined if the matter under consideration is physical or logical in relation to the data dictionary. Recall that the structured specification must be logical, with no footing in the physical implementation. It is contended here that the consideration of intentional versus accidental data exposure is indeed a physical consideration, relating to the motive of the person or machine precipitating the threat. As such, these physical parameters cannot be a consideration of the logical modeling phase of structured design. There are, therefore, only three classes of logical risk: *destruction, modification* or *disclosure.*

Data Controls

It would be appropriate that the data dictionary refers to the controls provided against each risk class threatening the data structure described in the entry. In determining the construction of such a reference, the nature of the required control information must be considered. Controls have been classed throughout much of the security literature as detective, preventative and corrective. What details should the data dictionary contain to annotate the design of these controls?

The controls must take the form of a process (or a part of a process). There may also be a requirement for additional data. For example, suppose the data structure under consideration is an order entry system customer-order dataflow. A risk under consideration must be "modification" of the data. A detective control could involve batch totals. The batch total control would involve a data element (the BATCH-TOTAL-AMOUNT) and a process (BALANCE TO CONTROLS).

Placing the details of both control data and control processes in the data dictionary under the entry for the CUSTOMER-ORDER dataflow would violate the principle of non-redundancy, since both the BATCH-TOTAL-AMOUNT data structure and the BALANCE TO CONTROLS process must also be members of the data dictionary or transform description documentation.

Clearly, it may only be necessary to enter the control data and control processes into the logical model in order to describe the controls. However, the model will not provide any concise indication of the completeness of the control set. To explicitly reflect the thread of controls through the design, it would be necessary to enter a cross-reference into each data dictionary entry. This cross-reference would list both the threat classes and the processes which provide the controls for each threat class. (It is unnecessary to refer to the data structure used in the control processes, as these are documented in the data flow diagram and functional primitives relating to the control processes.)

For example, the data dictionary entry for a file containing customer account numbers might contain the following cross-reference notes:

Modification Risk Control:	CHECK-DIGIT VERIFICATION
Destruction Risk Control:	GENERATE CUSTOMER-BACKUP-FILE
Disclosure Risk Control:	ENCRYPT CREDIT-ENTRY

In this example, CHECK-DIGIT VERIFICATION is a process documented elsewhere in the specification (as are the backup and encryption processes). The design of the controls and control data structures are detailed as other elements of the system under analysis.

Notice that a logical view of the risk/control design is achieved which transcends physical limitations. Check digits, encryption and backup offer protection against intentional or accidental destruction.

The cross-referencing of the controls is necessary for the completeness of the specification, as the security of the element is *not* documented elsewhere in the structured model. The inclusion in each data dictionary entry of a list of risk classes and their controls insures the completeness of the security system design. Figure 4.7 offers examples of such cross-reference entries.

Process Controls

Documenting the risks and controls for each process continues along similar lines: processes can be destroyed, disclosed or modified. However, the effects of these risks are more obscure when directed toward processes than when directed toward data. It may be useful to briefly consider such process-directed risks in the logical model of the system.

Logical Nature of Process Risks

Destruction. The destruction of a process is likely to be physical consideration (e.g., shooting the bookkeeper or burning the computer), and would seem to be dependent on the physical implementation of the design. From the logical view, however, destruction of a process would entail the loss of the "state" of a system. Controls for such a processing-state loss could involve the use of restart data and processes; e.g., a job completion log or an independent incoming message file and the associated restart processes.

Another logical control for process loss could involve logical (as well as physical) duplication of a process for fail-safe operation. For example, a credit card verification process could be logically separated into "stolen card check" and "credit-limit validity check". The logical separation could be implemented as physically distinct processes. Newton [1985] suggested just such an example of this division. In Newton's example, credit card checking for point-of-sale terminals is carried out at two levels: first, the tendered card is checked against a local stolen card list; second, the card is verified via telecommunications with a national bureau for credit amount limitations and validity. The loss of either portion of the process permits the system to continue operation in a degraded, but acceptable state.

Disclosure. In a different vein, the disclosure of a process involves a risk to a data structure introduced into the system upon its design (e.g., compromising an encryption algorithm is also the disclosure of the design system data structures). Logical controls can be specified for such threats; e.g., selecting random encryption algorithms.

Both destruction and disclosure of processes must be carefully divorced from the "control flow" which is present in many functional designs. Dependence on control flows can introduce physical elements into the logical design. Such control flows are usually physical implementations of a logical reference. Consequently, within the logical model, it must be acceptable to specify destruction and disclosure control *within the process being protected.* The essential control asset is the control data structures (which permit failure restarting) or disclosure recovery control flows (which restore operational status). When a process is controlling its own destruction or disclosure risk, this should be clearly documented, using the footnotes described below.

Modification. The most critical risk class for consideration in our logical specification process elements is modification; e.g., a process which produces purchase orders may accidentally or intentionally alter the data improperly. A "footnote" on the process's transform description which provides a cross-reference to a control process must be provided; e.g., control "feedback" by the routing of confirming copies of purchase orders to the requisition originators. Unlike the former two risk classes, it would be essential that no process be permitted to provide the controls over its own modification. Obviously, any element subjecting a process to modification can modify the controls portions as well as the transform portions of the process. This consideration must be observed in both the logical and physical design stages.

Logical Process Controls

The security system control function can be noted in transform descriptions in the following manner:

WRITE PURCHASE-ORDER

Modification Control:	APPROVE PURCHASE-ORDER
Destruction Control:	LOG PURCHASE-ORDER
Disclosure Control:	SEAL PURCHASE-ORDER

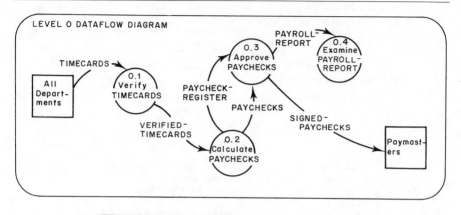

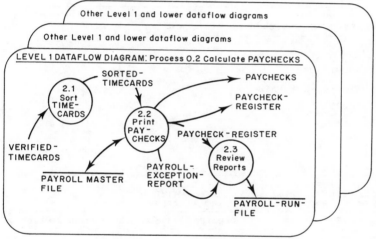

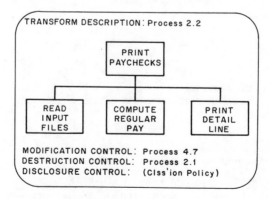

FIGURE 4.7 Data flow diagrams with security

DATAFLOW NAME: VERIFIED-TIMECARDS

COMPOSITION:

TIMECARD-HEADER-RECORD

+ { TIMECARD-RECORD }

+ TIMECARD-HASH-RECORD

MODIFICATION CONTROL: Process 2.2 (Print PAYCHECKS)
DESTRUCTION CONTROL: Process 1.3 (Transcribe TIMECARDS)
DISCLOSURE CONTROL: Process 2.1 (Sort TIMECARDS)

ALIASES: None   CREATED BY: Process 1.3 (Transcribe TIMECDS)

DATA ELEMENT NAME: TIMECARD-HASH-RECORD

COMPOSITION:

CURRENT-DATE

+ TIME-EMPL #-HASH

+ HOURS-HASH

MODIFICATION CONTROL: Process 2.3 (Review Reports)
DESTRUCTION CONTROL: Process 1.3 (Transcribe TIMECARDS)
DISCLOSURE CONTROL: Process 2.1 (Sort TIMECARDS)

ALIASES: None   CREATED BY: Process 1.3 (Transcribe TIMECDS)

DATA ELEMENT NAME: TIME-EMPL #-HASH

COMPOSITION:

1 { digit } 8

Possible values: 0 to 99999999
                 (total of all TIME-EMPL # in SORTED-TIMECARDS)

MODIFICATION CONTROL: Process 2.3 (Review Reports)
DESTRUCTION CONTROL: Process 1.3 (Transcribe TIMECARDS)
DISCLOSURE CONTROL: Process 2.1 (Sort TIMECARDS)

ALIASES: None   CREATED BY: Process 1.3 (Transcribe TIMECDS)

FIGURE 4.8 Data dictionary entries with security

The processes APPROVE PURCHASE-ORDER and LOG PURCHASE-ORDER are found elsewhere in the specification, and contain transformation steps which prevent modification and provide failure restart, respectively. The process SEAL PURCHASE–ORDER would contain transformation steps which insulate the process from disclosure. SEAL PURCHASE-ORDER and LOG PURCHASE-ORDER may be sub-processes of WRITE PURCHASE-ORDER.

By including one or more control cross-references in each process transform description, the design is assured of a very complete control set. Figures 4.7 and 4.8 illustrate the introduction of security into the logical specification examples from the appendix which reviews structured specification.

Strengthening Logical Security

Current security design techniques seek to identify complete sets of controls for information systems. It is usually left to risk analysis to eliminate unnecessary controls. A more dynamic approach might permit the designer latitude at the logical level in determining the strength of the control set identified in the design. For example, the design for a military intelligence analysis system requires the strongest of control sets. It would seem inadequate to approach such a system with a technique used to identify "mere commercial" control sets.

The identification of controls in the above process might be extended by the provision for entry of additional control processes for each risk class in the data dictionary and transform descriptions. For example, the traditional control classes "preventative," "detective" and "corrective" could be provided for each risk class (destruction, disclosure and modification). Instead of identifying three control processes, the designer is forced to consider nine of these controls. Alternatively, the more orthogonal control classes suggested in chapter two (avoidance, tolerance and mitigation) may provide an even better framework for strengthened security.

Modeling Strong Security

The control entries in the data dictionary or transform descriptions can be expanded in systems requiring strong security to explicitly indicate the process providing each of the three types of control for each threat class, whether using the preventative – detective – corrective scheme, or the avoidance – tolerance – mitigation scheme. The level of detail in the design would be increased, providing improved thoroughness of the control set specification, and thus offering stronger security for critical systems. Figures 4.9 and 4.10 illustrate a "strengthened" logical security specification.

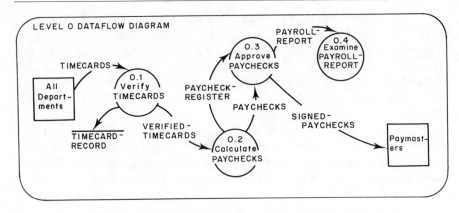

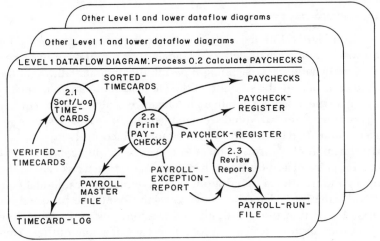

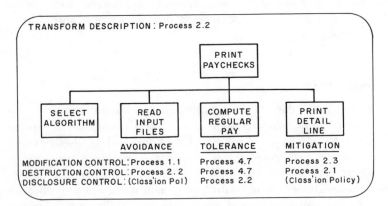

FIGURE 4.9 *Data flow diagrams with strengthened security*

DATAFLOW NAME : VERIFIED-TIMECARDS

COMPOSITION:

     TIMECARD-HEADER-RECORD

   + { TIMECARD-RECORD }

   +   TIMECARD-HASH-RECORD

ALIASES : None   CREATED BY : Process 1.3 (Transcribe TIMECDS)

DATA ELEMENT NAME : TIMECARD-HASH-RECORD

COMPOSITION:

     CURRENT-DATE

   +   TIME-EMPL≠-HASH

   +   HOURS-HASH

ALIASES : None   CREATED BY : Process 1.3 (Transcribe TIMECDS)

DATA ELEMENT NAME : TIME-EMPL≠-HASH

COMPOSITION:

     1 { digit } 8

Possible values: 0 to 99999999
          (total of all TIME-EMPL≠ in SORTED-TIMECARDS)

ALIASES : None   CREATED BY : Process 1.3 (Transcribe TIMECDS)

FIGURE 4.10 Data dictionary entries with strengthened security

Physical Specification

Logical specifications for information systems are necessarily incomplete. In the case of computer implementation, logical elements such as data dictionary entries and transform descriptions must be translated into Data-Sub-Language statements and computer programming statements. Similar specifications must be provided for manual elements in the physical specification. As discussed in the appendix, the actual man–machine boundary must be defined. Additional physical specifications, such as actual computer hardware and software RFPs (Requests For Proposals), are beyond DeMarco's methodology.

Certain physical controls must also be dependent on the man–machine boundary. The environmental controls are often different for human and machine "processors". The logical controls specification is *incomplete,* just as is the logical system specification.

However, it is clear that the task of physical control design is greatly reduced in complexity. Those controls which can be conceived at a logical level are in the specification, and have only to be translated into physical specifications with the remainder of the logical system specifications. This process eliminates one of the most difficult problems in existing methodologies: "mapping" of controls. This step, found in all of the current formulated security methodologies, is precipitated by the overlap of risks and controls in physical specifications. This overlap is thought to materialize because the current methodologies operate on the system's physical specifications. This overlap is not present at the logical level — the principle of non-redundant specification prevents it. Thus, the complex "mapping" stage found in current security practices would be unnecessary in the proposed approach.

In addition, the implementation of controls in the logical model reduces the complexity of control verification and testing. The logical behavior of the control set is defined *before* physical design features are specified. It can be expected that test plans can more effectively consider such complex problems as control independence and controls deadlock. Newton [1985] attributes many deadlocking difficulties to the inability to comprehensively test the operational situations. The concise nature of the logical system model would provide a strong tool in the design of such comprehensive tests.

At the physical level, the designers need only consider the physical controls (see the discussions in chapter two). These physical controls are a consequence of the physical design, and specifications for these controls must be integrated into the physical specification. Since the structured design process is removed from this stage, such physical controls are a consequence of the physical design. As has been shown in the discussion of computer security, these controls can be adequate when properly implemented.

It is appropriate to offer "strengthened" physical security by considering the inclusion of all three types of controls (avoidance, tolerance, and mitigation) in protecting particularly sensitive physical elements of the system.

Structured systems analysis and specification techniques may provide a very good solution to problems found in information systems security design. Narrowly focused security techniques fail to consider every facet of an information system. The structured technique, with the minor addition of security cross-references, will provide an elegant security design process, more complete than any presently in existence. This process is couched in concepts familiar to both security specialists and "general" systems analysts and designers.

Additionally, the final control set will have strong roots in the logical model of the information system. It can be expected that the controls will be more suitable to "flow" across the man–machine boundary where necessary, and to "flex" with the information system when required. This approach to the implantation of controls into modern information systems — systems rich in man–machine boundaries and flexibility — may solve the looming security problems in office automation, decision support systems and expert systems.

The structured design and specification approach, however popular, is certainly not the *only* approach. It may not even be contended that the structured approach is a dominant approach. It was selected for use above owing to its thorough logical modeling, and growing popularity. It is thought that any approach which embraces an abstract logical modeling stage in its design phase can be modified to explicitly define complete control sets. The ESPRIT Office Systems Methodology, currently being studied and developed, is considering features which include explicit consideration of controls.

The important concept which must be applied in any design methodology is the inclusion of controls definition in the logical modeling stage.

FOURTH GENERATION SECURITY DESIGN

Experience with systems design approaches which focus on human values is growing. However, practically no serious work exists on this approach to security design. One farsighted exception is a suggestion in Victor Lane's Security of Computer Based Information Systems [1986]. Lane prescribes the use of Checkland's Soft Systems Methodology as a preliminary study for Parker's Program. In doing so, Lane's approach achieves the holistic and humanistic concerns which dominate Checkland's work. However, the application of Parker's program as a follow-on to such a study is still likely to specify predominantly physical solutions to security problems. A more interesting approach would be the entire integration of some of Parker's tools (such as the occupational vulnerability analysis) into Checkland's Methodology.

In chapter six, some of the growing social implications of information systems security are discussed. It is felt that, as analysts grow more keenly aware of these problems, the trend toward fourth generation systems design may lead to the development of usable fourth generation security design methodologies.

REFERENCES

AFIPS (American Federation of Information Processing Societies). *Security: Checklist for Computer Center Self-Audits.* Arlington, Va.: AFIPS Press, 1979.

Ahlsen, M; Bjornerstedt, A.; Briffs, S; Hulten, C; and Soderlund, C. "An architecture for object management in OIS," *ACM Transactions on Office Information Systems* **2** (July 1984).

Aklilu, T. "Office automation productivity — the missing link," *1981 Office Automation Conference Digest.* Arlington, Va: AFIPS Press, 1981.

Bracchi, G. and Pernici, B. "Trends in office modelling," paper presented to IFIPS TC8 Working Conference on Office Information Systems, Helsinki, 1 Oct 1985.

Carroll, J. and MacIver, W. "Towards an expert system for computer facility certification," in *Computer Security: A Global Challenge* edited by J. Finch and E. Dougall. Amsterdam: North-Holland, 1984, pp. 293–306.

Checkland, P. *Systems Thinking, Systems Practice.* Chichester: J. Wiley, 1981.

Computer Security Institute. *Computer Security Handbook: The Practitioner's "Bible."* North borough, Mass: Computer Security Institute, 1985.

Couger, J. "E pluribus computum," *Harvard Business Review* **64** (Sept–Oct, 1986) pp. 87 – 91.

Courtney, R. "Security risk assessment in electronic data processing." *AFIPS Conference Proceedings NCC* **46**, 1977, pp. 97–104.

Croft, W. and Lefkowitz, L. "Task support in an office system," *ACM Transactions on Office Information Systems* **2** (July 1984): pp. 197-212.

DeMarco, T. *Structured Analysis and System Specification.* New York: Yourdon, 1979.

Dumas, P.; du Roure, G.; Zanetti, C.; Conrath, D. and Mairet, J. "MOBILE-Burotique: prospects for the future," in *Office Information Systems* edited by N. Naffah. Amsterdam: North-Holland, 1982, pp. 385–402.

Ellis, C. "Information control nets: a mathematical model of office automation flow," *Proceedings of the 1978 Conference on Simulation, Measurement and Modelling of Computer Systems.* Arlington, Va: AFIPS Press, 1978.

Fisher, R. *Information Systems Security.* Englewood Cliffs: Prentice-Hall, 1984.

FitzGerald, J. "EDP risk analysis for contingency planning." *EDP Audit Control and Security Newsletter* **I** (Aug, 1978): pp. 6–8.

FitzGerald, J. *Internal Controls for Computerized Systems.* San Ceandro: Underwood, 1978.

Fugini, M. and Martella, G. "ACTEN: a conceptual model for security systems design," *Computers and Security* **3** (Aug 1984): pp. 196–214.

Gane, C. and Sarson, T. *Structured Systems Analysis: Tools and Techniques.* Englewood Cliffs: Prentice-Hall, 1979.

Hammer, M. and Zisman, M. "Design and implementation of office information systems," *Proceedings of NYU Symposium on Automated Office Systems.* New York: NYU, 1979.

Hellman, M. "Beyond War: implications for computer security and encryption," in

Computer Security: A Global Challenge edited by J. Finch and E. Dougall. Amsterdam: North-Holland, 1984, pp. 41–47.

Hemphill, C. and Hemphill, J. *Security Procedures for Computer Systems.* Homewood: Dow Jones–Irwin, 1973.

Hirschheim, R. *Office Automation: A Social and Organizational Perspective.* Chichester: J. Wiley, 1985.

Hoffman, L. "Impacts of information system vulnerabilities on society", *1982 NCC Conference Proceedings.* Arlington, Va: AFIPS Press, 1982.

Hoffman, L.; Michelman, E. and Clements, D. "SECURATE — Security evaluation and analysis using fuzzy metrics." *AFIPS National Computer Conference Proceedings* 47, 1978: pp. 531–540

Krauss, L. *SAFE.* New York: Amacom, 1972.

Ladd, I. and Tsichritzis, D. "An office form flow model," *Proceedings of the 1980 National Computer Conference.* Arlington, Va: AFIPS Press, 1980.

Lane, V. *Security of Computer Based Information Systems.* London: Prentice-Hall, 1986.

Lucas, H. *The Analysis Design and Implementation of Information Systems.* Tokyo: McGraw-Hill Kogakusha, 1976.

Lundeberg, M.; Goldkuhl, G. and Nilsson, A. *Information Systems Development: A Systematic Approach.* Englewood Cliffs, NJ: Prentice-Hall, 1981.

Montini, S. and Sirovich, M. "Office access control objects," in *Computer Security: A Global Challenge* edited by J. Finch and E. Dougall. Amsterdam: North-Holland, 1984.

Mumford, E. *Designing Secretaries.* Manchester: Manchester Business School, 1983.

NBS (National Bureau of Standards), "Guideline for Automatic Data Processing Risk Analysis," Federal Information Processing Standards Publication 65, Aug 1979.

Newton, J. "Strategies for problem prevention," *IBM Systems Journal* 24 (Nos 3/4, 1985): pp. 248–263.

Ockham, W. *Philosophical Writings: A Selection.* Translated by P. Boettner. Indianapolis: Bobbs-Merril, 1964.

Parker, D. *Computer Security Management.* Reston: Reston, 1981.

Saltmarsh, T. and Browne, P. "Data processing —risk assessment," in *Advances in Computer Security Management* Vol 2, edited by M. Wofsey. Chichester: J. Wiley, 1983.

Sirbu, M.; Schorchet, S.; Kunin, J. and Hammer, M. "OAM: An office analysis methodology." MIT OA group memo OAM-OIG, 1982.

Smith, S. and Lim, J. "An automated method for assessing the effectiveness of computer security safeguards," in *Computer Security: A Global Challenge* edited by J. Finch and E. Dougall. Amsterdam: North-Holland, 1984, pp. 321–328.

Sutherland, J. *An Office Analysis and Diagnosis Methodology.* MIT M.S. Thesis, Febr, 1983.

Tapscott, D. *Office Automation: A User-Driven Method.* Plenum Press, 1982.

Wallenius, M-E. D. "Applying the data processing tools of structured systems analysis to an office automation systems study," *1985 Office Automation Conference Digest.* Reston, Va: AFIPS Press, 1985, pp. 187–195.

Weber, R. *EDP Auditing: Conceptual Foundations and Practice.* New York: McGraw-Hill, 1982.

Wong, K. *Risk Analysis and Control.* Manchester: National Computer Center NCC Publications, 1977.

Yourdon, E. *Managing the Structured Techniques.* Englewood Cliffs: Prentice Hall, 1979.

Yourdon, E. and Constantine, L. *Structured Design*. Englewood Cliffs: Prentice-Hall, 1979.

Zisman, M. "Use of production systems for modeling asynchronous concurrent processes," in *Pattern Directed Inference Systems* edited by D. Water and R. Hayes-Roth, New York: 1978.

Chapter 5

IDENTIFYING EFFECTIVE CONTROLS

In the preceding chapter, the application of structured techniques in designing system security may have appeared alluringly simple. In practice, however, alluringly simple approaches manage to mire quickly in unexpected bogs. The structured techniques for security are, unfortunately, not exceptional in this regard.

Structured techniques help channel the designer's efforts away from total dependence on physical controls. In addition, the cross-referencing helps build a complete logical control set in the design. However, the approach grows less complete as the design effort enters the physical design stage. This stems from two weakly treated problems:

The control identification problem arises during both the logical and the physical design stages. Many different controls can often be conceived during each stage for the protection of a particular element from a specific threat. Which of these candidate controls is the "best?"

The control selection problem arises during the last iterations of the physical design stages. Controls will find their way into a complete specification which are indeed unnecessary. For example, a control to prevent disclosure of a published process (such as the insurance rate calculation in the case study found in the appendix). Are all controls in the specification to be selected for implementation?

In the discussion below, these two aspects of controls design are explored. The second problem, that of selection of appropriate controls is discussed first, and the model developed as a tool in this area is used in the second section as a taxonomy underlying formal heuristics useful in identifying the most appropriate controls.

INVERSION MODEL OF INFORMATION SYSTEMS SECURITY

Unlike the physical methodologies discussed earlier, the logical control process does not identify every possible control. However, it does specify a *complete* control set (strengthened designs specify *very complete* control sets). There are frequently alternative controls which could be specified for the same elements. The improper selection of controls could include control processes and control data-elements which protect very low-value data against highly unlikely risks. The designer should not be abandoned to a complete dependence on risk analysis tools as the ultimate selection heuristic during the benefits analysis stage of the system approval process. The integrated nature of the control set makes it difficult to isolate the benefits of a single control process or its data. In addition, the problems of risk consequences make risk analysis as problematic on logically designed controls as it is on physically designed controls.

The search for an alternative to risk analysis might begin with a reconsideration of the fundamental views of threats and controls. The construction of a useful model of the interaction between threats and information system elements below can lead to a substantially new approach to controls justification.

Models, philosophers explain, have two main uses: *logically*, models offer heuristic guidance or enable certain inferences; and *epistemologically*, models permit expression or extension of knowledge through explanation [Harre, 1972]. The construction of a model of information security may be of immense benefit in preparation for reconsideration of the controls selection process.

In the discussion below, we will briefly discuss extant models underlying computer security practices. Following this, the literature will be combed for a new model; one appropriate for the more modern types of information systems security as well as traditional computer data processing systems security.

Science uses two types of models. Formal, sentential, or theoretical models are carefully constructed of quantitative variables or statements of logic. Analogical or iconic models are real or imagined things or processes which are similar to other things and processes in various ways [Hempel, 1965 or Harre, 1972]. It is the iconic model that most often occupies information systems scientists. Checkland [1981] defines a model as "an intellectual construct, descriptive of an entity in which at least one observer has an interest. The observer may wish to relate his model and, if appropriate, its mechanisms, to observables in the world. When this is done, it frequently leads — understandably, but not accurately — to descriptions of the world couched in terms of models, as if the world were identical with models of it."

EXISTING MODELS

It is possible that the security methodologies in current use suffer from a basis on inappropriate models. Indeed, most of the current methodologies do not pronounce security models as such. However, there do seem to be models underlying the existing methodologies (intentionally or unintentionally). These different models can be roughly amalgamated into three general models: the security *ring*, the security *matrix*, and the *data life cycle*.

Ring models. These models seem to have originated in computer operating system design. Operating system architecture often follows a "layered kernel" construction, with security provided in several of the layers [Deitel, 1983]. If additional security layers are added surrounding the computer system, security "rings" develop. Ring models seem to underlie most of the "checklist" approaches to computer security (see chapter four). Wong [1977], for example, calls this "the onion skin" approach. Martin [1973], AFIPS [1979], and Hsiao *et al* [1979] have comparable constructs. Figure 5.1 illustrates the threats and defense model from the AFIPS security checklist.

Matrix models. Another framework for organizing concepts relating to computer security is the matrix. Courtney's risk analysis is modeled on an array of *threats* and *measures* [NBS, 1979], trusted systems use the *lattice* model of non-discretionary controls (see chapter two), and Parker [1981] uses a four–dimen-

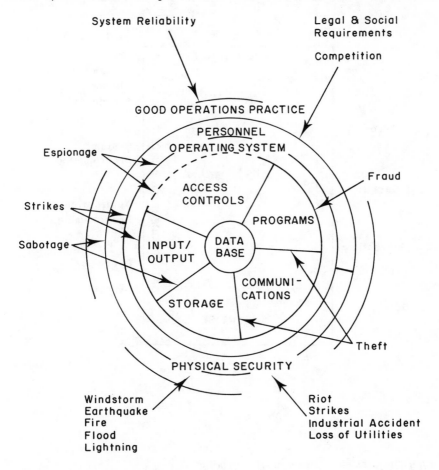

FIGURE 5.1 AFIPS threats and defenses
(Adapted by permission of AFIPS.)

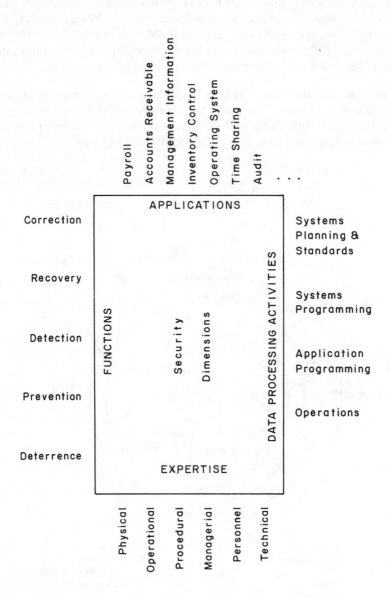

FIGURE 5.2 *Parker's security dimensions*
(Donn B. Parker, Computer Security Management, © 1981, p. 56. Reprinted
by permission of Prentice-Hall, Inc., Englewood Cliffs, New Jersey.)

sional "security dimensions" model in his methodology. Figure 5.2 illustrates Parker's model.

Data life cycle models. The SPAN and Fisher methodologies were both based on a data life cycle model originally defined in the "SAFE" project [IBM, 1972]. The eleven basic information processing steps defined in this model were wholly adopted by Fisher as "data exposure control points," and are discussed in detail in the appendix.

In addition, the *Threat–Feature–Object* database security model underlies SE-CURATE (see chapter three), but this tool is not accepted as a complete methodology, and therefore the model is unlikely to be useful in the present discussion.

Security Model Problems

The chief failing of these conceptual models lies in their passive attributes. These models are static, categorical, and typological. That is, as iconic models, it is assumed that all information systems will exhibit the same or very similar traits and behavior. Perhaps what is needed is a logical model which is more dynamic, fluid, or active; a model which allows varying information systems to be considered.

Harré [1972] refers to models in which both the subject model and the particular source are identical as *homeomorphs*. Harre identifies models in which the subject model and source are different as *paramorphs*, and notes that explanatory theories demand paramorphic models. Consider, for example, a model of an aircraft carrier, such as HMS *Hermes*. A homeomorph would attempt to exactly reflect the attributes of this ship. This homeomorphic model could be used to prescribe needed features for other aircraft carriers by carefully comparing other such ships with the model; identifying, for example, a missing aircraft launch ramp. However, such prescriptions would fail in the case of helicopter carriers, which do not necessarily require ramps. A paramorph, however, could be more abstract, including such aspects as the mission and environment of the ship. The paramorph might be able to identify the *need* for an aircraft launch ramp, permitting prescription for both fixed-wing or rotary-wing aircraft carriers.

The current security models described above tend to be homeomorphic, and may actually be the cause of the difficulty underlying benefits analysis. Methods based on these models will tend to identify *all* controls, rather than *necessary* controls. What is sought here is a paramorphic model which would permit the qualities of the specific information system being modeled to be reflected by the qualities of the model's security attributes.

In seeking a dynamic model, it would seem reasonable to base this on the dynamics of the subject. For example, risks threaten targets. Perhaps a more suitable, paramorphic model would result from the identification of risk "vectors," i.e. sources from which risks emanate, and targets toward which risks are directed.

RISK SOURCES

In chapter two, the common risk classifications (destruction, modification, and disclosure) helped identify a number of major discrete risks. These were *sabotage, fraud, espionage, integrity loss,* and *environmental* risks. Tendencies can be established in the directions from which most of these threats arise.

The security literature contains a number of references to "the enemy within" [Martin, 1973 or Batt, 1983], but the thought is never completed to include a contrasting "enemy without". A possible framework is offered here for classifying the source of risks as *internal* versus *external* risks; i.e., risks arising from within the organization versus risks arising from outside of the organization.

Internal Risks

Two of the information system risks identified above tend to arise from within the organization: fraud and integrity risks. This is by no means offered as an absolute, but rather a tendency found in documented cases.

Fraud. Fraud is most often an inside job. A 1983 study by a New York research institute attributed three-quarters of computer-related fraud and embezzlement to "insiders" [Batt, 1983]. A survey of U.S. government computer-related fraud reported in the October, 1984, *Computer Crime Digest* found two-thirds were perpetrated by functional users; and 75% of the cases involved a single, non-supervisory federal employee. Parker's 1976 study agrees: "Perpetrators are almost always involved in some form of trust violation in the acts they perform." This seems intuitively reasonable since close familiarity with the system being violated is necessary to avoid quick detection of the fraud. Usually members of the organization must be involved in order to provide this familiarity.

Integrity loss. Martin [1973] lists seven types of reasons for computer errors: (1) hardware errors, (2) software errors, (3) errors in application programs, (4) operator errors, (5) data-input errors, (6) inappropriate program design and (7) questionable system philosophy. He goes on to argue that the largest cause of computer errors is incorrect input. These types can be generalized somewhat to permit consideration of both manual and computer systems by reducing to the following four types:

Equipment errors. Martin states that these errors are rare today. Improved electronic designs include error-detecting circuits which clearly warn of possible electronically induced errors. However, when such errors do occur, these can be considered to be internally generated in many cases: poor preventative maintenance, use which exceeds equipment specifications, or poor equipment selection. These could all be considered faults of the organization rather than purely faults of any external entity.

Processing errors. Computer program errors are becoming less frequent as improved software design techniques proliferate [Yourdon and Constantine, 1979]. An exception to this trend may be in end-user-developed applications which were discussed in chapter two. Martin points out that program errors are especially subtle in early versions. The active use of such early versions is mandated when software is developed in-house. Many authorities agree that there is less likelihood of program errors in packaged software especially when a large base of installed systems exists [Kroenke, 1984 or FitzGerald *et al*, 1981]. The error-free quality of such packages is usually credited to careful design and testing by professional vendors. However, Scherer [1984] contends "custom" software is dangerous because "... the paths of data flow tend to be more numerous and complex than in standard software. Both the processes and data which a user needs may be quite unique. Common data [required by packaged software] has a universal quality to it."

If program errors tend to be more likely in internally-developed or customized programs, what of manual errors? If we accept the premise that virtually all manual processing is carried out by members of the organization, it necessarily follows that virtually all manual processing errors result from actions by members of the organization.[1]

Data capture errors. Martin considers data-entry errors to be the most common source of computer errors. Tremendous gains have been achieved in the reduction of these errors in the past decade through the use of source data capture devices, turnaround documents, and real-time validation. When it is recognized that the organization captures its own data in the majority of systems, it necessarily follows that errors in this process are most often internally generated.

Inappropriate policies. Martin considers inappropriate program design as a type of error distinguished from program errors. According to Martin, an example is the use of an inappropriate formula in calculating airline overbookings. This can be interpreted as being similar to DeMarco's idea of "policy" as distin-

---

[1] Martin's fourth type of error *operating error*, would be a form of manual processing error when considering the more global concept of information (rather than computer) security. For example, mounting an incorrect disk volume can be considered a manual processing error. Unless the organization is using a service bureau, such errors are internal to the organization.

guished from "procedure" [DeMarco, 1979]. In both computer and manual systems, management must convey — and system designers must understand — the appropriate policies on which to base the procedures. If the policies are incorrect, processing errors (e.g., flight overbooking) can result. Where management and system designers are members of the organization, such errors are internally generated.[2]

Integrity problems can be most often traced to problems within the information system itself. Errors in processing, data entry, system design, and restart procedures are all necessarily risks commonly arising from operating the information system, and therefore tend to swell from within the organization, rather than from outside of it.

External Risks

Two of the major information system risks identified above can be established as *usually* arising from outside of the organization: sabotage and espionage risks.

Sabotage. Intentional damage to an information system chiefly emanates from several sources: disgruntled employees, vandals, and terrorists. Traditionally, disgruntled employees were emphasized as the chief sabotage threat. However, current thought (see chapter two) is found to be shifting toward vandalism and terrorism as the rising source of this risk. This may be due to a combination of the perceptible increase in vandal or terrorist incidents, and the embracement of office automation by many clerical workers as a vehicle for job enrichment [Gill, 1983]. Vandalism presently dominates the literature (see the panel discussion on "hacking" in the April, 1986 *Communications of the ACM* [Lee *et al*] for an example). This is possibly due to the lack of existing controls to protect systems from violation through dial-up access. It is believed that such controls are gradually being implemented in these poorly protected systems. It is the rising vulnerability of society to terrorist sabotage of information systems that is threatening to be the major issue in this area, and controls to protect against this risk (such as protecting or backing-up key personnel) are rarely in place.

Espionage. Colonel William Kennedy *et al* [1983] commence the chapter in *Intelligence Warfare* which treats espionage thus: "ESPIONAGE — spying — has been an aspect of human affairs since society began, so much so that when formal diplomacy was established aspects of espionage were given the protection of international law. The military attache system by which uniformed representatives of foreign military establishments are permitted to 'spy' openly in the countries in which they are stationed is the most open expression of this curious

---

2 Martin's seventh error type, *questionable system philosophy*, is easily encompassed by the more global concept of inappropriate policies, rather than inappropriate procedures.

arrangement." Few would dispute the importance of the power conveyed by foreknowledge of an enemy's (or a friend's) position. In government circles, espionage connotes sinister and deadly risks to both perpetrator and victim, toppling governments or preventing a war.

In a commercial environment, this risk is most damaging when it involves the compromise of trade secrets, marketing strategies, new product data, or other confidential information. Such compromises can cripple an organization and assure the success of its competitors. Often the product of such industrial espionage simultaneously benefits competitors and drastically reduces the value of the victim's information assets.

In addressing the issues of espionage in the community of nations, Kennedy *et al* [1983] identify three levels of espionage: *diplomacy, quasi-official,* and *the spy*. Parallels to these levels can be drawn in the commercial arena.

Diplomacy. In government circles, military attaches and scientific delegations gather information. Additionally the host nation's literature is combed for intelligence. Industrial parallels could include social exchanges, information freely exchanged in technical conferences, and examination of the target organization's marketing literature, press releases, investor prospectus or other public information.

Quasi-official. For governmental espionage, unofficial representatives, such as journalists, scholars and missionaries, report observations noted when visiting the host country. Industrial equivalents could include the acquisition of indirect information from the target organization's customers or vendors, or the close examination of an indirectly acquired specimen of the competing product.

The spy. This includes the insertion or recruitment of agents within the host country or, in industrial terms, the target organization. Open solicitation of a key defection with valuable information can be included in both governmental and industrial circles.

Bamford [1982] asserts that the volume of Western espionage intelligence gleaned through the agent-spy is surprisingly tiny. The greatest volume is, by far, obtained from legitimate sources (categorized above as *diplomatic* and *quasi-official*). The parallel carries forth into the industrial arena: an executive who fails to consider the marketing publications of competitors would likely be considered negligent. However, only a few cases of "criminal" industrial espionage are actually reported each year.

Variations

The arguments above support the view of *tendencies* in the source direction of certain risks. There are obvious exceptions, such as the use of bank automatic teller machines in creating an external fraud risk, or the hiring away of a key design engineer in creating an internal espionage risks. However, these are clearly the exceptions, not the most usual source of such risk types.

In addition, the environment is a risk type which can emanate from inside or from outside of the organization. Dust, for example, can be attributed to the environment (Arizona is a miserable place for disk drives), or to the organization (as in a plaster factory). Water, static, noise, fire, and other environmental threats can be traced to internal and external sources.

However, the non-environmental risk tendencies provide an interesting and potential attribute for use in studying the interaction of risks and controls. But what of the direction *toward* which these risks are directed? In the section below, the targets of these risks will be examined for tendencies in comparison to the risk sources.

RISK TARGETS

The previous discussion centered on the direction from which risks are felt by an information system. These delineations are not categorical, and *should* be qualified as "tendencies." Still, the classification of internal and external risks yields a useful frame on which to organize a further discussion of tendencies of risks and controls. Consider now the opposite view. Rather than organizing the risks and controls on the basis of the direction *from* which the risk tends to approach, could the basis of such organization be the direction *toward* which the risk tends to approach? Can we classify risks according to the elements of the system which are subjected to certain risks? The discussion below will explore the implications of classification of risks by risk-subject.

Absolutes are as doubtful an occurrence in this classification scheme as they were in the internal–external scheme discussed earlier. Still, some general tendencies or clustering will surface if the concept is pursued.

Identification of Elements

What are the elementary components of an information system? There are several popular categorizations commonly encountered in response to this question. Several authorities find these three basic elements are useful classes: *people, procedures,* and *equipment* [Murach, 1980]; sometimes further broken out to include data [Ahituv and Neumann, 1982 or Kroenke, 1984]. Another popular scheme identifies these basic elements as *input, output,* and *processing* [Parker, 1984 and Brabb and McKean, 1982].

The above organizations of elements in the information system may be useful in explanatory texts introducing the student to data processing or the automation of information systems. However, these structures are not particularly useful in documenting risks in any practical way, just as they would not be useful in documenting the entire design of a system. For example, it would be difficult to discuss threats to the procedures without considering threats to the people or to the machinery which is following the procedures. It would be equally hard to delineate input threats from processing threats when the input and processing tend to merge during a single transaction; e.g., a data entry clerk who rejects "questionable" input.

It is necessary to use a more practical classification scheme to clearly identify the elements of a system which are victimized by risks. There are several established methodologies for designing and documenting information systems. Many of these methodologies could be adapted to establish a verifiable classification scheme. However, the word "verifiable" will immediately highlight the design methodology selected earlier for exemplary purposes. DeMarco's "structured" system specification is well-known for its concise and maintainable system documentation [Hicks, 1984].

DeMarco's approach involves partitioning the system in a structured manner, using a number of tools. DeMarco's toolbox includes data flow diagrams, data dictionaries, transform descriptions (decision tables, decision trees and structured English) and data structure diagrams [DeMarco, 1979]. The high-level document, the data flow diagram, documents the elements of the information system without regard to automation or computerization (although in practice, computerized functions were forcibly concentrated). This diagram delineates the flow of information from input to output, and the processes under which the transformation takes place. Transform descriptions, the data dictionary and leveled data flow diagrams are used to support this top-level data flow diagram.

The elements of the diagram included *sources/sinks, processes, dataflows* and *files* (data repositories). DeMarco shows the usefulness of this methodology for creating a maintainable system design. There is very little vagueness in the documentation. Since it is this vagueness which creates problems with some of the other schemes for classifying system elements, data flow diagram elements could provide both a practical and concise classification scheme for which one might classify the elements of the system as risk-subjects.

The data flow diagram elements may be further reduced for our purposes. By nature, the source/sink element is external to the system under consideration, and is identified only as a reference point. The dataflow attached to this element is germane to our discussion, but the actual source/sink as a risk-subject may be eliminated as a peripheral consideration.

It is to be noticed that without an integrated database system, both the dataflows and files are documented in the data dictionary in a very similar form. DeMarco further remarks that dataflows are "data structures in motion" and files or data stores are "data structures at rest." In keeping with these views, it is possible that the elements of an information system might be further reduced for our purposes to two general categories of risk-subjects: processing elements and data-elements.

Differentiating the Process-element and the Data-element as Primary Risk-subjects

Risks which threaten processes do ultimately threaten data flows and files. It is perhaps for this reason that most of the risks do threaten most of the system elements to some degree. It is rare that a process can endure a disruption without affecting the data flowing through it. However, the difference in the nature of the risks can be explained in this manner: data which is exposed to risk without subjecting the processing elements to any exposure would be considered primarily a risk to the dataflow or file element itself. If the data was subjected to risk exposure by attacking it through the exposing of the processing element to risk, this processing element would be considered the primary risk-subject.

Data-elements as Risk-subjects

The risks we have identified are: environment, sabotage, espionage, fraud and integrity loss. Clearly all of these are data risks. But are they balanced equally in their threat to both automated and manual systems? A closer examination of each risk and its relationship directly to data files and flows now follows.

Environmental Data Risks

Smith and Lim [1984], in constructing their threat–target model, recognized that environmental risks applied equally to all system elements. No claim should be made that the environment is gentler to either manual or automated data-elements. Data can be easily destroyed in a direct manner by acts of nature in both manual and automated systems. Fire has little respect for tape *or* paper. A PTT (PSTN) switch failure will terminate voice or data communications.

Sabotage Data Risks

Automated systems. Purposeful or intentional disruption of an information system by destruction or alteration of the data is rare in automated systems. Graffiti *has* been inserted in databases and files changed by vandals, but these instances are rare. In most cases, legitimate system programs are illegally accessed in order to alter the files (e.g., file update utility program) [BBC,1984]. In other words, a lack of controls on the procedures or processes exposed the data to alteration. Thus the process is the primary risk-subject.

Manual systems. When considering the sabotage of manual information systems, it is almost always the data which is attacked. This could be because sabotage of the processing system involves human injury or murder. An example is the occupation of the U.S. Bureau of Indian Affairs headquarters in Washington, D.C. by American Indian protesters. While equipment damage did result when the protest was carried out (typewriters, etc.), it was the burning of the files which caused irreparable harm ["Wardrums," 1972]. It is important to note the data elements were directly at risk, not damaged by normal processes under improper engagement.

Espionage Data Risks

Automated systems. The risk of unauthorized access to data without process - elements also aligns itself with manual systems. Automated systems are almost always subverted in order to illegitimately access data files or flows. This may be because the information is often maintained in a form which must be converted to portable or human-decipherable form before it can be perused (e.g., from binary ASCII codes to printed alphabetic text). Thus the processing system must be violated rather than merely the data.

Manual systems. Direct espionage against the manual data element is more common. Eavesdropping by "bugging" in order to overhear human conversations, browsing through files, or copying printed documents does not involve attacking the processing system at all, merely the data repositories and flows. Witness to this vulnerability is found in a study of the confidentiality of British census data by the British Computer Society. The society stepped beyond its charge in its final recommendation: that the retention of the manual data file be "reviewed" in consideration of alternate forms of storage. The Society's working party considered the mere existence of the manual store to be a privacy threat [BCS, 1981].

Recent oil company industrial espionage cases reveal the nature of the manual system espionage risk-subject. For example, a Shell Oil Company engineer hand-copied a geological survey map worth $40 million to competitors. The investigators noted that the map had no connection with the engineer's job. The employee was not connected with the manual "processing" of the geological maps [Obbie, 1984].

Fraud Data Risks

Automated systems. Another surprising alignment can be found when data as a victim of fraud is considered. The most common "computer fraud" involves manipulation of input data, rather than the processing system. Actual involvement of programmers and analysts is comparatively rare. Wong's survey of computer fraud found fewer than 5% of U.K. cases involved unauthorized program amendments. It is important to note that 63% of the U.K. cases resulted from manipulation of input data or source documents [Wong, 1983]. Further, Wong reports that only about one quarter of the cases involve any data processing staff at all. A study by the U.S. Department of Health and Human Services reached the same conclusion: typical perpetration of fraud was by "manipulating the input data to trigger the issuance of government checks..." [Betts, 1985]. Further confirmation of this tendency is found in an analysis of 1000 computer abuse cases by SRI International. This study found 37.6% of the abuse cases resulted from direct modification of the data, while only 9.5% involved program modification [Straub and Widom, 1984]. A 1976 report by the U.S. General Accounting Office also confirms this tendency: 62% of the computer-related crimes in government resulted from fraudulent input data [Whiteside, 1978]. Thus we see that most often, the fraud is perpetrated by someone outside of the process-element (computer system), and the fraud is executed by juggling the input data-flow (data-element).

Manual systems. Manual system frauds are more often "inside" jobs, often involving a second set of records to permit juggling figures in the official books in such a manner that there is an appearance of propriety. While the incorrect data may be part of the crime, its cause was the subversion of the processing system, perhaps by the clerk or cashier. For example, a cashier may inflate "deposits in transit" to misdirect cash, covering the fraud by underfooting receipts of later days.

There is substantial evidence supporting this process-element orientation of fraud in manual systems. Parker, for example, contrasted his survey of computer-related embezzlements with "general" embezzlement cases. His analysis indicated that these manual information system frauds were centrally perpetrated by persons processing negotiable instruments. Fully 90% of the cases involved persons acting in their official functions as clerks, loan officers, bank tellers, etc. Here the human "process element" is subverted in attacking the data [Parker, 1976]. James Finch [1985] agrees: "The dishonest clerical employees only very rarely cross organizational lines and steal from functional areas to which they are not assigned. ... Most employees are limited by their skills to stealing from those parts of the system they know best."

Auditing experience also supports the data risk-subject orientation in manual frauds. Brink and Witt [1982] list fifteen most common fraudulent practices derived from experience in manual systems. Of the practices cited, twelve involve illegitimate data manipulation during normal, authorized processing:

1.   Non-recording of revenues.
2.   Withholding receivables collections.

3.   Padding payrolls.
4   Misuse of credit cards.
5.   Payment of personal expenses.
6.   Purchase kickbacks.
7.   Misuse of petty cash.
8.   Transfer of assets.
9.   Excessive allowances to customers.
10. Conflict of interest.
11. Theft of materials.
12. Misappropriation of receipts.

Some of the items on the above list may seem surprising as products of an information system fraud. Brink and Witt go on to illustrate that these frauds involve the manipulation of the information processing in "covering up" the occurrence. For example, theft of materials will often involve intentional misrequisitioning to disguise the disappearance of the items.

Brink and Witt's list does include two items which often do not involve the information system, viz., bribes and diversion of securities. Only one fraud on their list is chiefly data element oriented: falsification of disbursement documents.

Integrity Data Risks

Automated systems. Program errors can cause integrity problems, but these are not the most common cause. One reason is the nature of data transformation resulting from an erroneous program. The output data is often so *spectacularly* stupid that it commands correction [Martin, 1973]. Program testing design techniques have also vastly improved program reliability.

Integrity risks in automated systems cluster around data, both flowing and reposed. The classic conflict arises when multiple occurrences of a data item is permitted, such as in central and regional files. Problems can also develop upon interruption of a dataflow. Transactions must be protected against loss by a real-time recovery method. Even these must accept a certain degree of loss.

Manual systems. By contrast, rarely is the integrity risk to data files and flows serious in manual systems. Inconsistencies will arise in duplicate manual files, and improperly resumed processing following an interruption may cause some data loss, but these are insignificant compared with integrity errors resulting from faulty processes (e.g., math errors).

Authorities often observe that any task which can be reduced to inflexible rule-following is less accurately performed by humans [Grindley, 1975]. Much work attesting to this idea is found in systems analysis literature, such as Paul

Fitts' list of human and machine specifications (applied in the "ergonomic" division of human and computer functions) [Singleton, 1966]. It is sometimes advised to use the presence of inflexible rule-following as the impetus for the consideration of automating a manual function [Grindley and Humble, 1973]. System design methodologies are particularly keen to eliminate transcription of input data through the use of real-time source data capture techniques. Martin [1973] notes a typical improvement of an 80% error rate drop by use of point-of-action terminals on a factory shop floor.

Process-elements as Risk-subjects

The arguments above have dwelled upon those risks which cluster around data flows and files. The following discussion examines each of the risks discussed above with particular reference to the exposure of the system processes to risk.

Environment Process Risks

The environment threatens both manual and automated information system processes. Fires, floods, and windstorms can damage both computer systems and people who are using adding machines. Some environmental hazards are more severe on one system or the other, such as magnetic fields on computers, or carbon monoxide on humans. However, no argument can be advanced to claim that environment risks, as a group, cluster about any of our risk-subjects, as a group.

Sabotage Process Risks

Automated systems. While sabotage risk is most often felt to be a data threat in manual systems, it is the processing element which deserves the controls for this risk in automated systems. The easiest element to attack is the computer hardware. The SRI study cited earlier [Straub and Widom, 1984] supports this view. Under the intentional destruction class, twice as many hardware and program assaults (9.9%) were identified than were direct data assaults (4.8%). Interestingly enough, in Pollak [1983] the terrorist attacks were aimed at both computer systems and personnel — elements of the process — rather than directly toward the files or data. When Eriksson [1979] complains of the new vulnerability of society to loss of vital functions due to trivial events, it is the lack of manual processing back-ups which he inculpates. Automated process-elements are at easy risk to saboteurs in contrast to their manual alternatives or backups.

Manual systems. As argued above, manual system sabotage is more often directed toward the data itself, rather than the processing system. In those instances where manual process elements are sabotaged, they are often internally motivated rather than external. Gerald Mars [1982] studied *Cheats at Work,* and delineated jobs according to "grid" (autonomy of job control, insulation from fellows, etc.) and "group" (frequency of worker interaction, mutuality of workers, etc.). Mars' "B" group (nicknamed "donkey jobs") represents those individuals who perform manual data processing: strong grid (many rules, insulation from fellows), and weak group (no interaction with fellow workers, no group reference-frame). Mars finds these workers prone to sabotage as a form of gaining psychological control over their lives.

Espionage Process Risks

Automated systems. Hsiao *et al* [1979] discuss at length the use of the data complexity to protect the data element from wrongful access. To process the stored values, programs must know the attributes of the values, and the values must be manipulated in accordance with their types. Unauthorized access to data maintained on a computer system is most often accomplished by illegitimate access through the use of legitimate programs which manipulate the data properly. "Hacking" involves invading the computer by breaking its security protection scheme to gain access to legitimate processes. These are then used to access the data.

Eavesdropping on automated systems is possible, and worries in this arena have led to much work being done in cryptographic data communication techniques. The current encryption techniques are proving adequate for today's industrial needs. This is leading to an interesting twist in industrial espionage techniques. Davies and Price [1984], in discussing the need for data security in computer networks, explain how information can be derived from the volume of communications, rather than the content of the messages transmitted. Known as "traffic analysis" in military communications intelligence, this technique is widely applied to analyze indecipherable enemy messages [Baker *et al*, 1983; Bamford, 1982; and Alem, 1980]. Notice that as the information system moves deeper into the technology for protection, we find the risk shifting away from the data entirely and focusing on the process alone. Not even the nature of the process is scrutinized, it is *how busy* the system is being kept that compromises the organization's private information.

Manual systems. As argued earlier, the nature of manual system data lends itself more easily to direct perusal. It is more difficult to store in encrypted form, and its organization and access methods must be comprehensible. For example, if a spy can get close enough to estimate the volume of manual message traffic, the message content is probably also exposed.

Fraud Process Risks

Manual systems. The threat of fraud by attacking processes in the system draws itself along the lines of manual systems. Most frauds are revealed when the perpetrator "slips up" in processing. The data is being perverted while proceeding through an illegitimately altered process. Often fraudsters are unable to take leave or go on holiday during the period of the fraud in order to remain in control of the consistently perverted processes. Lack of segregation of duties is also a usual factor. The error detection functions which would reveal the fraud must be reduced to the perverted processing element; e.g., the fraudulent bookkeeper himself. Existing manual system audit control practice attests to these elements of manual frauds.

Automated systems. As argued above, fraud in automated systems is rarely known to pervert processes. Donn Parker [1976], in *Crime by Computer*, agrees: "A crook confronted with an unfamiliar computer or telecommunications system containing his target would have great difficulty achieving his goal without a great volume of printed information or working programs and instructions for use." The process becomes too complex to pervert. It is the input data which is manipulated illegitimately prior to processing through reliable processing elements. Parker's survey of U.S. bank embezzlements quantitatively supports his view. An analysis of 39 computer-related bank embezzlements found only 7 programmers among the perpetrators; i.e., fewer than 20% of the surveyed cases.

Additional support is found in the 1976 report by the U.S. General Accounting Office on government computer-related crime. Of the 69 cases in these files, 50 were committed by functional users, not computer personnel [Whiteside, 1978]. More recent evidence is found in a profile of computer criminals offered by the National Center for Computer Crime Data (NCCCD) in California. Preliminary results from a 1985 survey of 130 prosecutor's offices in the U.S. found only 13 of 43 defendants who were charged with computer crimes were programmers [Mayo, 1985].

Integrity Process Risks

Automated systems. Errors or omissions in data caused by faulty processing is in the realm of manual systems. Automated systems, when properly designed and tested, are known to be extremely reliable in performing calculations and thoroughly proving the data collection to be complete and intact [Martin, 1973]. Batch and hash totals, check-digits, parity checks and similar techniques are well-known. Incomplete and inaccurate data can often be prevented from entry into a system by good data validation and data entry design. An example is the data entry screen which will not permit the operator to continue until all entries have some legitimate value; e.g, NAME field is not blank.

Manual systems. Manual systems allow processing errors to regularly damage input and output data. Transcription errors abound, errors in arithmetic may remain even after some manual checks. Forms may easily be left incomplete through the oversight of a busy clerk. Documents become lost through misfiling. Even "lost in the mail" is a problem in manual mail handling processes which is rendered virtually impossible by most electronic mail systems' error handling features.

Data Risks Versus Process Risks

Sabotage and espionage are risks to both processes and data, but were shown to be most severe in manual system data flows/files and automated system processes. By contrast, fraud and integrity threaten data flows/files strongly in automated systems, and processes in manual systems. Environmental threats seem to lurk about this structure and must be considered as a thing apart ... a category of threat which is universal to all elements of the system.

Figure 5.3 illustrates the tendencies of two risks, sabotage and espionage, in

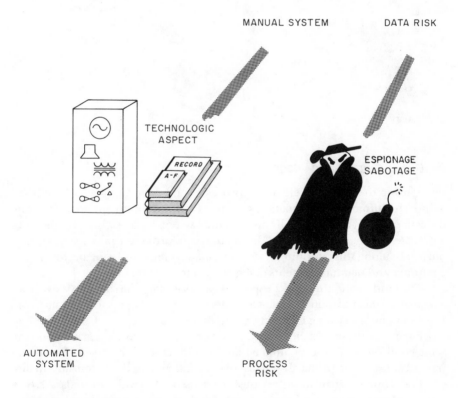

FIGURE 5.3 Sabotage and espionage

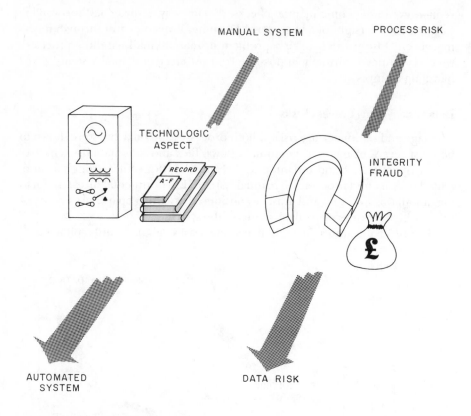

FIGURE 5.4 Fraud and integrity

relationship to the system elements, processes and data, along a continuum of manual to automated information systems. The continuum is used to illustrate the separation of a theoretically pure manual system at the right, from the pure automated system on the left. All functional information processing systems must exist along this continuum, with automated elements being performed by computer and manual elements being performed by humans.

The tendency of these risks, espionage and sabotage, has been to move from a primary concentration on data-elements in manual systems to a primary concentration on processing elements in automated systems.

Figure 5.4 illustrates the remaining two risks, fraud and integrity, along the same continuum. However, notice that the orientation is reversed. Fraud and integrity move from primarily process risks to data risks as the system automates.

Fraud and integrity have previously been associated with internal risks. Sabotage and espionage have been associated with external risks. Therefore, these models may be used at a higher plane to show that internal risks tend to cluster

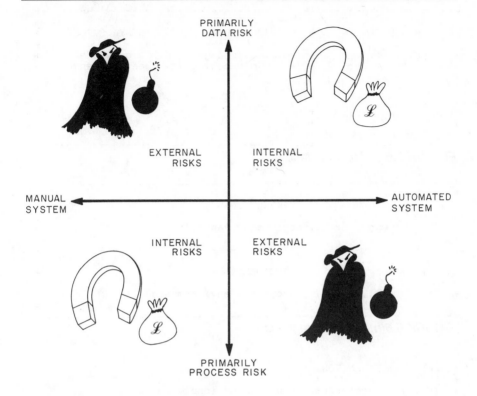

FIGURE 5.5 Internal–external risks

around *processes* in manual systems. In automated systems, internal risks tend to cluster around the *data* instead. The opposite orientation occurs with external risks, clustering around data in manual systems and processing elements in automated systems. See figure 5.5.

FORMAL HEURISTICS FOR CONTROLS IDENTIFICATION AND SELECTION

The inversion model of computer security offers a powerful aid in the solution of the selection problem during final physical control design iterations. The problem first mentioned, however, still remains: that of identifying the most appropriate control. Further, the context for application of the inversion model has not been clarified.

The two problems can both be assaulted from a single foundation of formal heuristics in controls identification and selection. Prior to a discussion of these details, however, a brief summary of five previously elucidated discoveries concerning information security and its design methodology would be useful.

```
+--------------------+----------------------+---------------------+
+                    +                      +                     +
+    MODIFICATION    +     DISCLOSURE       +    DESTRUCTION      +
+                    +                      +                     +
+    e.g., fraud,    +   e.g. espionage,    +   e.g. vandalism,   +
+        error       +       misrouting     +   environmental     +
+                    +                      +                     +
+                    +                      +                     +
+                    +                      +                     +
+                    +                      +                     +
+                    +                      +                     +
+                    +                      +                     +
+--------------------+----------------------+---------------------+
```

FIGURE 5.6(a) Threat categories

```
+------------------------------------------------------------------+
+                                                                  +
+                          INTENTIONAL                             +
+                                                                  +
+          e.g., fraud, espionage, vandalism.                      +
+                                                                  +
+------------------------------------------------------------------+
+                                                                  +
+                          ACCIDENTAL                              +
+                                                                  +
+          e.g., error, misrouting, environmental                 +
+                                                                  +
+------------------------------------------------------------------+
```

FIGURE 5.6(b) Threat categories

```
^
+   PHYSICAL DIMENSION
+
+   (Motive:  Accidental versus Intentional)
+
+
+
+
+                                              LOGICAL DIMENSION
+                  (Nature: Modification, Destruction, Disclosure
+
+
+------------------------------------------------------------------->
```

FIGURE 5.6(c) Threat categories

```
+--------------------::-------------------------------------------+
+                    ::                                           +
+                    ::           CHIEFLY EXTERNAL THREATS        +
+                    ::                 e.g. vandalism,           +
+                    ::                        espionage.         +
+                    ::                                           +
+              ::::::::::::::::::::::::                            +
+                                    ::                           +
+   CHIEFLY INTERNAL THREATS         ::                           +
+      e.g. fraud, error.            ::                           +
+                                    ::                           +
+                                    ::                           +
+------------------------------------::---------------------------+
```

FIGURE 5.6(d) Threat categories

1. Threats

Threats can be categorized in the dimension "modification–destruction–disclosure", or in the dimension "accidental–intentional", or in the dimension "logical–physical", or in the dimension "internal–external". See figure 5.6.

To a *limited* extent, these threat dimensions have common boundaries. For example, as argued above, the logical category is comprised of the modification—destruction—disclosure dimension, while the physical category overlays the intentional–accidental dimensions. The overlaying of these categories is summarized in figure 5.7.

```
         <--------------- Logical Dimension ---------------->

             MODIFICATION        DISCLOSURE          DESTRUCTION

           ::::::::::::::::::::::
           +----------------::----------------+----------------+
           +                ::                +                +
INTENTIONAL +    e.g.        ::    e.g.        +    e.g.        +
           +    fraud        ::    espionage   +    vandalism   +
    /\     +                ::                +                +
 Physical  +                ::                +                +
 Dimension +----------------::::::::::::::::::::::----------------+
    \/     +                +                ::                +
           +    e.g.        +    e.g.        ::    e.g.        +
ACCIDENTAL +    error        +    misrouting   ::    environment+
           +                +                ::                +
           +                +                ::                +
           +----------------+----------------::----------------+
                                              ::        Chiefly
              Chiefly Internal Threats        ::        External
           :::::::::::::::::::::::::::::::::::::::::::     Threats
```

FIGURE 5.7 Summarized threat categories

2. Targets

Targets have been illustrated above as having two important dimensions: Data–Process and Automated–Manual. See figure 5.8.

	MANUAL	AUTOMATED
DATA	e.g. order forms	e.g. disk files
PROCESS	e.g. decision-making	e.g. payroll

FIGURE 5.8 Target categories

3. Controls

Controls can be categorized on the dimension of logical– physical. Logical controls can be represented in an abstract logical model of an information system. See figure 5.9.

```
+-----------------------------------------------------------------+
+                                                                 +
+                         LOGICAL                                 +
+                                                                 +
+           e.g., access logging, checkpoints.                    +
+                                                                 +
+-----------------------------------------------------------------+
+                                                                 +
+                         PHYSICAL                                +
+                                                                 +
+        e.g., building access control, media backup.            +
+                                                                 +
+-----------------------------------------------------------------+
```

FIGURE 5.9 Control categories

4. Controls Design Context

The process of design, selection and specification of controls for an information system can take place in either a physical or logical context. It is an essential premise of the structured approach to controls design that the contexts are orthogonal, that is, the logical design process is isolated from the physical design process. In this manner, the physical controls are "layered" around the logical controls. See figure 5.10.

```
                              ****
     >>                     **    **                    ((
     >>>>                  **      **                   ((((
     >>>>                 **        **`                  (((((
     >>>>                **          **                  (((((
     >>>>               **            **                 (((((
     >>>>              **              **                (((((
     >>>>             **      ::::      **               (((((
     THREATS         **     ::    ::     **              (((((
     >>>>           **     ::      ::      **      INFORMATION
     >>>>          **     ::        ::      **        SYSTEM
     >>>>         **     ::          ::      **        (((((
     >>>>        **     ::            ::      **        (((((
     >>>>       **     ::              ::      **       (((((
     >>>>     **     ::                ::      **       (((((
     >>    **     ::                    ::      **       ((((
     >    **     ::                      ::      **        ((
        **     ::                        ::      **        (
       **     ::                          ::      **
      **     ::                            ::      **
     **       ::::::::::Logical Layer:::::::::::     **
     **                                              **
     ****************Physical Layer*******************
```

FIGURE 5.10 Control design layers

5. Orthogonal Control Classes

Earlier, a classification scheme of avoidance–tolerance–mitigation was employed in discussion of the effects of controls. Avoidance controls reduced risk of a threat, tolerance reduced severity of a threat, and mitigation reduced costs of recovery. While this scheme is convenient for discussing the effects of controls, notice that it has not been mentioned here under control categories. This is because the consideration of the effects of a control in isolation from the specifics of the threat or of the element being shielded is too simplistic from the standpoint of practical heuristics.

Thus, for present purposes, this scheme becomes more adequate when avoidance, tolerance, and mitigation qualities are assigned to specific threat-control-target triads, such as those employed in the SECURATE approach [Hoffman *et al*, 1978, see chapter 4]. See figure 5.11.

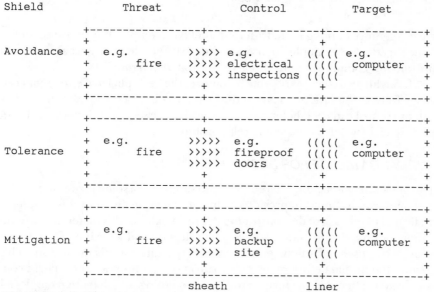

```
Shield              Threat              Control              Target

            +-----------------+-----------------+----------------+
            +                 +                 +                +
Avoidance   +   e.g.          >>>>> e.g.        ((((( e.g.       +
            +        fire      >>>>> electrical ((((( computer   +
            +                  >>>>> inspections (((((           +
            +                 +                 +                +
            +-----------------+-----------------+----------------+


            +-----------------+-----------------+----------------+
            +                 +                 +                +
            +   e.g.          >>>>> e.g.        ((((( e.g.       +
Tolerance   +        fire      >>>>> fireproof  ((((( computer   +
            +                  >>>>> doors       (((((           +
            +                 +                 +                +
            +-----------------+-----------------+----------------+


            +-----------------+-----------------+----------------+
            +                 +                 +                +
            +   e.g.          >>>>> e.g.        ((((( e.g.       +
Mitigation  +        fire      >>>>> backup     ((((( computer   +
            +                  >>>>> site        (((((           +
            +                 +                 +                +
            +-----------------+-----------------+----------------+
                              sheath            liner
```

FIGURE 5.11 Shield triads

As in the SECURATE model, the boundaries between the controls and other elements are significant and have propagative effects. Controls are Janus-faced, outward toward the threat, inward toward the target. The face of a control which is directed toward a threat (represented as a jagged line above) is labeled a "sheath", and the face which is directed toward the target (represented by a wiggly line above) is labeled a "liner".

A sheath–liner pair represents a single threat–control–target triad, and is labeled a "shield." It is the SHIELD which can be categorized as either avoid-

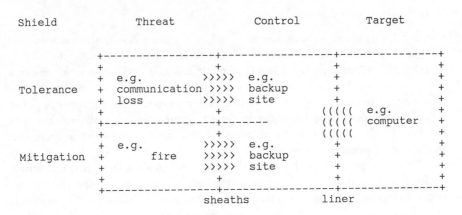

FIGURE 5.12 Overlapping liner use

ance, tolerance or mitigation. Different shields can employ the same liner or the same sheath. For example the use of a "hot" backup site to protect against both fire and lost communications threats is illustrated in figure 5.12.

It can be seen that this scheme recognizes the multiplicity of effects that can ensue from consideration of any of the elements discussed above. A threat, target, or control can each belong to its respective classes. Additionally, each can participate in widely varied shield relationships.

FORMAL DATABASE FOR DESIGN HEURISTICS

The preceding discussion offered a concise summary of some major discoveries and implications found in previous chapters. The remainder of this chapter is dedicated to the task of demonstrating the practicality of this material as a foundation for formal heuristics in control identification and selection. The context of an "expert system" will be employed as a structure for this discussion. This permits the formal definition of a database and rules for selection. These concepts can be offered in the form of the "pseudo Prolog" which is often employed by expert system shells[3]. The purpose of the discussion below is NOT the technical description of an expert system or its shell (although to some extent, this will be a side-effect). Rather, the purpose is the demonstration of the feasibility of formal expressions of these heuristics. This demonstration is felt to be as useful to decision-makers who would employ the methodology above WITH or WITHOUT expert systems support.

---

3   The examples here are consistent with either the Teknowledge "M.1" or Paperback Software "VP Expert" knowledge-based system development tools, although minor modifications would be necessary for compatibility with any specific syntax.

The five constructs listed in the section above can be translated into a Prolog-style database useful in defining rules in an expert system. However, one additional capstone structure should be added. This structure would store the confidence which can be placed in the ability of any shield to perform its function (such confidence structures are usually built into expert system shells). Thus the following database could be defined (see figure 5.13):

ELEMENT	MEANING
threat(Thname)	"Thname" is the name of some threat.
control(Cname)	"Cname" is the name of some control.
target(Tgname)	"Tgname" is the name of some target.
modification(Thname)	"Thname" is the name of some modification threat.
destruction(Thname)	"Thname" is the name of some destruction threat.
disclosure(Thname)	"Thname" is the name of some disclosure threat.
intentional(Thname)	"Thname" is the name of some intentional threat.
accidental(Thname)	"Thname" is the name of some accidental threat.
logical(Cname)	"Cname" is a logical control.
manual(Tgname)	"Tgname" is the name of some manual target.
automated(Tgname)	"Tgname" is the name of some automated target.
data(Tgname)	"Tgname" is the name of some data target.
process(Tgname)	"Tgname" is the name of some process target.
sheath(Cname,Thname)	"Cname" is a control which protects against a threat named "Thname".
liner(Cname,Tgname)	"Cname" is a control which protects a target named "Tgname".
avoidance(Sheath,Liner)	"Sheath" and "Liner" combine to provide an avoidance shield.
tolerance(Sheath,Liner)	"Sheath" and "Liner" combine to provide a tolerance shield.
mitigation(Sheath,Liner)	"Sheath" and "Liner" combine to provide a mitigation shield.

shield = avoidance;   "shield" refers to either "avoidance",
      tolerance;   "tolerance" or "mitigation" relations
      mitigation

confidence ("shield",Cnf)   "Cnf" is a confidence factor expressing
      the reliability of the shield "shield".

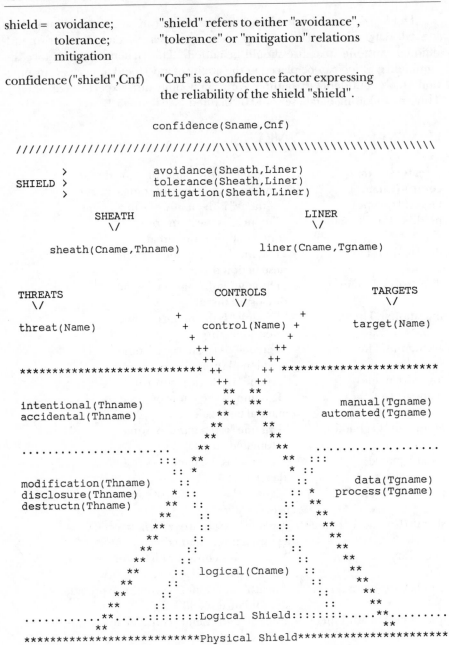

FIGURE 5.13 Expert system database model

Several interesting aspects of this database structure deserve consideration before proceeding further.

First, it is unnecessary to represent all elements discussed in the five summaries above, since two can be derived. One of the simplest rules would be: a control which is not logical must be physical:

RULE 1
  IF   control = Ctrlname AND
        NOT logical = Ctrlname
  THEN
        physical = Ctrlname

Further, internal and external threats can be *generally* implied by other categories:

RULE 2
  IF   threat = Thrtname AND
        modification = Thrtname
  THEN
        internal = Thrtname
RULE 3
  IF   threat = Thrtname AND
        disclosure = Thrtname AND
        accidental = Thrtname
  THEN
        internal = Thrtname
RULE 4
  IF   threat = Thrtname AND
        NOT internal = Thrtname
  THEN
        external = Thrtname

```
+--------------------------------------------------------------------+
+                                                                    +
+  physical(C) :- control(C),                        /*RULE 1*/      +
+                 not(logical(C)).                                   +
+  internal(T) :- modification(T).                   /*RULE 2*/      +
+  internal(T) :- disclosure(T),                     /*RULE 3*/      +
+                 accidental(T).                                     +
+  external(T) :- threat(T),                                        +
+           not(internal(T)).                        /*RULE 4*/      +
+                                                                    +
+--------------------------------------------------------------------+
```

FIGURE 5.14 Prolog implementation of physical/internal rules

The remaining database structures could not be easily simplified into rules. Certain threats could be intentional *and* accidental. Data or process elements at the boundary between automation and manual must be considered *both* automated and manual.

A further inspection of figure 5.13 can reveal another very important aspect of the model. The faces of the logical and physical aspects of the shields are different. A logical sheath faces three categories of threat: modification, destruction and disclosure. However, as motive has been cast as a physical implicandum, a physical sheath faces all SIX categories of threat. Additionally, a logical liner faces only two categories of target: process or data. However, as the automated–manual dimension is entailed by physical design, the physical liner faces a four-element taxonomy of targets.

The implication found here is that the logical design process is much simpler in the constructs with which it must deal. Further, the information security model proposed earlier is clearly illuminated as a property of the physical model of an information system.

Figure 5.15 is a short extract from a small database created to design controls for a small, desktop-computer budgeting system. Even a small function can generate a very large database.

```
-------------------------------------------------------------------
confidence
    (mitigation
        (sheath("Backup site","Windstorm"),
            liner("Backup site","Computer system unit")),0.8)
confidence
    (tolerance
        (sheath("Encryption","Vandalism"),
            liner("Encryption","Budget file")),1)
confidence
    (avoidance
        (sheath("Spot audits","Fraud"),
            liner("Spot audits","Checkbook register")),0.4)
confidence
    (tolerance
        (sheath("Data classification","Browsing"),
            liner("Data classification","Checkbook register")),0.5)
mitigation
        (sheath("Backup site","Windstorm"),
            liner("Backup site","Computer system unit"))
tolerance
        (sheath("Encryption","Vandalism"),
            liner("Encryption","Budget file"))
avoidance
        (sheath("Spot audits","Fraud"),
            liner("Spot audits","Checkbook register"))
tolerance
        (sheath("Data classification","Browsing"),
            liner("Data classification","Checkbook register"))


-------------------------------------------------------------------
```

FIGURE 5.15 (a) *Extract from controls database*

```
------------------------------------------------------------------
sheath("Backup site","Windstorm")
sheath("Encryption","Vandalism")
sheath("Spot audits","Fraud")
sheath("Data classification","Browsing")
liner("Backup site","Computer system unit")
liner("Encryption","Budget file")
liner("Spot audits","Checkbook register")
liner("Data classification","Checkbook register")
threat("Browsing")
threat("Fraud")
threat("Vandalism")
threat("Windstorm")
control("Encryption")
control("Backup site")
control("Data classification")
control("Spot audits")
target("Computer system unit")
target("Checkbook register")
target("Budget file")
logical("Spot audits")
logical("Data classification")
logical("Encryption")
modification("Fraud")
destruction("Windstorm")
destruction("Vandalism")
accidental("Windstorm")
intentional("Vandalism")
intentional("Fraud")
intentional("Browsing")
disclosure("Browsing")
data("Budget file")
data("Checkbook register")
process("Computer system unit")
manual("Checkbook register")
automated("Budget file")
automated("Computer system unit")
------------------------------------------------------------------
```

FIGURE 5.15 (b) Extract from controls database (continued)

FORMAL DESIGN HEURISTICS

It can be seen that, to a large extent, the basis for controls identification and selection can be reduced to relational data structures and a few simple rules. It remains to be seen whether it is possible to convey the principles of controls identification and selection in additional rules. In the sections below, these principles are defined according to control significance, control potential, selection of controls, and analysis of remaining exposures.

Inversion model significance. An established database permits the formal definition of rules for decisions which can be derived from the data. For example, a significant control might be defined as one which shields targets against common threats such as those shown in the discussion of the inversion security

model (see figure 5.5). For example, a rule which defines those controls shielding manual data from external threats as being significant would be:
RULE 5
> IF   external = Thrtname AND
> target = Trgtname AND
> manual = Trgtname AND
> data = Trgtname AND
> is_shield = (Thrtname,Ctrlname,Trgtname,Cnf) AND
> Cnf > 0.5

> THEN
> significant_control = Ctrlname

RULE 6
> IF   avoidance = (Thtname,Ctrlname,Trgtname,Cnf) OR
> tolerance = (Thtname,Ctrlname,Trgtname,Cnf) OR
> mitigation = (Thtname,Ctrlname,Trgtname,Cnf)

> THEN
> is_shield = (Thtname,Ctrlname,Trgtname,Cnf)

A more conversational translation of this rule would be, "A control CTRLNAME is significant if there is an external threat THRTNAME, and there is a target TRGTNAME, and TRGTNAME is both manual and data, and CTRLNAME exists as a shield relation with TRGTNAME and THRTNAME, and the confidence in that shield is acceptable." Similar rules could be written for the other three quadrants of the inversion model. (Figure 5.16 is a Prolog translation of this rule.)

```
+----------------------------------------------------------------+
+                                                                +
+   sig_ctl(C) :- external(Th),                     /*RULE 5*/   +
+                 target(Tg),                                     +
+                 manual(Tg),                                     +
+                 data(Tg),                                       +
+                 a_shield_exists(Th,C,Tg,Cnf),                   +
+                 Cnf > 0.5.                                      +
+   a_shield_exists(Th,C,Tg,Cnf) :-                 /*RULE 6*/    +
+        confidence(avoidance(sheath(C,Th),liner(_,Tg)),Cnf).    +
+   a_shield_exists(Th,C,Tg,Cnf) :-                              +
+        confidence(tolerance(sheath(C,Th),liner(_,Tg)),Cnf).    +
+   a_shield_exists(Th,C,Tg,Cnf) :-                              +
+        confidence(mitigation(sheath(C,Th),liner(_,Tg)),Cnf).   +
+                                                                +
+----------------------------------------------------------------+
```

FIGURE 5.16. Prolog implementation of inversion significance (manual data illustrated)

Plurality significance. An additional definition of a significant control could reference the plurality of targets or threats protected by a particular control. For example, a control which provided security for 30% of the possible targets would be more important than a similar control which protected a single target. A rule which defines such a control would be:

RULE 7

    IF   population = Thrtpop AND
            part_pop = (Ctrlname,Ctlthrtpop) AND
            Ctlthrtpop/Thrtpop > 0.30
    THEN
            significant_control = Ctrlname

where population(Thrtpop) equals the number of known threats. and part_pop(Ctrl,Ctlthrtpop) equals the number of known threats sheathed by control Ctrl.

Which could be read "Control CTRLNAME is a significant control if the count of the population of threats is THRTPOP, and the count of that part of the known population of threats which is shielded by CTRLNAME is CTLTHRTPOP, and the ratio is greater than 0.30." Figure 5.17 illustrates the Prolog version of this rule.[4]

```
+-------------------------------------------------------------------+
+                                                                   +
+   sig_ctl(C) :- ctlthtpop(_,T),               /*RULE 7*/   +
+               ctlthtpop(C,Tc),                             +
+               Tc/T > 0.3.                                  +
+   ctlthtpop(C,Cnt2) :- retract(threat(Tht)),               +
+               ctlthtpop(C,Cnt1),                           +
+               asserta(threat(Tht)),                        +
+               count(C,Tht,Cnt1,Cnt2).                      +
+   ctlthtpop(_,0).                                          +
+   count(C,Tht,Cnt1,Cnt2) :- sheath(C,Tht),                 +
+               Cnt2 = Cnt1 + 1.                             +
+   count(_,_,Cnt,Cnt).                                      +
+                                                                   +
+-------------------------------------------------------------------+
```

FIGURE 5.17 Prolog implementation of a plurality rule

---

4   The manner in which an expert system shell handles such problems as list manipulation or finding the population of threats often involves language keywords ("metafacts") and procedural requirements which approach the complexity of third generation programming languages. For example, finding the count of the population of threats for RULE 7 above in VP-Expert might require:

    ACTIONS
      Thrtpop = 0
      WHILEKNOWN threat = Thrtname
         Thrtpopl = Thrtpop + 1
         RESET Thrtpop
         Thrtpop = Thrtpopl
         POP threat = Thrtnamel
    END;

Identifying potential controls. Similar rules could establish the significance of controls which protect a target against more than 30% of the possible threats. More sophisticated plurality effect rules would consider the confidence factors as a measure of whether a control protects well enough to be counted.

More interesting, perhaps, are rules which select controls from the database in consideration of the possible targets and threats. Thus far, it has been shown that rules establishing the significance of controls can be formulated. But what of rules which decide which of these significant controls deserve implementation?

First, the design stage must be established in order to avoid recommending the wrong type of control for the design model at hand. Thus, controls would be selected in either a "logical" or "physical" mode. This permits the use of the heuristics in the logical design stage as well as in the physical design stage.

Second, the rule should define a comprehensive collection of controls. Thus, in the logical design, one would expect a dependable control to protect each target against every type of threat.

One approach to this process is to assert one list[5] of all controls in each type for every target. Thus if there were six targets undergoing a logical design, three lists would be constructed (modification, destruction, and disclosure) for each of the six targets. The resulting eighteen lists could be analyzed to identify those controls which are most significant, provide the greatest plurality of effect, and yet together will comprise complete coverage against all types of threat.

The rule for constructing such a list of controls for modification risks would be:

RULE 8
     IF   target = Trgtname AND
               threat = Thrtname AND
               modification = Thrtname AND
               is_shield = (Thrtname,Ctrlname,Trgtname,Cnf) AND
               Cnf > 0.5 AND
               possible_control = Ctrlist
    THEN
               possible_controls = [Ctrlname | Ctrlist]

               where is_shield is defined by RULE 6.

Which might be read "control CTRLNAME belongs to a list of possible con-

---

5   Lists are commonly illustrated within brackets with elements separated by commas: ["Fire", "Flood", "Famine"], or the first element separated from the trailing elements by a bar (|): ["Fire" | Others].

trols name CTRLIST if there is a target TRGTNAME and a threat THRTNAME and THRTNAME is a modification threat and a shield relation exists such that control CTRLNAME protects target TRGTNAME against modification threat THRTNAME with acceptable confidence." Figure 5.18 illustrates a Prolog version of this rule.

```
+------------------------------------------------------------------+
+                                                                  +
+  build_mod  :- target(Tg),                        /*RULE 8*/     +
+                start_list,                                        +
+                modification(Tht),                                +
+                a_shield_exists(Tht,Ctl,Tg,Cnf),                   +
+                Cnf > 0.5,                                         +
+                add_to_list(Ctl),fail.                            +
+  build_mod.                                                      +
+  start_list :- asserta(possible_controls([])),!.                 +
+  add_to_list(Ctl) :- possible_controls(Ctlist),                  +
+              not(member(Ctl,Ctlist)),                            +
+              retract(possible_controls(Ctlist)),                 +
+              append(Ctlist,[Ctl],Newctlist),                     +
+              asserta(possible_controls(Newctlist)),!.            +
+  add_to_list(_).                                                 +
+  member(E,[E|_]).                                                +
+  member(E,[_|Ts]) :- member(E,Ts).                               +
+  append(_,Ls,Ls).                                                +
+  append([H|Ts1],Ls2,[H|Ts3] :- append(Ts1,Ls2,Ts3).            +
+                                                                  +
+------------------------------------------------------------------+
```

FIGURE 5.18 Prolog implementation of modification list construction

Similar rules could define lists for destruction and disclosure controls. Physical analysis would require six lists for each target, considering both accidental and intentional threats in each of the three categories. Thus, lists would be constructed with controls for accidental destruction, intentional destruction, etc.

Selecting controls. Controls selection process could take place in which a recommended control set is derived from the set of possible control lists. One approach to this would involve finding any control which appears in more of the lists than any other control. This control could then be recommended, and any lists in which it appears could be deleted (since this type of risk would be shielded). The process could then repeat until all lists (and thus all controls) are exhausted. This process would require a series of rules: (9) defines a candidate control, (10) select the control for recommendation, (11) add this control to a list of recommended controls, (12) delete lists containing this control, (13) repeat this process.

RULE 9
    IF   control = Ctrlname AND
           possible_controls = Ctrlnamelist AND
           member = (Ctrlname,Ctrlnamelist)
    THEN
           candidate = Ctrlname

RULE 10
    IF   possible_controls = Ctrlnamelist AND
           member = (Ctrlname,Ctrlnamelist) AND
           (NOT make_recommend = Ctrlname) AND
           high_frequency= Ctrlname
    THEN
           make_recommend = Ctrlname
RULE 11
    IF   make_recommend = Ctrlname
    THEN
           recommended_control = Ctrlname

RULE 12
    IF   make_recommend = Ctrlname AND
           possible_controls = Ctrlistname AND
           member = (Ctrname,Ctrlistname) AND
           recommended_control = Ctrlname
    THEN
           DELETE possible_controls = Ctrlistname

RULE 13
    IF   make_recommends = Ctrlnamelist AND
           recommended_control = Ctrlname AND
           member = (Ctrlname,Ctrlnamelist) AND
           NOT candidate = Ctrlname
    THEN
           DELETE make_recommend = Ctrlname

    where high_frequency equals the name of the control which appears
        in more of the possible_controls lists than any other control
        (a procedural counter)

    RULE 9 defines a candidate control as any control in the list of possible controls. This definition is required by RULE 13 which forces the inference engine to continue to recommend controls as long as possible control lists remain.

RULES 9 and 13 are complications for expert system shells but are easily implemented with recursion in Prolog (RULE 9 is not even necessary).

RULE 10 reads, "If there are existing lists of possible controls and a control is not presently being recommended, recommend the control of highest frequency."

RULE 11 reads, "If a control is being recommended and it is not already a recommended control, then make this a recommended control."

RULE 12 reads, "If a control is being recommended, and it is a member of a list of possible controls, then delete that list of possible controls."

```
make_rec :- high_freq(C,_),                        /*RULE 10*/
            add_rec(C),
            remove_list(C),
            make_rec,!.                             /*RULE 13*/
make_rec.
remove_list(C) :-  possible_controls(Cs),
                   member(C,Cs),
                   retract(possible_controls(Cs)),
                   remove_list(C).
remove_list(_).
add_rec(_) :- not(recommend_ctl_list(_)),          /*RULE 11*/
              asserta(recommend_ctl_list([])),fail.
add_rec(C) :- recommend_ctl_list(Cs),
              not(member(C,Cs)),
              retract(recommend_ctl_list(Cs)),
              append(Cs,[C],Newcs),
              asserta(recommend_ctl_list(Newcs)).
add_rec(_).

/*---(Remainder of code finds high frequency control)---*/

high_freq(_,_) :- retract(possible_controls([])),fail.
high_freq(_,_) :- not(possible_controls(_)),!,fail.
high_freq(C2,N2) :- retract(control(C)),
                    high_freq(C1,N1),
                    asserta(control(C)),
                    number_of_lists(C,N),
                    highest(C,N,C1,N1,C2,N2),!.
high_freq(_,0).
highest(_,N,C1,N1,C1,N1) :- N1 > N,!.
highest(C,N,_,_,C,N).
number_of_lists(C,Cnt1) :- retract(possible_controls(Ps)),
                number_of_lists(C,Cnt2),
                count1(Cnt1,Cnt2,C,Ps),
                asserta(possible_controls(Ps)).
number_of_lists(_,0).
count1(Cnt,Cnt2,C,Cs) :- member(C,Cs),
                Cnt = Cnt2 + 1.
count1(Cnt,Cnt,_,_).
```

FIGURE 5.19 Prolog implementation of control selection

RULE 13 reads, "If a control is being recommended, and it is no longer a candidate control, delete it as a recommendation." This rule eliminates the further consideration of any control whose original lists have all been deleted, and forces the rules to consider further high frequency controls under RULE 10.

The rule base described above can now be adjusted to select significant controls FIRST, and then complete the control list with those less significant controls necessary to provide comprehensive coverage against all threat types. For example, RULE 8 described above could be modified to execute differently upon a second "pass" at the database.

RULE 8
    IF   significant_recommended = yes AND
             target = Trgtname AND
             threat = Thrtname AND
             modification = Thrtname AND
             is_shield = (Thrtname,Ctrlname,Trgtname,Cnf) AND
             Cnf > 0.5
             possible_controls = Ctrlist
    THEN
             possible_controls = [Ctrlname I Ctrlist]

RULE 8A
    IF   NOT(significant_recommended = yes) AND
             target = Trgtname AND
             threat = Thrtname) AND
             modification= Thrtname AND
             is_shield(Thrtname,Ctrlname,Trgtname,Cnf) AND
             Cnf 0.5,
             significant_control(Ctrlname)
             and possible_controls = Ctrlist
    THEN
             possible_controls = [Ctrlname I Ctrlist]

where significant_recommended is a procedural setting which indicates an execution of the recommendation rules.

Now RULE 8 would not be applied until after RULE 8A had been used in the construction of the possible controls list. The two rules are similar, except that RULE 8A only considers those *significant* controls that otherwise meet the requirements of RULE 8. The order of application of rules is a procedural problem handled differently by different systems. Figure 5.20 depicts a Prolog ver-

```
+-----------------------------------------------------------------+
+                                                                 +
+   build_mod2 :- target(Tg),                      /*RULE 8A*/    +
+                 start_list,                                      +
+                 modification(Tht),                               +
+                 a_shield_exists(Tht,Ctl,Tg,Cnf),                 +
+                 Cnf > 0.5,                                       +
+                 sig_ctl(Ctl),                                    +
+                 add_to_list(Ctl),fail.                           +
+   build_mod2.                                                    +
+                                                                 +
+-----------------------------------------------------------------+
```

FIGURE 5.20 Prolog implementation of significant recommendtion construction priority (only modification shown).

sion of RULE 8A, and Figure 5.21 illustrates how the sequencing of RULE 8A and RULE 8 can be enforced.

```
+-----------------------------------------------------------------+
+                                                                 +
+   recommend_ctls :- build_mod2,   /* Recommend Significant */   +
+                     build_des2,    /* and effective controls*/  +
+                     build_dis2,    /* of all three types    */  +
+                     make_rec,                                    +
+                     build_mod,     /* Recommend additional  */  +
+                     build_des,     /* effective controls    */  +
+                     build_dis,     /* all types if required */  +
+                     make_rec.                                    +
+                                                                 +
+-----------------------------------------------------------------+
```

FIGURE 5.21 Prolog implementation of logical recommend rule

Exposure analysis. Finally, while these and other similar rules can suggest the best candidate controls for different classes and categories, the eventual control set will still be incomplete. This is because, during physical controls design, the designer must consider specific threats within the different categories. For example, both fire and earthquake would be classified as accidental destruction threats, and rubber shock-mounting and halon fire control systems are two very different controls which would compete for recommendation from the same list. This does not invalidate the approach above, since a recommendation for the most significant and frequently useful control is certainly still valid. But this does mean that there will be physical exposures remaining after the first set of recommendations. There are two possible solutions to this problem.

First, the recommended controls can be removed from the controls database temporarily, and a complete second pass through the recommendation process could be made. This process would recommend a second "layer" of controls, independent and supportive of the first layer; yet probably the most significant and important controls excluded from the first recommendation.

Second, an exposure analysis can be conducted by which defined rules are applied to all the possible threats in the database to determine if any are ignored

by the recommended controls. Such an exposure analysis can be defined as in
RULE 14 and RULE 15 below:

RULE 14

    IF   recommended_control = Ctrlname AND
              threat = Thrtname AND
              target = Trgtname AND
              shield_exists = (Thrtname,Ctlname,Trgtname,Cnf) AND
              Cnf > 0.5
    THEN
              protected = (Thrtname,Trgtname)

RULE 15

    IF   threat = Thrtname AND
              target = Trgtname AND
              NOT protected = (Thrtname,Trgtname)
    THEN
              exposure = (Thrtname,Trgtname)

RULE 14 might read, "A target TRGTNAME is protected against a threat
THRTNAME if there is a recommended control CTRLNAME and a shield relation exists with TRGTNAME, THRTNAME and the control CTLNAME is
among the recommended controls."

```
+------------------------------------------------------------------+
+                                                                  +
+  covered(Th,Tg) :- recommend_ctl_list(Cs),        /*RULE 14*/    +
+                    control(C),                                   +
+                    member(C,Cs),                                 +
+                    a_shield_exists(Th,C,Tg,Cnf),                 +
+                    Cnf > 0.5.                                    +
+  exposed(Th,Tg) :- not(covered(Th,Tg)).           /*RULE 15*/    +
+                                                                  +
+------------------------------------------------------------------+
```

FIGURE 5.22 Prolog implementation of exposure/covered rule

RULE 15 might read, "A target TRGTNAME is exposed to a threat
THRTNAME if it is not protected against THRTNAME."

Rules can then be defined which suggest any specific controls needed to
eliminate the exposure. RULE 16 identifies significant controls for an exposure, and RULE 17 adds any other effective controls.

RULE 16

    IF   exposure = (Thrtname,Trgtname) AND
              control = Ctrlname AND
              shield_exists = (Thrtname,Ctrlname,Trgtname,Cnf) AND
              Cnf > 0.5 AND
              significant_control = Ctrlname

THEN
        specific_recommend_control = (Thrtname,Ctrlname,Trgtname)

RULE 17
    IF   exposure = (Thrtname,Trgtname) AND
           control = Ctrlname AND
           shield_exists = (Thrtname,Ctrlname,Trgtname,Cnf) AND
           Cnf > 0.5 AND
           NOT specific_recommend_control =
            (Thrtname,Ctrlname,Trgtname)
    THEN
        specific_recommend_control = (Thrtname,Ctrlname,Trgtname)

RULE 16 might read, "A control CTRLNAME is specifically recommended in protecting the target TRGTNAME against the threat THRTNAME if a shield relation exists between THRTNAME, CTRLNAME, and TRGTNAME, the confidence in the shield is adequate, and CTRLNAME is a significant control."

```
+------------------------------------------------------------------+
+                                                                  +
+  spec_recommend(Tht,C,Tgt,Cnf) :-                                +
+               exposed(Tht,Tgt),                    /*RULE 16*/   +
+               a_shield_exists(Tht,C,Tgt,Cnf),                    +
+               recommend_ctl_list(Cs),                            +
+               not(member(C,Cs)),                                 +
+               Cnf > 0.5,                                         +
+               sig_ctl(C),!.                                      +
+  spec_recommend(Tht,C,Tgt,Cnf) :-                                +
+               exposed(Tht,Tgt),                    /*RULE 17*/   +
+               a_shield_exists(Tht,C,Tgt,Cnf),                    +
+               recommend_ctl_list(Cs),                            +
+               not(member(C,Cs)),                                 +
+               Cnf > 0.5,!.                                       +
+  spec_recommend(Tht,C,Tgt,Cnf) :- exposed(Tht,Tgt),             +
+               a_shield_exists(Tht,C,Tgt,Cnf),      /*RULE 17A*/  +
+               recommend_ctl_list(Cs),                            +
+               not(member(C,Cs)),!.                               +
+  spec_recommend(Tht,C,Tgt,0) :- exposed(Tht,Tgt),               +
+               C = "No known controls",!.           /*RULE 17B*/  +
+                                                                  +
+------------------------------------------------------------------+
```

FIGURE 5.23 Prolog implementation of specific control rules

RULE 17 is almost the same, except it specifies the adequate, but insignificant controls. The ordering of the two rules assures that the significant controls precede any insignificant controls during any reference to specific controls.

Figure 5.23 lists a possible Prolog implementation of rules 16 and 17. This version includes additional rules which recommend less-effective controls (RULE 17A) and note unprotected exposures (RULE 17B). Because these

```
+-----------------------------------------------------------------+
+                                                                 +
+   analyze :- recommend_ctls,                                    +
+              print_recommends,                                  +
+              check_coverage.                                    +
+   print_recommends :- nl,                                       +
+              write("The following controls are recommended:"),  +
+              recommend_ctl_list(Clist),                         +
+              nl,write(Clist).                                   +
+   check_coverage :- target(Tgt),                                +
+              threat(Tht),                                       +
+              spec_recommend(Tht,C,Tgt,Cnf),nl,nl,               +
+              write("Exposure remains of ",Tgt," to ",Tht),nl,   +
+              write("Recommendation: ",C," CNF ",Cnf),fail.      +
+   check_coverage.                                               +
+                                                                 +
+-----------------------------------------------------------------+
```

FIGURE 5.24 Prolog implementation of analysis rules

rules will recommend poorer controls when nothing better in known, the confidence factor CNF is included in the specific-recommend-control relation .

Organizing the expert system. Figure 5.24 lists a Prolog program which would perform an analysis by utilizing the rules defined earlier. Figure 5.25 illustrates a sample of the output from the program. The full listing of this "tiny" Prolog version of the expert system will also be found in the appendix.

While the preceding discussion illustrates the practicality of the methods and models discussed above in their usage as heuristics for security decision making, it must be recognized that the composite illustration is still too simple for professional application. Many improvements must be added:

- Logical and physical models in isolation should be handled in the analysis.[6]
- The definition of an adequate control (Cnf > 0.5 above) should be adjustable depending on the target and the specific application.
- Effectiveness of multiple controls against an exposure should be handled through an accumulation of their non-overlapping coverage. This overlap factor must be adjustable.
- The system should optionally consider different control types individually, i.e., avoidance, mitigation, and tolerance.
- Percentage of population of threats or targets deemed to be "significant" (0.30 above) should be adjustable.
- Recommendations and exposure analysis would have to be interactive to allow an expert to consider a set of recommendations and remaining exposures repeatedly.

---

6   These are easily isolated as different databases during the two design phases; a merged database capability would permit a more effective exposure study.

```
+--------------------------------------------------------------------+
+                                                                    +
+  The following controls are recommended:                           +
+                                                                    +
+  ["Access logging",                                                +
+   "Separation of duties",                                          +
+   "Password access control",                                       +
+   "Perimeter fencing",                                             +
+   "Separation of duties",                                          +
+   "Encryption",                                                    +
+   "Audit trail report"]                                            +
+                                                                    +
+  Exposure remains of Computer system unit to Water damage          +
+  Recommendation: Dust covers CNF 0.8                               +
+                                                                    +
+  Exposure remains of Filing cabinets to Fire                       +
+  Recommendation: Fire alarm system CNF 0.8                         +
+                                                                    +
+  Exposure remains of Filing cabinets to Misrouting                 +
+  Recommendation: No known controls CNF 0                           +
+                                                                    +
+  Exposure remains of Filing cabinets to Arithmetic error           +
+  Recommendation: No known controls CNF 0                           +
+                                                                    +
+  Exposure remains of Filing cabinets to Power spikes               +
+  Recommendation: No known controls CNF 0                           +
+                                                                    +
+  Exposure remains of Filing cabinets to Dust                       +
+  Recommendation: No known controls CNF 0                           +
+                                                                    +
+  Exposure remains of Personnel to Fraud                            +
+  Recommendation: Background investigations CNF 0.7                 +
+                                                                    +
+  Exposure remains of Floppy diskettes to Fire                      +
+  Recommendation: Fire alarm system CNF 0.7                         +
+                                                                    +
+  Exposure remains of Floppy diskettes to Misrouting                +
+  Recommendation: Data classification CNF 0.9                       +
+                                                                    +
+  Exposure remains of Checkbook register to Fire                    +
+  Recommendation: Fire alarm system CNF 0.5                         +
+                                                                    +
+  Exposure remains of Checkbook register to Misrouting              +
+  Recommendation: No known controls CNF 0                           +
+                                                                    +
+  Exposure remains of Checkbook register to Power spikes            +
+  Recommendation: No known controls CNF 0                           +
+                                                                    +
+--------------------------------------------------------------------+
```

FIGURE 5.25 Report produced by Prolog rules (partial)

- "Because" explanations must be stored and available for recommendations and exposures.
- An editor is required for the database which permits the entry or modification of the original data, and the removal of targets, threats or controls which are inappropriate in a particular application.
- Confidence factors should be added to the rules, perhaps most especially to the significance rules.

SUMMARY

It has been shown that a model can be developed which is based on the more dynamic aspects of information systems security. This model can be applied practically in selecting controls, as suggested by the discussion of controls selection heuristics.

Tendencies can be discovered in creating a dynamic security model for information systems and may be applied as a heuristic aid in translating the logical design into a physical design. DeMarco advises experimentation with various man–machine boundary alternatives in identifying the most feasible physical system. The selection of logical controls can be allowed to follow this boundary according the tendencies of risk sources and subjects. Consider the general guidelines below:

"Machine" processes. Implement controls oriented toward external risks, particularly sabotage and espionage.

"Human" processes. Implement controls oriented toward internal risks, particularly fraud and integrity problems.

"Machine" data. Implement controls oriented toward internal risks, particularly fraud and integrity problems.

"Human" data. Implement controls oriented toward external risks, particularly sabotage and espionage.

These general guidelines can be applied as aids in the identification and selection of appropriate controls for implementation. If a competent designer possesses an awareness of the nature of the threat–control–target dynamics, and is cognizant of both the sensitivity of the data or process and the strength of the threat, these general guidelines and the specific rules above can be interpretatively applied in the controls identification process. The designer is thus enabled to take a more hermeneutic approach to controls selection, rather than the empiric risk analysis approach.

As an alternative, however, the database and rules can be implemented as an expert system to permit a more empirical approach which observes the principles suggested here. In this manner, the rules could be applied during the logical design phase to identify controls for use in the logical model security. During the physical design phase, the rules are not only useful as an aid to physical controls identification, but may additionally supplant risk analysis as the primary tool available in both logical and physical control selection decisions.

An example of the expert system usage in the mode of logical controls identification and selection will be found in the case study in the appendix. In addition, the text describes the rationale underlying the expert system recommendations using the hermeneutic guidelines suggested above.

Chapters 4 and 5 have provided insight into the complex problems which face computer security, and how concepts adapted from general information systems analysis and design may provide useful alternatives to present techniques. But systems analysis, like computer science, may be perceived to be too narrow in its perspective of the problem. In the following chapter, an even broader viewpoint is presented.

REFERENCES

Ahituv, N. and Neumann, S. *Principles of Information Systems for Management.* Dubuque: Brown, 1982.

Alem, J-P. *L'espionnage et le contre-espionage.* Paris: Presses Universitaires de France, 1980.

AFIPS (American Federation of Information Processing Societies). *Security: Checklist for Computer CenterSelf-Audits.* Arlington, Va: AFIPS Press, 1979.

Baker, D.; Friedman, R. and Miller, D. *Intelligence Warfare.*New York: Crescent Books, 1983.

Bamford, J., *The Puzzle Palace.* Boston: Houghton Mifflin, 1982.

Batt, R. "White collar crime: the enemy within," *Computerworld* **17** (26 Dec 1983): pp. 51–52.

BBC, "Spies in the Wires," *Horizon*, BBC2, 30 Jan 1984.

BCS, (The British Computer Society). *1981 Census of* Population: Confidentiality and Computing. Cmnd 8201. London: HMSO, March, 1981.

Betts, M. "Federal DP crooks profiled," *Computerworld* **19** (1 June 1985): p. 2.

Brabb, G. and McKean, G. *Business Data Processing.* Boston: Houghton Mifflin, 1982.

Brink, V. and Witt, H. *Modern Internal Auditing: Appraising Operations and Controls.* New York: J. Wiley, 1982.

Checkland, P. *Systems Theory, Systems Practice.* Chichester: J. Wiley, 1981.

"Computer security seminar," *Computer Crime Digest* (Oct, 1984): p. 6.

Davies, D. and Price, W. *Security for Computer Networks.* Chichester: John Wiley, 1984.

Deitel, H. *An Introduction to Operating Systems.* Reading, Mass: Addison-Wesley, 1983.

DeMarco, T. *Structured Analysis and System Specification.* New York: Yourdon, 1979.

Eriksson, A. "The vulnerability of society." *Transnational Data Regulations: The Realities.* Wellesley, Mass: Online Conferences Ltd, 1979.

Finch, J. "Security of office systems," *IFIPS Working Conference on Office Systems*, Helsinki, 30 Sept, 1985.

FitzGerald, J.; FitzGerald, A. and Stallings, W. *Fundamentals of Systems Analysis*. New York: J. Wiley, 1981.

Gill, P. "Electronic offices please personnel, poll shows," *Information System News* (16 May, 1983): pp. 74, 77.

Grindley, K. *Systematics: A New Approach to Systems Analysis*. London: McGraw Hill, 1975.

Grindley, K. and Humble, J. *The Effective Computer*. London: McGraw Hill, 1973.

Harre, R. *The Philosophies of Science, An Introductory Survey*. London: Oxford Univ. Press, 1972.

Hempel, C. *Aspects of Scientific Explanation*. Toronto: Collier MacMillian, 1965.

Hicks, J. *Management Information Systems: A User Perspective*. St. Paul: West, 1984.

Hoffman, L.; Michelman, E. and Clements, D. "SECURATE — Security evaluation and analysis using fuzzy metrics", *AFIPS National Computer Conference Proceedings* **47**, 1978.

Hsiao, D.; Kerr, D. and Madnick, S. *Computer Security*. New York: Academic Press, 1979.

IBM, *"Secure Automated Facilities Environment" Study 3*. Part 2 (May, 1972).

Kennedy, W.; Baker, D.; Friedman, R. and Miller, D. *Intelligence Warfare: Today's Advanced Technology Conflict*. New York: Crescent, 1983.

Kroenke, D. *Business Computer Systems: An Introduction*. Santa Cruz: Mitchell, 1984.

Lee, J.; Segal, G. and Steir, R. "Positive alternatives: a report on an ACM panel on hacking," *Communications of the* ACM **29** (April, 1986): pp. 297–299.

Mars, G. *Cheats at Work*. London: Allen and Unwin, 1982.

Martin, J. *Security, Accuracy and Privacy in Computer Systems*. Englewood Cliffs: Prentice Hall, 1973.

Mayo, K. "Fingering data thieves," *Business Computer Systems* **4** (Nov, 1985): pp. 11–12.

Murach, M. *Business Data Processing*. Chicago: SRA, 1980.

M.1 Reference Manual. Palo Alto, Calif: Teknowledge, Inc. 1986.

NBS (National Bureau of Standards). "Guidelines for Automatic Data Processing Risk Analysis," Federal Information Processing Standards Publication 65. Washington: US Department of Commerce, 1 Aug, 1979.

Obbie, M. "Engineer indicted for theft of oil map." *Houston Post*, 11 Apr 1984.

Parker, D. *Computer Security Management*. Reston: Reston Publishing Co., 1981.

Parker, D. *Crime by Computer*. New York: Chas Scribners Sons, 1976.

Parker, C. *Understanding Computers and Data Processing: Today and Tomorrow*. New York: Holt, Rinehart and Winston, 1984.

Pollak, R. "Implications of international terrorism on security of information systems." *Proceedings of IEEE INFOCOM 1983*. New York: IEEE, 1983.

Scherer, M. "Unsafe software — the missing security perspective," *Computer Security Journal* (Summer, 1984).

Singleton, W.T. "Current trends toward systems design." Ergonomics for Industry **12**. London: Ministry of Technology, August, 1966.

Smith, S. and Lim, J. "An automated method for assessing the effectiveness of computer security safeguards," in *Computer Security: A Global Challenge* edited by J. Finch and E. Dougall. Amsterdam: North-Holland, 1984, pp. 321–328.

Straub, D. and Widom, C. "Deviancy by bits and bytes: computer abusers and control measures," in *Computer Security: A Global Challenge* edited by J. Finch and E. Dougall. Amsterdam: North-Holland, 1984, pp. 431–442.

Turbo Prolog Owner's Handbook. Scotts Valley, Calif: Borland International, Inc. 1986.

VP-Expert Rule-Based Expert System Development Tool. Berkeley, Calif: Paperback Software International, 1987.

"Wardrums across the Potomac," *Newsweek* (18 April, 1972): p. 14.

Whiteside, T. *Computer Capers: Tales of Electronic Thievery, Embezzlement and Fraud.* Toronto: Fitzhenry and Whiteside, 1978.

Wong, K. "DP fraud: a revealing look at the criminal mind." *Computing* 11 (19 May 1983)

Wong, K. *Risk Analysis and Control.* Manchester: National Computer Centre, 1977.

Yourdon, E. and Constantine, L. *Structured Design.* Englewood Cliffs: Prentice-Hall, 1979.

Chapter 6

Reflecting on the importance of the preceding chapter on selecting controls, it would be tempting to conclude that the significance of the model and its heuristics lies in their practical prospects of providing simplification in a very complex process. However, something fundamentally more important can be learned from the experience. The entire controls selection process suggested above is conducted from the perspective of the interaction between controls, targets and threats. The overall methodology proposed enforces consideration of complete logical control sets before physical design is begun. Both of these attributes serve to reduce dependence on risk analysis as a controls selection process.

"What is the Role of Information Systems Security?"

Before addressing this topic, it should be pointed out that this innocuous question conceals a sinister implication. The mere use of the term "role" suggests that the application of information systems security is an entity quite discrete from its nature, like the personality of the thespian as discriminated from their character portrayal. To draw the theatrical analogy further, the character portrayal is a temporary and changeable state. The character exists without the actor and the actor exists without the character. It would seem from the preceding chapters that information systems security exists without information systems, but should information systems exist without security? Naturally this is possible, but it is suggested that one of the strongest pitfalls of security design is the fact that the conceptual isolation of security from its subject information systems has become such a severe premise. It entails the assured preexistence of an information system before its security.

For example, the expert system described in the previous chapter, while founded on an alternate philosophy, is not, in its functional technology, dissimilar to such previous work as SECURATE or the Carroll and MacIver system described in chapter 4. Carroll and MacIver [1984], in particular, discovered a feasibility challenge in the acquisition of an adequate database to effectively analyze an information system. Does this problem confront the system above?

No. The reason that this problem does not confront this system lies in the methodological context in which the system is presented. Further, the philosophical context underlying the methodology is an essence of this reasoning. Philosophically, the design of the safety of the information system is NOT a thing to be considered apart from its functional design. Insecure elements are not permitted to exist. Methodologically, this appears in the security structures which are required in the definition of every logical or physical component of the system. The heuristic tool presented above is NOT intended to analyze a complete information system (which indeed would require an enormous database). Rather, the rules and database are easily applied (during the design process) in selecting controls for the small components of the overall information system. The scale should never be much larger than the example suggested in the appendix.

In civil engineering, the design of the safety of a bridge would never be an afterthought. Structural safety is a consideration in every pier, every span, every member, and every bolt. This is because the engineer recognizes that the bridge is destined to become an essential structure of the community it serves. Human life, as well as the investment of the state, is a consequence of the design. Historically, such dramatic concerns have not been a part of information systems design. But as our society becomes more dependent on these systems, the body of opinion is undergoing a metamorphosis.

The original body of opinion on the security components of information systems consisted of the system owners and the designers. In the past decade, other groups have developed interests (or "stakes") in the security attributes of information systems and begun to influence the arena. These stake-holder groups include users, clients, human entities and the state [Baskerville, 1987].

THE OWNER

The system owner is the original stake-holder in the security of information systems. The perspective of the system owner is usually assumed in security management technical studies. From this view, risk analysis is one of the critical decision making tools with regard to computer security. One of the most important aspects of the preceding chapter is considered to be the reduced requirement for risk analysis in selecting controls for implementation. This is because risk analysis is so strongly founded on the concept of insecure AND feasible information systems. The risk analysis technique is frequently attacked, yet remains embedded in the practitioner's repertoire.

Risk Analysis: A Management Problem

The problem of probability. Risk analysis is an exercise in guesswork. The approach is to provide the best scientific structure in which to couch the guesswork. Almost all variations of the technique have been challenged on their approach to the original quantification of threat probabilities and costs. For example in Saltmarsh and Browne's [1983] extensive review, advantages and disadvantages of the various approaches are listed. Consider their comments on comparative disadvantages:

Courtney's Method:

> "Insofar as orders of magnitude are utilized, little credence can be placed in the far ends of the scales; in other words, a great difference exists between $100,000 and $1,000,000, for example."

CITIBANK Method:

> "Results are inexact at best, if not merely guesses."

Relative–Impact Measure (RIM) Method:
> "RIM is only useful in a relative sense. it can only be compared with other RIM values."

Jerry Fitzgerald and Associates Method:

> "Demands much guesswork. Is susceptible to 'garbage in, garbage out'."

Perhaps the last comment summarizes the danger most clearly. If the original estimations are invalid, then the probability arithmetic which follows these is complete nonsense. Yet, little work has been attempted in validating the use of estimated "probability of threat occurrence" or "cost of threat occurrence". The use of experts, committees or Delphi techniques is sometimes advocated [Parker, 1981]; however, it would be extraordinarily difficult to establish the usual accuracy of the estimations. Too many variables exist, such as duration of consideration, decision environment, skill and experience of estimators, and number of estimators.

Therefore, it can be seen that risk analysis is a technique which, while widely accepted, is commonly applied in an environment devoid of any strong feedback as to the success of its use. Knowledge as to the effectiveness of this approach is too easily buried beneath the oppressing dependence on good or bad "luck." For example, the probability of a particular data center's damage owing to a major civil disruption (e.g., rioting) could be estimated to be "once in 500 years." But, as riot damage to data centers is a dramatically uncommon threat, such an estimation is very arbitrary. However, suppose controls were rejected under this evaluation. If the disaster should strike the following month, the inclination would be to shrug off the loss due to lack of substantial controls as "bad luck."[1] Rather than admit that the controls selection process is flawed,

---

1 Certainly one might factor in such concepts as the elapsed time since the last major riot, but nothing eliminates the pure "bad luck" of the occurrence of two major riots 30 days apart. "Good luck" could be said to have the opposite effect.

"luck" allows risk analysis to retain its credibility as a vehicle for properly reaching a "scientific" decision. Thus, the impact of strong negative feedback as to the effectiveness of this technique is virtually eliminated.

The problem of crisis design environments. The inability to establish feedback for the effectiveness of a controls design and specification method permeates the entire spectrum of current computer security practice. Typically, computer security is a low priority of management until something awful occurs [O'Mara, 1985]. Then (appropriately) a highly visible effort is made to improve the controls: risk analysis, security consultants, security hardware, security software, etc. Slowly, the problem moves from central focus to the periphery and frequently, further to oblivion. What remains, like the echo from the abrupt conclusion of a military band, are some controls, some security hardware, some security software, an operationally more complex system and some interesting statistical fantasies. Often, however, the system functioned perfectly for years without these "improvements." Unless the disaster reoccurs, management never really receives effective feedback to indicate that the effort has actually provided security. Indeed, Providence may be merely providing "good luck."

It can be seen, therefore, that the effectiveness of techniques for designing computer security is a bit more difficult to establish than that of techniques for designing computer systems. There is a suspicion that there may be some questionable practices in common use, such as the checklist approaches discussed in chapter 4. The result may be that ineffective control designs are encumbering existing information systems with unnecessary (and perhaps ruinous) modifications. However, the cloudy feedback prevents effective measurement of the success or necessity of the controls.

The problem of profitability. Cost justification of new information systems is often a difficult process. DeMarco's design methodology, for example, deftly skirts this crucial element by declaring it to be subordinate to the particular organization's customary tactics [DeMarco, 1979]. The "return on investment" for improved information systems sometimes involves quantified estimates at least as dubious as those involved in risk analysis. Company directors are appropriately guided by their obligation to shareholder profitability. Security controls, such as access control software, may fare badly in the comparative light of "return on investment," particularly when presented as an "option" on the proposed system which may be added later.

When a proposed information system is dramatically infeasible if controls were in place, consideration of the system without the required controls automatically ensues. Rather than recognizing that the system is ultimately infeasible, it is considered feasible in light of certain "risks." Risk analysis can be applied in statistically reducing the importance of these controls.

The ultimate result may be that management will proceed with the creation of an unsafe information system without truly understanding the implications of the risks involved in the investment. John Newton points out that many organizations are becoming operationally dependent on complex, interdependent information systems; e.g., automated tellers (ATMs) or point-of-sale (POS) terminals. This dependence renders the continual availability of the system elements as essential to the survival of the organization. For example, the loss of a POS system for a week might bankrupt the organization:

> "Risk analysis techniques (financial costs of event multiplied by probability of event equals exposure) are not appropriate where business survival is at issue. This point can be illustrated by looking at the financial cost of losing an entire enterprise valued at, say, $1 billion as the result of an event whose probability of occurrence is 10 million to 1 — an exposure of $100." [Newton, 1985]

In the costs dimension of the risk analysis methods, only the direct implementation and operation costs are usually considered. As was shown in chapter 3, this is an artificially narrow view of the true cost of controls, ignoring interference costs, flexibility and maintenance costs, and the costs associated with system lifespan curtailment.

Both major dimensions of the risk analysis approach can be subjected to strong criticism, yet this technique persists as the major selection criterion for computer security controls in industry.

Risk Analysis: A True Champion of Management.

Is it to be concluded from the foregoing discussion that problems with information systems' security can be directly traced to avaricious, narrow-sighted managers and incompetent, obsequious systems analysts? No; to narrowly accept the harsh criticism above without considering the practical foundations of the problems facing management would be unforgivable.

First, management cannot ignore its essential loyalty to its ownership. Implementation of unnecessary, expensive controls without due investigation would be an incompetent dissipation of the resources with which management is entrusted.

Second, the earliest applications of automated information systems were fragmented functions buried deep within individual organizations. The importance of those systems was imperceptible outside of the organization. Thus, if the organization chose to implement a dangerous system, it was certainly its prerogative.

Third, the genesis of information system design was an arena of critically forecasted financial benefits contrasted with major initial investments. It was an arena filled with the glory of management science. There were disasters, but there were many triumphs. The roots of risk analysis are firmly planted in management science. It offers an algebra that management understands, relates to, and can easily adopt as a basis for decision making. However questionable the results, risk analysis offers a sharp foundation for decision making, AND THERE IS PRESENTLY LITTLE TO OFFER MANAGEMENT AS A PRACTICAL ALTERNATIVE.

Even the design methodology offered above can only be said to reduce the importance of risk analysis by embedding controls structures deep in the logical model of the information system. During the final practical design, expensive physical controls are liable to face the scrutiny of probability arithmetic.

Thus, everyone currently involved with information security winces when risk analysis is questioned. Its shortcomings are easily recognized, its alternatives are unknown. It is a technique by which, at least, many security features are justifiable.

The discussion of the risk analysis problem offers a well defined summary of the perspective of the owner stake-holder group. The chief benefit of security is its improvement to the performance dependability of the information system. The chief cost is perceived to be the added initial and operational expenses associated with the controls.

THE DESIGNER

The second of the stake-holder groups which influence information security is the system designer. The design of the system's security presents extremely difficult conflicts to these professionals. A consideration of the conflicts from the designer's perspective helps to reveal the motivation which has promoted the continued use of checklist design methods.

Conflicts of the Designer

The problem of designer motivation. In many respects, system designers become advocates of the system being designed. Such systems often become intertwined with the designers' egos, and challenges to the system's feasibility can expect to be received as personal challenges to the designers. This attitude often leads designers to share management's view of controls as "optional" when system costs approach infeasibility.

The problem of simplified methodologies. Design methodologies sometimes seem to invite security oversights. Dominant concerns with logical modeling, effective socio-technical solutions, or the "world view" of the user seem remote from security control design. Security is rarely ignored by design methodologies, but it is often a mere "footnote" — tacked on as something the designer should consider (without detailed tools for integrating the security into the design). One of the great misfortunes of security research is that it has been "left behind" by information systems researchers.

The problem of technological dependence. Systems designers are quick to defer security problems to the technology. Yet the technology (such as access control software, communications security devices, or physical security) may well turn the system into a human misery for the user. Whereas, if controls are considered from the earliest moments in analysis and design, there may be a considerable reduction in technological "overlays," and improvements in the organizational and human "fit" of the system controls.

The problem of unrealistic expectations. Frequently, discussions of security design will treat the topic of "security and people." Here will be discovered a diatribe on "organizational involvement" or "security is everybody's business." There is no question of the importance of this issue; however, designers too often underpin security with a complete dependence on the expectation that end users of the information system will behave with absolute consistency, responsibility, and predictability.

Checklists: A True Champion of Designers

However, it must be accepted that designers are responsible, intelligent stakeholders. The problems listed above do not stem from any fondness for "the easy way out." Rather, like the situation confronting management, designers are forced to take "the only way out." Checklists provide comprehensive anthologies of possible threats and controls. These provide known, dependable security and are founded in the accumulated expertise of a number of designers. What are the alternatives?

Techniques such as Fisher's, SPAN, and Parker's (see the appendix) have not drawn widespread practice. Although it is felt that the methodology presented above offers a real alternative, it does not yet exist outside of the limited experience of the author's close associates.

The review of the first two stake-holder groups (owners and designers), reveals that two easily criticized techniques in information security (the checklist and risk analysis), do indeed represent responsible, professional and intelligent practices from these stake-holders' perspectives. However, the body of opinion is broadening rapidly as other stake-holders begin to recognize their interests in the arena.

THE HUMAN ENTITY

Auditors frequently verify the existence of "entities," purportedly represented by data in information systems. The *persons* represented by data, the "human entities" constitute a third stake-holder group in the body of opinion on information security. Their interests have now been widely propounded. In the discussion of managerial problems, the privacy issues surfaces as a motivational challenge. This issue represents a perspective from the individuals or organizations who are the subjects of information which is retained and processed by information systems.

The problem of privacy. This one issue overwhelms all other social questions in security of information systems. The debate swirls around problems devolving from the rights of the persons represented by data, and the obligations of system owners to those persons.[2] Privacy is a prominent argument concerning public rights in privately designed information systems. The public is becoming aware of the astonishing capabilities of databases. When those databases contain personal information, the implications are disturbing. Currently, government systems may be the most visible, but private systems may be next: Schmitt [1982] cites a survey conducted by the Sentry Insurance Company in which 52% of their sample of computer executives expressed the opinion that privacy was inadequately safeguarded by computer systems.

The problem of data integrity. Far less debate envelops the social aspects of data integrity, but it may be expected that future attention will be focused here. For example, an error in the U.S. FBI database containing suspected criminal information precipitated the arrest, strip-search and imprisoning of an innocent New Jersey woman [Babcock, 1985]. This is not surprising in the light of a study on behalf of the U.S. Office of Technology Assessment. Researchers examined the data quality of automated criminal history systems in the U.S. The two major Federal Bureau of Investigation (FBI) criminal history systems and three sample state systems were evaluated. In one major FBI file, 75% of the records were significantly inaccurate. The other four systems were found to contain over 50% inaccurate, incomplete or ambiguous records. The findings included the following interpretation: "The constitutional rights of due process are not well-protected ... and the efficiency and effectiveness of any law-enforcement or criminal-justice programs that use or rely on such records must be considerably impaired." [Landon, 1986]

Other work has concentrated on the social implications of computer errors. One study investigated the impact of computer errors on consumer households [Sterling, 1979], discovering that some 20% of such errors absorbed more than 20 man-hours of household labor in attempts to resolve the ensuing problems (indeed, 7% of the errors prevailed after the household yielded in its attempts at correction while another 8% of the consumers did not even attempt to effect a correction).

---

2   Publications from this viewpoint abound: see Turn [1982] or Kling [1980] for examples.

THE USER

The viewpoints of owners, designers and data entities are well-expressed in the published work in this area. However, very little work is being directed toward a fourth major stake-holder group, the users, and their interests in security. What little thinking exists on this plane is usually motivational, found in articles entitled, "Security is everyone's business". As mentioned above, this thinking ensues weak security designs which are dependent on the user for proper operation.

User concerns seem to concentrate on three issues: (1) security should not interfere with system operation, (2) users will frequently bypass operationally complex security, and (3) user job satisfaction often suffers in stiff security.

The first issue, that of interference with system operation, is embedded in the concept of controls design being an "overlay" or modification of existing systems. Much of the attention in this area is demanded by the original system designers as often as it is by the users.

The second issue is directly related to the first, as experience has shown that operationally cumbersome controls will soon be defeated by users. The more motivated users, anxious to complete their tasks, will seek the most direct routes to completion. Unmonitored controls are easily discarded [Finch, 1985], and the lost protection can go unnoticed until a major loss or an embarrassing audit report ensues.

The third issue is less straightforward. It might be expected that increased controls within an information system could lower job satisfaction. For example, this might be perceived by the users as "lack of faith" by management, or alienation may increase as users lose some control over their functions. Opposing this view, however, is a recognition that an increasing pride or sense of wellbeing could directly result from more safe and accurate work.

However, these may only be the most superficial of concerns. Organizational politics may be a more critical issue confronting the user in relation to information security. From this view, information security mediates the intra-organizational power of various stake-holder groups.

Security can be used to impose a poor design on users (a conflict between the designer and user stake-holder groups). For example, controls are sometimes considered as techniques which prevent systems from behaving in undesirable ways. During systems implementation, such controls may be perceived as "constraints" which suppress user resistance. Where such resistance is an unhealthy symptom, as in a bad design feature, the controls may sustain a system which is otherwise humanly unacceptable [Markus, 1984].

Lyytinen and Hirschheim [1987], in their study of computer-based information systems as a means of managerial and social control, suggest that information systems can deliver or deny social emancipation. Present design techniques can only present a very real threat to the social environment in which the system intervenes by dominating instrumental reason and tightening social control. It is the security components of such intervention which assure that these effects are preserved. From this viewpoint, the security enforces information designs which restrain the user's social freedom. Without these controls the user would likely modify the system and introduce such social freedom.

Newer technologies are bringing information systems security into the working life of higher level professionals, a process Gurstein [1987] refers to as the mechanization of intellectual crafts (such as language translators or meteorologists). Gurstein cites a case in which the introduction of a computer-based information system reduced the differentiation between professionals (meteorologists) and semi-professionals (weather briefers). The political balance (and the differentiation) had to be restored by means of system controls which prevented briefers from accessing the meteorologist's capabilities.

THE CLIENT

A fifth stake-holder in the security arena is rarely recognized. The client is an organization or individual who may be dependent on the system without necessarily being the owner. For example, a bank could be a client of a credit bureau system. This perspective entails concerns which overlap both the owner and human entity views. Since the client may be making decisions based on the system, integrity is certainly a concern. From the viewpoint that the client is often contributing financially to support the operation of the system, the financial feasibility of any security becomes an indirect concern. Further, the client may well be concerned that information about the client maintained in the system is held safe from competitor or public scrutiny.

The problem of dependability. Initially, it may be perceived that a client's interest in the performance dependability is a simple overlap of the owner stakeholder group. But this may be narrow-sighted. In certain situations, a client may be more fundamentally dependent on the information system than the owner. For example, a number of major international firms are broadening their in-house electronic mail networks by selling access to these systems. These include McDonnell Douglas, General Electric, Computer Sciences and RCA [Krasnoff, 1987]. These organizations may well survive an extended network outage by relying on their major profit centers to offset the loss. However, a less financially stable client, dependent on the system reliability, could possibly fail as a result of the loss.

There are certain fundamental similarities in the nature of some information services being offered today and other essential utilities such as telecommunications or electrical power. The rising influence of client opinion may soon affect this arena

The problem of confidentiality. Privacy interests of clients as entities represented by data would also seem to overlap the interests of another stake-holder group, the human entities. However, these two groups differ in that the client is a "business partner" whose rights are adjusted somewhat by contract law. The obligations of the owner to the client outside of any contract are ill-defined at present.

The problem of access. There may be a rising conflict between the interests of clients and the data entity. It can be argued that a major new information market is about to surface: data vending. Data vending is one of the latest developments in the sphere of information products. An example is the Lotus Corporation offering of some 20 years of historical financial data on laser disks. In other words, their latest product is not a program, or a system, it is data. Obviously, financiers investing in this latest Lotus product will be making a capital investment with strong prospects of high returns on that investment.

On the surface, this may seem commonplace, as vendors such as Compuserve have been selling data for years. However, it is the packaging assumed by data vending that makes this information area so new and exciting. Lotus, like other recent data vendors, is selling the *actual, physical* data, not just access to it. Data is being sold as an asset rather than as an operating expense. This is a new viewpoint; data is becoming "product" to its vendors.

Historically, this is very significant. It is essentially a new commodity that is entering the information systems marketplace. Originally, this marketplace was dominated by computing machinery. That is, hardware was the focus of strategic purchase decisions. Indeed, it was the "computer" marketplace in those times. In the microcomputer world, this computer marketplace era was the scene of the battle between the IBM PC, the Apple III and the DEC Rainbow (among others). In later times, the marketplace has become more of a systems contest. Displaywriter versus Wordstar, Framework versus Symphony, and Lotus versus Supercalc represented certain strategic considerations; the supporting computing machinery decisions are relegated to tactical decisions.

The market has developed from hardware alone to software *and* hardware. But information systems are not dichotomous. Information systems are trichotomous: hardware, software *and* data. A market with its strategic focus centered on data may well develop into a dominant segment of the information product marketplace.

A problem confronting this market is the assured conflict between the data entities and the clients. An example is the case cited in chapter two in which a California concern marketed a database ("Physicians Alert") containing identities gleaned from public court records of medical malpractice suits ["Row brews ...", 1985]. This database of 1.3 million lawsuit records from Los Angeles and

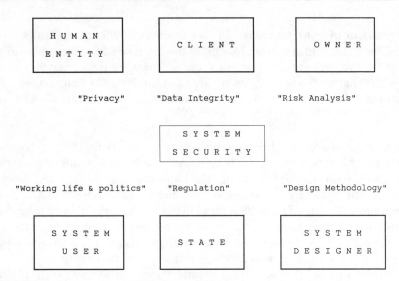

FIGURE 6.1 Human perspectives on information system security

Orange County is made available to medical practitioners for use in the review process of new patients at a cost of $5 – $10 per search. The obvious function is to permit rejection of patients known to have issued a malpractice suit in the past. A direct conflict arises between the rights of the client and the data entity over this sort of service.

Freedom of access to data is an important public issue when the prospect of an "information society" is considered. Here, the general public may be perceived in its role as client, and the conflict between data entity rights to privacy and public rights to access is presenting intense demands for resolution through information security.

THE STATE

In the current climate of information systems development, the owner is probably the "ultimate" stake-holder. The owner, by power of property rights, exercises virtually unrestrained control over the structures of information systems security. Thus, risk analysis and checklists have continued to dominate the design techniques. However, the abuse of this unrestrained domination may eventually lead to the intervention by the state as the new "ultimate" stakeholder. Indeed, the state is beginning to assert its role in information security in several ways.

Computer crime laws. Legislation has been demanded by owners to protect such "property" as computing access and data. In the United States, a federal statute (18 USC 1029 and 1030) specifically address electronic and computer frauds; most states in that country have supporting statutes [Ingram, 1986]. In this respect, the state is entering the arena to assert the rights of its subjects who are owners, and to defend those rights against criminals.

Privacy laws. Legislation, such as that discussed in chapter two, has been demanded to protect individual rights to privacy. Further, some financial data reporting laws require owners to respond to audits from data subjects. This public attitude creates a nuisance for owners by requiring controls for data access and accuracy which, without the legal requirements, may not have been cost-justifiable. In this respect, the state is entering the arena to assert the rights of its subjects who are data entities, and to defend those rights against owners, users, or clients.

To some extent, the intervention of the state may devolve from the managerial emphasis on risk analysis. Controls dedicated to the "public weal" simply can not survive the internal microeconomics of the organization, and state intervention follows. This intervention can be expected to grow tremendously in future.

The problem of managerial motivation. The shift in the importance of information technology to a position of prominence with regard to the survival of the organization may have escaped the notice of management. Indeed, it may also have escaped the notice of our society as a whole. This could be far more important as an issue than any previously discussed.

Organizational management usually recognizes its responsibilities to "public welfare" in conducting its affairs. For example, building construction must not only be profitable, but the public can expect the resulting building to be *safe*. However, management may not yet have projected this responsibility into its information system design projects. Does the public have a right to expect these systems to be safe? There are growing arguments that the time has arrived for the shouldering of this obligation.

One argument notes that our social fabric has become more critically dependent on the thread of technology as its binder. If this technology is fragile, it is an obvious terrorist target. Hoffman [1982] writes of this threat: "As computer applications in many countries have become increasingly sophisticated, the operators of these systems have become increasingly concerned about the unforeseen consequences of total reliance on them ..." Menkus [1983] argues that there is no guarantee that computer facilities will continue to escape the notice of terrorists groups as an ideal target for the disruption of the basic structural elements of a society. Indeed, Pollak [1983] catalogs some 54 published cases, and estimates that over 100 terrorist acts against computer targets and DP personnel took place prior to 1983. Since that survey the attacks have continued. For example, in 1985 two German software houses (Scientific Control Systems and Mathematischer Beratungs und Programmierungsdienst) had major computer center bombings. The credited terrorist group considered the development of DP systems as oppressive to workers [Lamb and Etheridge, 1986].

Presently, however, management is unmotivated to treat the safety of new information system projects as a matter of "public responsibility." Martin Hellman [1984], writing of the implications of the Beyond War movement to computer security, compared efforts in obtaining computer controls to the efforts in securing nuclear weapons treaties. The principals seem unwilling to work to obtain the desired result on *reasonable* terms. In the case of computer security, this commodity is only desired strongly enough to warrant acquisition when it is available at virtually no cost. Hellman singles out the security of many electronic funds transfer systems as examples. These, he finds, seem to discover the implementation of adequate controls to be fraught with impossible costs and barriers. Hellman contends that the organization needs to reorient its values to account for the inevitable importance of security.

Motivation for future state intervention. As social structures become more directly dependent on the internal information systems of organizations, it can be expected that the state must assume additional powers directly over these systems. This is the only possible mechanism to inject controls which are macroeconomically sound, but could not survive organizational microeconomic justification. Groups on whose behalf the state would be likely intervene would include:

The public. The state must recognize and correct deep-seated vulnerabilities to terrorism, war, espionage or natural disasters which result from poorly secured, yet critical private information systems. Further, the state can be expected to recognize the critical nature of the developing "information utility," and mandate measures to promote uninterruptable service to the public.

The client. This stake-holding group may involve the state as an ally in assuring the dependability of systems offered for commercial use. Sanctions (probably using existing statutes) could develop against negligent system operation.

The data entity. Further intervention may be demanded from the state as data vending proliferates, establishing individual rights over the use their personal data. This may take the form of legal requirements to inform data entities when and to what purpose their data is being used. This concept could develop in some cultures into royalty payment rights obligated to the data entity. In addition, further sanctions against misrepresentation may develop, with formalized damages recovery mechanisms.

The user. In many countries, the state has already intervened to mandate user influence in new systems design. The use of security controls to force successful implementation of operationally miserable systems may lead to limitations in the use of physical security controls where logical controls are an option.

Forms of state intervention. In some Scandinavian countries, it might be feasible that the dominant humanistic concerns in the government for the social welfare of its subjects (in relation to computers and automation) might permit successful legislation and enforcement of laws directly regulating such issues as those above. This possibility is not as strong in every state, however. The United States federal government is not likely to create many statutes directly regarding such demands as those listed above. But in such countries, the necessities of the stake-holders are likely to be supported in other ways. For example, utility licensing and regulation may be invoked for information vendors, or common law decisions may apply existing statutes to protect the new interests (e.g., applying copyright statutes to personal data). However, the most critical form this may take from the security designer's perspective would be the implementation of industrial standards.

INDUSTRIAL STANDARDS AND PROFESSIONAL LICENSURE

One of the easiest, and most likely intervention techniques which could be expected in countries dominated by capitalism would be through construction standards. Presently, there are only peripheral standards for the design of information systems. "Peripheral" refers to such standards as accounting Standards of Practice [Weber, 1982], or encryption and communication standards such as the Data Encryption Algorithm (ANSI X3.92) or the Financial Institution Message Authentication standard (ANSI X9.9) [Davies and Price, 1984]. In addition, several de facto standards can be found, such as the U. S. Defense Department's "Trusted Computer System Evaluation Criteria" [Department of Defense, 1985].

Perhaps the information systems field has matured to an age where standards of practice in information systems analysis and design are both feasible and essential. Such standards could address tools (such as data flow diagrams) and system attributes (such as back-up and recovery). In addition, and pertinent to the present subject, the standards could define *attestation*.

Attestation would entail a practice in which a recognizably qualified individual (such as a CDP or MBCS) must certify that a new information system design meets minimum industry standards for performance and safety. The same principle is applied when a PE or CEng certifies a civil structure design, or a CPA certifies an external audit. The institution of attestation would immediately propel the information systems industry toward resolution of the problems discussed above.

Motivation for standards. The demand for coordinated and recognized standards would surge as designers confront certification of their work. The present potpourri of peripheral and de facto standards would have to be integrated under an umbrella of information systems standards.

Diminution of emphasis on probability. Performance standards in information systems must replace probability arithmetic when defining controls. The search for these standards would begin with attestation, since the feedback loop for the effectiveness of controls design and specification closes. The performance of a control would be studied from an industry viewpoint, rather than conjectured in isolated cases.

Defocussing profitability. Attestation would begin the process of elevating systems analysis and design to the same plane as engineering and accounting. Information systems professionals would shoulder direct responsibility to shareholders as well as management; and to society as well as the organization. Attestation would certify the public safety of the design of the information system, removing, for example, managerial discretion over the protection of privacy of personal information. In addition, the designers' direct accountability to shareholders through attestation would dislodge risks and controls involving the survival of the organization from nonsensical cost justification.

Redirecting managerial motivation. Attestation also curtails the complete bondage of the designer to managerial perception. Essential elements of the information system's security and integrity could be removed from an "optional" status in the presentation of the design to management. Civil engineers are not permitted to offer minimum building safety (such as adequate fire exits) as an option. Management, through this process, recognizes its responsibility to the public in creating a safe building. Similarly, designers should not be permitted to offer minimum privacy protection as an option. By removal of the option, management would begin to recognize its responsibility to the public in creating a safe information system.

SUMMARY

Much of the work in computer security has taken a very technical perspective. Even when people are considered respective to security, the view has been more instrumental than beneficial. The only strong views to attract the attention of security designers, outside of the interests of the owners, have been the mandated privacy concerns of the data entity.

If, indeed, society is entering the "information age", it can be expected that the state will begin to assume a stronger position of influence in the arena of information security. It is very likely that the brunt of that influence will fall directly on the shoulders of systems analysts and designers who are charged with the specification of security features of information systems critical to society.

Thus, the influence of owners over security features is likely to diminish. Techniques such as risk analysis and checklists must surrender to standards and attestation. Loyalty of the designer will splinter: the system owner, the state, and the profession will share this loyalty. Through the state and the profession, the designer will be forced to recognize obligations directly to clients, data entities and users.

The diminishment has begun. Privacy legislation, computer crime legislation, and professional certification programs are in place. In the United States, the federal government has broadened the scope of the National Computer Security Center to consider standards for publicly held information systems.

REFERENCES

Babcock, C. "Online crime suspect system implicated in false arrest," *Computerworld* **19** (19 August 1985): p. 12.

Baskerville, R. "Logical controls specification," *Information Systems Development for Human Progress in Organizations*, IFIP TC WG 8.2 Conference, Atlanta, Georgia, May, 1987.

Carroll, J. and MacIver, W. "Towards an expert system for computer facility certification," in *Computer Security: A Global Challenge* edited by J. Finch and E. Dougall. Amsterdam: North-Holland, 1984, pp. 293–306.

Davies, D. and Price, W. *Security for Computer Networks*. Chichester: John Wiley, 1984.

DeMarco, T. *Structured Analysis and System Specification*. New York: Yourdon, 1979.

"Department of Defense trusted computer system evaluation criteria," DOD 5200.28-STD, Washington: National Computer Security Center, Dec, 1985.

Finch, J. "Security of office systems," paper presented to *IFIP WG 8.4 Working Conference on Office Systems*, Helsinki, October, 1985.

Gurstein, M. "The politics of intelligence: micro- technology and micro-politics," *Information Systems Development for Human Progress in Organizations*, IFIP TC WG 8.2 Conference, Atlanta, Georgia, May, 1987.

Hellman, M. "Beyond war: implications for computer security and encryption," in *Computer Security: A Global Challenge* edited by J. Finch and E. Dougall. Amsterdam: North-Holland, 1984, pp. 41–47.

Hoffman, L. "Impacts of information system vulnerabilities on society," *1982 NCC Conference Proceedings*. Arlington, Va: AFIPS Press, 1982.

Ingram, D. "Investigating and prosecuting computer crime and network abuse," *13th Annual Computer Security Conference*, Atlanta, Georgia, Nov, 1986.

Kling, R. "Social analyses of computing: theoretical perspectives in recent empirical research," *ACM Computing Surveys* **12** (Mar 1980), pp. 61–110.

Krasnoff, B. "Corporate E-Mail: The Electronic Mailroom", *PC Magazine* 6 (12May87), pp. 295–301.

Lamb, J. and Etheridge, J. "DP: the terror target", *Datamation* (1 Feb 1986), pp. 44–45.

Landon, K. "Data quality and due process in large interorganizational record systems," *Communications of the ACM* **29** (Jan, 1986): pp 5–11.

Lyytinen, K. and Hirschheim, R. "Information systems and emancipation: promise or threat?" *Information Systems Development for Human Progress in Organizations*, IFIP TC WG 8.2 conference, Atlanta, Georgia, May, 1987.

Markus, L. *Systems In Organizations: Bugs + Features.* Boston: Pitman, 1984.

Menkus, B. "Notes on terrorism and data processing," *Computers and Security* **2** (Jan 1983), pp. 11–15.

Newton, J. "Strategies for problem prevention," *IBM Systems Journal* **24** (Nos 3/4, 1985): pp. 248–263.

O'Mara, J. "Computer security, a management blindspot," *Computer Security Handbook.* Northborough, Mass: Computer Security Institute, 1985.

Parker, D. *Computer Security Management.* Reston: Reston, 1981.

Pollak, R. "Implications of international terrorism on security of information systems," *Proceedings of IEEE INFOCOM 83.* New York: IEEE, 1983, pp 270–276.

"Row brews in US over database of medical lawsuits," *Computing* (28 Nov 1985): p. 30.

Saltmarsh, T. and Browne, P. "Data processing — risk assessment," in *Advances in Computer Security Management* Vol 2, edited by M. Wofsey. Chichester: J. Wiley, 1983.

Schmitt, W. "Data security program development: an overview," *Computer Security Journal* (Winter, 1982).

Sterling, T. "Consumer difficulties with computerized transactions: an empirical investigation," *Communications of the ACM* **22**, (May 1979), pp. 283–289.

Turn, R. "Privacy protection in the '80s," *Proceedings of the 1982 IEEE Symposium on Security and Privacy.* Silver Springs Md: IEEE press, 1982, pp. 86–89.

Weber, R. *EDP Auditing: Conceptual Foundations and Practice.* New York: McGraw-Hill, 1982.

Chapter 7

CONCLUSION

The foregoing work has ranged widely over the issues surrounding information systems security, offering a redefinition of the field, treating computer security, varied management issues, and ultimately the societal responsibilities. Its *raison d'être* was its long pause over what is thought to be the immediate technical stumbling block of the arena: design methodological problems. It would be useful to summarize what is found above, and what is missing in the work.

SUMMARY

The technology of computer security has been shown to be a well developed, competent technology of computer science. Feasible controls can be identified for virtually every threat. Yet losses traceable to unspecified, minimum control features abound. This is not a simple, one dimensional problem with a solution lying in organizational involvement or better technology. The problem is multi-faceted, as is its solution.

Information security. A fundamental element of the problem is the narrow view held by many managers, analysts and designers, that the security problem is wholly a computer problem. Attempts to secure modern information systems applications such as office automation or decision support systems purely through computer security are misguided. The unpredictable, continuous flow of information across the man/machine boundaries makes computer security only a portion of the formula. Thus, a fundamental element of the ultimate solution must be a broadened definition of the problem. The approach must be reframed as an information systems security solution, rather than a computer security solution, availing itself of the decades of advances in systems analysis and design.

Adopting computer security. An element of the problem is the lack of awareness in many designers of the spectrum of controls available within computing technologies. Thus, a fundamental element of the solution has to be the adoption of the progressive excellence of computer security solutions. Automated processes and data are easily secured within their technological hosts. It is the availability of these solutions which substantiate the technical feasibility of information security in modern computer-based information systems.

Recognizing the burdens. An important, often-overlooked, aspect of the information security problem is the real costs of security controls. Without realizing the damage which can be inflicted to the long-term functionality of a new information system, the designer may be prone to depend the security upon constricting physical controls. Such controls are likely to limit the system's effectiveness and lifespan, and the immense unseen cost of this may actually dwarf the comparatively tiny costs of implementation and maintenance. These costs must be recognized and considered in modern applications demanding increased flexibility in computer-based information systems.

Accepting new generation methodologies. Computer security design methods, approaching the information system from the modification or overlay perspective, can operationally cripple the original system functionality. Information security need not be designed and specified as a process discrete from the original system design. Newer generation methodologies can be applied in designing security such that complete control sets are intrinsic elements of logical and physical models of the information system. Such specifications are seen as offering dramatic improvements in the effective security of the system, while reducing the damage to the flexibility and the consequent diminution of the lifespan of the system.

Applying effective heuristics in control set selection. Checklists for controls identification, and risk analysis for controls selection present the designer with inappropriate tools for selection of effective controls. Consideration of the nature of threats and controls behavior can provide feasible alternative heuristics to aid in the selection of an effective control set. When these tools are applied within microspheres created by third generation methodologies, the problem of feasible scale encountered in earlier generation approaches can be eliminated. Expert systems are shown to be feasible in this process.

Recognize the changing role of information security. The major stake-holder in information systems security is increasingly the society, rather than the system owner. Reflected by this change, the state can be seen as becoming more involved in the decision processes surrounding controls selection through regulated or legislated standards. The allegiance of the designer may soon be split with specific obligations to the profession and the public (as well as the owner). It is likely that many information systems being designed today will survive into this future. Management may be able to circumvent major systems renovations in the future by accepting design techniques and the subsequent systems specifications which entail responsible controls. Use of methodologies and tools such as those suggested above, which embed logical controls within systems, could add little to the initial or operating costs of an information system and yet permit the system to fulfill enforced societal requirements in future.

FUTURE RESEARCH

The work summarized above is not to be considered at its final terminus. Much research is needed to properly underpin and prove the continued practicality of the concepts presented above. Those avenues of future research which seem particularly important are suggested below.

Structured methodology. Additional experimentation with the structured methodology in various environments would provide evidence as to whether the approach is universally effective in all types of information applications. For example, will it work in a purely manual office information system, or a very small office system; would it be successful for highly secure office functions (e.g., diplomatic offices)? Does the structured security methodology work as successfully in large-scale data processing systems as it seems to work in office information systems? DeMarco's work is oriented toward these data processing systems originally. Perhaps this approach is even more applicable in identifying control sets in these systems. The structured methodology needs to be empirically applied in such systems to provide evidence of its applicability.

The opportunities above will probably demand a longitudinal "action" research project, studying the organizational function, designing and implementing the controls, and studying the effect of these controls. Such longitudinal studies as these face difficult problems in time consumption. Logical controls will sometimes thread ubiquitously through an information system. Implementation of such controls can require months, even years. For example, the Life Issuance Control Number recommended in the case study in the appendix, was projected to require at least a year to implement. Considering the longitudinal data collection and analysis, and the original structured modeling and design phase, and the enlistment of the voluntary host, such a project would occupy a minimum of three years.

Control effectiveness. While these studies could measure the success of organizational acceptance of the controls, measuring the success of controls in providing protection is particularly difficult. Many threats are creatures of probability. A longitudinal study of a particular implementation can be obfuscated by simple "good luck." There is a particular need for more cross-sectional empirical data on control effectiveness. In relation to the studies above, a particular logical control could be implemented in a number of similar organizations, and statistically tracked to determine probabilities of success.

The "morphs." Much of the unhappy pressure surrounding risk analysis was relieved by the introduction of a paramorph, rather than homeomorph as the underlying model of the subject. It would be interesting to broaden this idea into an examination of the usage of paramorphs in benefits analysis for information systems, rather than just their security. Cost–benefit analysis has always proved to involve tangled estimates of probability, forecasts of performance, and other projections for which management science has only been able to offer improved arithmetic manipulation and representation of the guesswork.

Other methodologies. DeMarco's methodology adapted itself easily to perform as a security design methodology. What of the myriad other design methodologies? Could Checkland's Soft Systems Approach, Mumford's ETHICS, or the ESPRIT Office Systems Methodology be equally well-adaptable? It would be most interesting to apply the fourth generation methodologies to an information security problem in an environment in which the user society is presenting the designer with difficult conflicts.

Behavioral controls. Large-scale data processing has found physical protection of its facilities as acceptable controls. The methodology above seeks to minimize that dependence in office systems. But certain physical controls must be added to the control set to complete the protection. In the case study, confidential documents were "classified" for disclosure control. This logical control is incomplete without the policies, physical access controls and locks which accompany such classification. What are the behavioral reactions to these physical controls outside of the computer room? What is the effect of these controls on the quality of the worker's life? More empirical work is needed in the study of the behavioral aspects of information systems security.

Organizations and security. Organizations differ in their nature. Organizations may be large, small, adaptable, rigid, informal, formal; as variable as individuals. Intuitively, certain controls would seem more appropriate for certain organizational qualities. Perhaps physical controls are more suitable for rigid, formal organizations, and logical controls for flexible, informal organizations. What is the interaction between organizational attributes and successful controls? Also, commitment of the organization to new controls implementation only seems to develop following a major loss. How can this commitment be raised prior to such losses?

Logical versus physical. The division between logical and physical controls has seen some exploration, but what of the controls inventory identified by logical versus physical methodologies? An interesting study might direct two design teams in specifying controls for the same (or similar) systems. The acceptability, cost, and effectiveness of the two control sets could then be compared in order to determine which methodology provides the most ideal control design. In addition, maintenance costs and the consequent lifespan of the two subsequent systems could be monitored to reveal the effects of the logical foundations of control sets.

ACHIEVEMENT

From the perspective of the preceding section, the work depicted in previous chapters can be seen to pose as many questions as it has offered answers. However, this should not be perceived as lacunae. Rather, the questions delineate the transition from this work to that which must follow. If there were no other achievement above than the clear statement of so many unanswered questions, then this alone could serve to celebrate the success of the science.

However, the overt purpose of this book is to illustrate techniques, tools, and methodologies which can be successful in identifying complete and effective controls for information systems without the necessity of checklists, risk analysis, or expensive automated support. It may be likely that these tools will find their way to the desks of the analysts, designers and managers who need such support in the face of a dramatically changing arena of information systems security analysis and design. This arena in the 1990's may be a complete metamorphosis of its precursor of the 1980's.

Perhaps the major achievement of the foregoing study is in the revelation that the current problems of information systems security may not be entirely a technological or management issue. Indicators revealed here seem to assert that these problems may presently be design and social issues. Until appropriate controls are regularly offered, management cannot be expected to blindly finance controls, nor can the knowledge workers be expected to completely accept controls. The information systems field has failed to discover all important perspectives from which to study security. The perspectives of management and the "human entity," may need to be joined by those of the designer, the user, the client and the state. Indeed, the "computer security" field may need to redefine itself and its essential purpose; and equipped with its impressive technological sophistication, adopt more sophisticated design approaches, and a more responsible social philosophy.

The research presented above suggests that such a redefinition may lead to dramatic improvements in system security, possibly without the interference that hounds present approaches. Should such improvements become widespread, the implication would be that the information system of the society as a whole could be made substantially safer.

The term "information society" is sometimes applied as a description of the immediate future of civilization. Should this future be realized, we must recognize that improvements such as those described above, would promote the stability of an essential, defining element of that future society. From this perspective, it is hoped that the foregoing work will inspire more responsible systems designs, and thus help to prepare the information systems field to fulfill its vast promise to society.

Appendix A

CASE STUDY: NEW LIFE ISSUANCE SYSTEM

The selection of the insurance company for this study was dictated by a number of factors. A prime factor was the availability of a highly automated office function (described below), in which controls were believed to be lacking. This provided one of the newer arenas of computer-based information systems for the subject study. Another factor was the enthusiasm with which the proposed work was accepted. A third factor was the less formal security "climate" of the insurance industry. Many organizations are able to impose a considerably larger degree of physical security in their office environments than would have been acceptable to the insurance industry offices.[1]

THE COMPANY: "XYZ INSURANCE"

XYZ Life and Accident Insurance Company is ranked among the twenty-five largest stock life companies in the United States, listing more than two billion dollars in assets on its consolidated balance sheet. It issues insurance policies covering life, health, accident, property and casualty risks. XYZ, like most major insurance companies, also provides pension plans in connection with its insurance packages. XYZ also envelopes a number of subsidiary companies. All six of these companies maintain corporate headquarters at a single XYZ office complex (where this study was conducted), and regional offices are maintained in major population centers across North America.

The corporate headquarters is organized into four major line departments and a number of staff and support offices. The line departments are (1) Life Insurance Department, (2) Accident Insurance Department, (3) Group Insurance Department, and (4) Franchise Department. The staff offices include Personnel, Information Systems, Audit, Legal, and Marketing (see figure A.1).

New Life Issuance

XYZ's vice-president for information systems, office information systems manager, and security administrator conferred in selecting a target system for this

---

1   It is interesting to note that this case study was originally completed without the benefit of the computer-based expert system. The heuristics were applied "manually" to the controls identification process. The findings were confirmed when Prolog-generated recommendations matched-up two years following the original study.

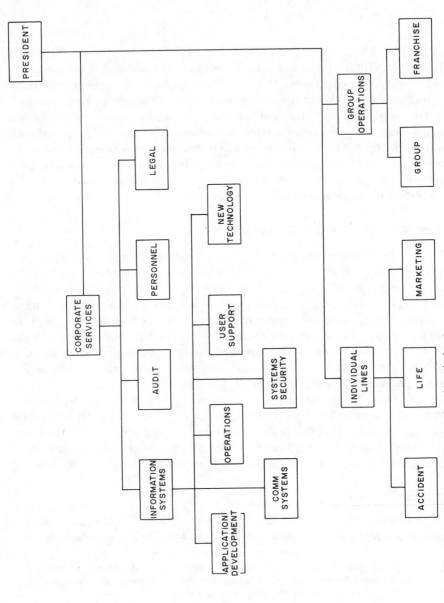

FIGURE A.1 Abridged XYZ organizational chart

study. Their New Life Insurance Policy Issuance System was selected for a number of reasons. First, it provided a complete fit to the research request, as this system involved a number of advanced office technologies. Second, the disparate technologies brought the maintenance of the integrity and privacy of the information flowing through the system into question. Third, the controls in the system had not been examined since the heavy automation had been introduced, denoting interest in the research results.

Technologies. The system being studied was jokingly called WIZARD by some of the systems analysts, as an acronym for "Wang, IBM, Xerox, And Related Devices". The processing of the new policies involved the use of an IBM mainframe computer in calculating premiums, payments, and value schedules; a Wang word processing system was used to select and organize clauses and paragraphs in the actual policy document; and a Xerox document digitizing scanner and laser printing system was used to integrate the final policy package. This final component was mandated by regulations which required exact facsimiles of the signed applications as attachments to the final policy.

SECURITY ANALYSIS AND DESIGN

DeMarco argues strongly that structured analysis and specification eliminates the necessity for the attachment of detailed text supporting the diagrams which portray the operation of the target information system. This is rightfully denoted as redundant information in this design methodology. However, for the purpose of this case study, the reader cannot be considered as one who is the slightest bit familiar with the target system. In addition, the purpose of this study is to illustrate the methodology, not merely the resulting controls. Therefore, it is felt necessary to provide adequate discussions of the current physical system, and the effects of the analysis activities on the system specification.

Current Physical Model

Figure A.2 is the current physical data flow diagram for the New Life Insurance Policy Issuance System. The insurance agent, who may or may not be a XYZ employee, creates a handwritten insurance application for the client, attaches the necessary medical records and forwards these to the New Life section. The agent receives the bound policy in return after the processing is completed. This policy is then presented to the client.

A New Business Assistant is assigned to each application received in the New Life section. The New Business Assistant marshals the application through the steps of its processing and verifies its integrity. The perspective of the New Business Assistant may provide the clearest insight into the operation of the system.

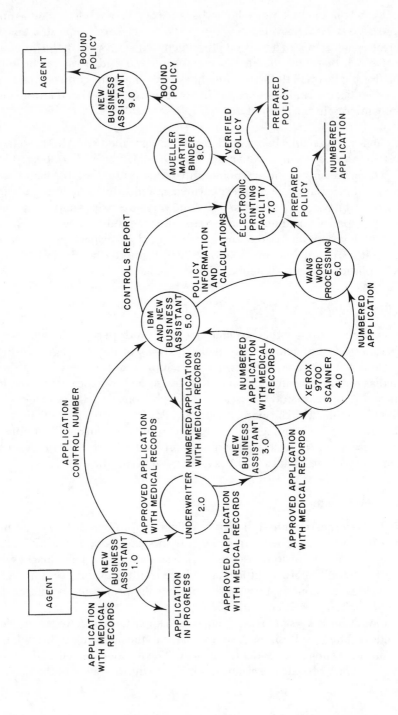

FIGURE A.2 Current physical data flow diagram

The application and medical records are checked by the New Business Assistant upon receipt from the agent (process 1.0), and passed to the underwriter. The underwriter approves the client as "insurable" (process 2.0) and returns the approved documents to the New Business Assistant. (Uninsurable applications are returned to the agent.) The approved application and records are then given by the New Business Assistant to the Xerox technician who digitizes these in a batch mode into a tape data file (process 4.0). The documents are returned to the New Business Assistant with an image number inscribed on the back of a photocopy of each application. The image number relates the documents to the digitized image in the Xerox system (see figure A.3). The New Business Assistant then keys the application data (including the image number) into a computer file (an IBM mainframe) using an interactive data entry program and a CRT terminal (process 5.0). The New Business Assistant then files the documents. This document file is periodically transferred to a permanent archive (required by regulation).

The New Business Assistant only has a minor involvement in the remainder of the process. Word processing technicians (using the Wang text processor) initiate a program which accesses the mainframe policy information and calculation files in order to select clauses in composing the policy (process 6.0). The program also reads the digitized image tape and appends the image data to the policy document file. This composite data is transferred by tape back to the Xerox system where the policy pages are printed from the tape (process 7.0). The image and composite data tapes are *temporarily* retained. The Xerox technician checks the policy for missing pages, and forwards the pages to the binding technician. The bound policy is returned to the New Business Assistant. The New Business Assistant distributes the policies to the agents (usually without any further verification).

```
SAMPLE PRINT OF IMAGE O31OOO

IMAGE FILE HEADER INFORMATION:

    IMAGE NAME -
    IMAGE HEIGHT (PIXELS) -  1288
    IMAGE WIDTH (PIXELS) -  996
    COMPRESSED IMAGE SIZE (BYTES) -  34845
    COMPRESSION FACTOR -  4
    IMAGE RESOLUTION (DOTS/INCH) -  300/1

STORAGE REQUIREMENTS:

    IMAGE MEMORY (K-BITS) -  272.25
    DISK BLOCKS -  70

SAMPLE SPECIFICATIONS:

    COMMAND LINE -  SAMPLE O31OOO.IMG,D,(.5,.5,2)

    POSITIONING MODE -  P
    ORIGIN -  150,150
    SCALING -  2
```

FIGURE A.3 *Specimen application image and number*

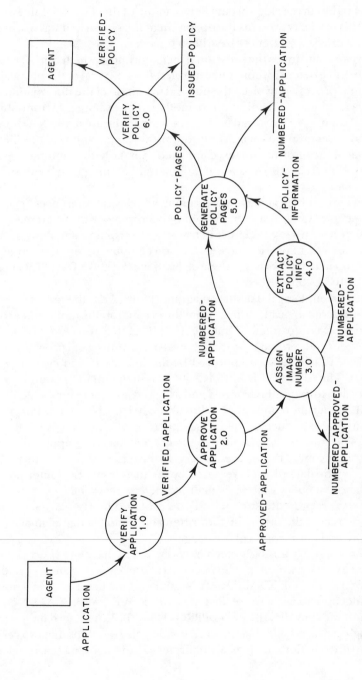

FIGURE A.4 Current logical data flow diagram

Current Logical Model

Figure A.4 is the current logical data flow diagram of the XYZ New Life Issuance System. This model represents the operation of the system as it was discovered; however, all physical references have been removed.

This system illustrates the substantial metamorphosis which can occur when viewing an office system without physical references. Several of the physical data flow diagram processes involved the physical transition of the information from one media or physical organization to another. For example, current physical process 3.0 (figure A.2) involved nothing more than the use of the New Business Assistant as a communication link for the approved application. No verification or approval of the information was conducted. Similarly, the binding step (current physical process 8.0) was a simple physical fastening of the information into its packet.

In the current logical data flow diagram, all physical references (e.g., New Business Agent, Wang, Scanner, etc.) have been removed. Additionally, processes which have no logical effect in translating incoming dataflows into outgoing dataflows (e.g., physical process 3.0) are eliminated, with the subsequent consolidation in dataflows (e.g., physical dataflow APPROVED-APPLICATION-WITH-MEDICAL-RECORDS).

In the current logical data flow diagram (figure A.4), the medical records are not considered logically distinct from the original applications, since this information is never separated. Thus the APPLICATION is received by the New Business Agent and verified for completeness in current logical process 1.0. The VERIFIED-APPLICATION is approved by the underwriter in current logical process 2.0. The APPROVED-APPLICATION is then sent to the scanner where the application form itself is scanned and assigned an image number.

The next transition presented a difficult analysis problem. The image number is a physical reference to the image data record in the Xerox 9700 system tape file. This number is appended to the documents of the application by attaching a photocopy of the *application image* to the other written documents (see figure A.3). The data which is required by the mainframe computer program for calculation of policy values is actually *keyed in from a second scanner photocopy*. The analysts were presented with several copies of the same logical data in different physical forms: the original handwritten application, a digital image of the application, and photocopies of the image.

The only logical transition which has occurred in the above processes is the creation of an image number. The next logical process is therefore considered only as ASSIGN IMAGE NUMBER. This number is included in the original application documents as these are filed. The APPROVED-APPLICATION consequently becomes the NUMBERED-APPROVED-APPLICATION dataflow and is filed in logical process 3.0. The curious situation also develops that two very different physical dataflows are logical duplicates. The image data (current logical dataflow NUMBERED-APPLICATION) exists in a digital tape file, and in printed hardcopy form. The logical information content is exactly the same, and must be shown as such in the current logical data flow diagram. The tape copy is sent directly to current logical process 5.0 (GENERATE POLICY PAGES) and the photocopy is used for data entry in process 4.0 (EXTRACT POLICY INFO).

The remainder of the current logical data flow diagram is less complex. The policy data and computed value information is conveyed by data communications link to the GENERATE POLICY PAGES process, where the policy clauses are selected, merged with the application image, and printed. The image tape is temporarily filed (NUMBERED-APPLICATION file). The policy is then checked for completeness (VERIFY POLICY process 6.0), and the composite policy printing tape is temporarily filed. The binding references are excluded due to their physical nature.

New Logical Design

It is necessary to establish the "domain of change" within the system; that is, define that portion of the system which requires alteration in adapting the system to its new requirements. The purpose of the study is to define controls necessary in protecting the system from the threats of modification, destruction and disclosure. It must be noticed that there are three control stages already present in the system. Current logical processes 1.0 (VERIFY APPLICATION), 2.0 (APPROVE APPLICATION) and 6.0 (VERIFY POLICY) are intended to capture errors or prevent improper policy issuance. Among these, it can be noticed that current logical process 6.0, in which the final policy is verified, is poorly implemented. During this process, the printing technician glances through the pile of documents in search of missing pages. Other than this gross error procedure, no attempt is made to ensure the policy reflects the application data prior to return of the document to the Agent. Since both the input and output stage of our system must be included in the domain, it will become very difficult to eliminate any of the processes or dataflows from the study. It would be in keeping with the goal of designing a complete control set to establish a domain of change over the *entire* system being studied. There are two exceptions: both incoming and outgoing data flows of the system (APPLICATION and VERIFIED-POLICY) cannot be controlled without involving the external process. Our study should therefore provide controls for the following elements:

Process Elements
1. Verify Application
2. Approve Application
3. Assign Image Number
4. Extract Policy Information

5. Generate Policy Pages
6. Verify Policy

Data Elements
1. Verified Application
2. Approved Application
3. Numbered Application
4. Numbered Approved Application
5. Policy Information
6. Policy Pages
7. Issued Policy

The analysis determining the controls for each of these process and data elements is briefly discussed before presenting the new logical model of the secured system. It is important to avoid any physical references or benefits analysis during this design stage. The only benefits consideration would be whether to design a "strengthened" or "normal" control set. A normal control set will be considered below, since no unusually strong threats are identifiable.[2] The insertion of the control processes and data into the new logical data flow diagram will then be illustrated.

Logical Data Controls

A logical destruction control would be the creation of a backup copy of the application material upon receipt. Logical disclosure controls include encryption, seals, or classification schemes. Modification controls could include classification (enabling access control), checksums, or audit trails.

Backup application file. Provision of a second copy of the raw input data for the system would protect against destruction of any dataflow within the entire process. This is because the original application material could be re-introduced into the system in order to restore any of the subsequent dataflows. (Logging may also be required, but this is offered as a control for restarting a destroyed process).

Classification. Classification is a logical control which can protect against both disclosure and modification, but it is invoked here as a disclosure control. Physi-

---

2   The logical processes of approving, calculating and issuing policies are a matter of public
     domain information. It is unlikely that process disclosure controls will be of use in this system.
     However, these will be discussed here in order to illustrate the potential for logical
     specification of these controls.

cal access controls are enhanced by classification, and classification schemes can flow easily across man–machine boundaries. Sensitive data elements within this system should be logically protected by the label "CONFIDENTIAL" or equivalent corporate term.

Life Issuance Control Number. The concept of checksum leads to a very attractive logical control for this system: a control number for use in logging, batch totals or verification. The critical data-elements being controlled in this system include: *Insured's Name, Date of Birth,* and *Face Value* (insurance amount). Modification of one of these three fields would be intrinsic to many fraud, integrity loss, or sabotage threats. The provision of a control code number derived from these three elements, would reduce the undetected modification risk considerably. For example, an applicant named John R. Smith, born 25 March, 1955 for a $100,000 life policy would be assigned a Life Issuance Control Number of *JRS250355000100.* In this example, the first three characters represent the insured's initials, the next six digits represent the birth date, and the final six digits represent insurance in thousands of dollars. The derivation algorithm could be adjusted to provide adequate detection levels in this system. For example, seven name characters could be used in the code: *JOHRSMI250355000100.*

   This control code can be used for audit trails, batch totals (using numerical encoding such as EBCDIC or ASCII for the characters), or for manual or automated verification of data consistency. Notice that the use of a logical control, such as this data-content-based control number, protects against modification regardless of motive: intentional or accidental. Further, the control protection can flow easily across the man–machine boundaries of this system.

Logical Process Controls

Logical controls against destruction would most likely entail logging in order to provide a restarting state after restoration of the processing capability. Logical controls for disclosure would require unpredictable variations in processing flow (i.e., random changes in the procedures, such as the use of several alternating coding schemes). A logical control against modification would be verification by independent audit trail.

Logging. The Life Issuance Control Number can be recorded by each process after completing work on the associated application. An interrupted process can use the log in state-restoration as a recovery technique. This logical control can apply to either manual or automatic systems.

Varying procedures. Each process could select from several procedural paths designed to accomplish the same task. This logically protects against procedural disclosure, as the exact procedure being used at any given time would be made to be unpredictable. This control can be effected in either manual or automatic systems. For example, the definition of the image number (usually based on the date), could be variously based on the time, or a random number, or Life Issuance Control Number. An automated example would be the use of two or three separately designed and coded policy value calculation programs. The process could be known, but its usage schedule would vary.

Very often, the use of such logical process disclosure controls will exceed practical limitations. After all, the disclosure of XYZ's procedure for calculating policy values amounts to disclosure of the minutiae underlying published product information. However, for the purposes of this case study, it should be demonstrated that such logical controls are specifiable at the modeling stage. Suitable applications (such as diplomatic encryption processes) will require logical process disclosure controls such as these.

Logical process division. Each functional process could be examined for possible division in the logical model to permit fail-safe, degraded performance following a risk occurrence. To a certain extent, this control is incorporated in the current design. For example, the application review is divided into two logical functions: verify and approve. The operation of the system without either one of these processes is conceivable as a temporary, degraded, but functional alternative. Thus, it can be seen from the existing logical data flow diagram that such controls may be specified at the logical level. However, like the preceding control, the additional logical division of processes is likely to be justifiable only when "strengthened" security is required.

Verification. This control can be used at the logical level to reduce the risk of either intentional or accidental modifications to either automatic or manual processes. After each process is completed, the outgoing dataflows can be verified upon reception by the next process to ensure that the process has not corrupted the information. The verification work can be minimized by positioning the checks only at critical stages, such as those subsequent to a crossing of the man–machine boundary or prior to distributing system output (the VERIFIED-POLICY).

Control Design Iterations

The controls discussed above were inserted in the logical model of the New Life Issuance System by iteratively inserting the control cross-reference entries into the data dictionary, and inserting new dataflows, files or processes into the data flow diagram when needed. The data dictionary was not extant, and was created for the purpose of designing controls. This dictionary is adequate for control specification, but would require further details for use as a complete system specification tool.

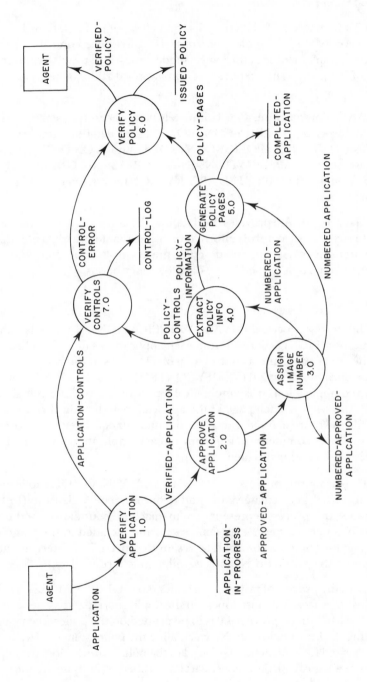

FIGURE A.5 New logical data flow diagram

New Logical Model

Figure A.5 is the new logical data flow diagram after control iterations had resolved insertion of the recommended controls. Disclosure controls for processes were not implemented at the logical model level, since these were, even at the outset of the project, not expected to win approval at the benefits analysis phase.

New logical data flow diagram. One completely new process has been added to the diagram: process 7.0 VERIFY CONTROLS. Three dataflows are new: APPLICATION-CONTROLS, POLICY-CONTROLS, and CONTROL-ERROR. There are two new files: APPLICATIONS-IN-PROGRESS and CONTROL-LOG. In addition, one file (COMPLETED-APPLICATION) is renamed to reflect its new logical purpose.

Data dictionary. Figure A.6 provides the dataflow, file and process transform descriptions to support the controls information in the new logical data flow diagram. The transform descriptions describe the controls operation, and the added controls' data is described in the dataflow descriptions.

Controls Operation

Process 1.0. During process 1.0 (VERIFY APPLICATION), the Life Issuance Control Number (LICN) is derived from each application's data. The LICN is added to the application, and a control total of all LICN's in the batch is calculated for use during process 7.0 (VERIFY CONTROLS). As the LICN is now included on the application, it is automatically part of most of the remaining dataflows in the system. Each page of the application and medical records, as well as the file jacket are marked with a "confidential" or equivalent XYZ corporate policy mark. A complete backup copy of each application (with medical forms, LICN, and markings) is filed.

Process 4.0. During this process (EXTRACT POLICY INFO), the application information is used to calculate values and determine policy clauses. (In the physical model, this process represents a man–machine boundary). Additionally, the LICN is derived *from the application data* and included in the outgoing dataflow. The LICNs and a control total is sent to process 7.0. There are now two independently derived LICNs and two independent control totals.

Process 5.0. In the process of printing the policy (GENERA}ICYPAGES), the initial LICN from process 1.0 must appear in the application image. The second version of the LICN from process 4.0 is to be printed on the policy "data page" (representing the information used in calculating the policy values). Two independently-derived LICNs can now be found in the policy. In addition, the application file's new logical purpose as a restart log is reflected in its new name.

Name: APPLICATION-IN-PROGRESS
Origin: PROCESS 1.0
□ Dataflow ☑ File
□ Process □ Element

Description:
{VERIFIED-APPLICATION}

Controls: PROCESS 7.0 Modification: PROCESS 3.0 Destruction: Disclosure: PROCESS 1.0

Name: APPROVE APPLICATION
Origin:
□ Dataflow □ File
☑ Process 2.0 □ Element

Description:
IF MEDICAL-RECORD IS UNACCEPTABLE
THEN RETURN VERIFIED-APPLICATION TO AGENT

AFIX APPROVAL TO MEDICAL-RECORD

Controls: PROCESS 7.0 Modification: PROCESS 1.0 Destruction: Disclosure: (MANY PROCEDURES?)

Name: APPLICATION
Origin: AGENT
☑ Dataflow □ File
□ Process □ Element

Description:
{APPLICATION-FORM + MEDICAL-RECORD}

Controls: Modification: Destruction: — SOURCE — Disclosure:

Name: APPLICATION-CONTROLS
Origin: PROCESS 1.0
☑ Dataflow □ File
□ Process □ Element

Description:
{APPLICATION-LICN + TOTAL-APPLICATION-LICN}

Controls: PROCESS 7.0 Modification: PROCESS 7.0 Destruction: PROCESS 1.0 Disclosure: PROCESS 1.0

FIGURE A.6.1 Data dictionary

Name: COMPLETED-APPLICATION   ☐ Dataflow ☐ File ☑
Origin: PROCESS 5.0   ☐ Process ☐ Element

Description:

{ NUMBERED-APPLICATION }

Controls: PROCESS 7.0   **Modification:**   **Destruction:** PROCESS 3.0   **Disclosure:** PROCESS 1.0

Name: CONTROL-ERROR   ☐ Dataflow ☐ File
Origin: PROCESS 7.0   ☐ Process ☐ Element

Description:

ERROR-NOTICE
+
{ UNMATCHED-APPLICATION-LICN }
+
{ UNMATCHED-POLICY-LICN }

Controls: PROCESS 6.0   **Modification:**   **Destruction:** PROCESS 7.0   **Disclosure:** PROCESS 7.0

Name: APPROVED-APPLICATION   ☑ Dataflow ☐ File
Origin: PROCESS 2.0   ☐ Process ☐ Element

Description:

{ APPLICATION-FORM
+
APPLICATION-LICN
+
APPROVED-MEDICAL-RECORD }

Controls: PROCESS 7.0   **Modification:** PROCESS 7.0   **Destruction:** PROCESS 1.0   **Disclosure:** PROCESS 1.0

Name: ASSIGN IMAGE NUMBER   ☐ Dataflow ☐ File
Origin: ☑ Process 3.0 ☐ Element

Description:

AFIX IMAGE-NUMBER TO APPROVED-APPLICATION

Controls: PROCESS 7.0   **Modification:** PROCESS 7.0   **Destruction:** PROCESS 1.0 (WHY PROCESS ONE?)   **Disclosure:**

FIGURE A.6.2 Data dictionary (continued)

Name: CONTROL-LOG
Origin: PROCESS 7.0
☐ Dataflow ☑ File
☐ Process ☐ Element

Description:
{ APPLICATION-CONTROLS }
+
{ POLICY-CONTROLS }

Controls: PROCESS 7.0 Modification: PROCESS 7.0 Destruction: PROCESS 1.0 Disclosure: PROCESS 7.0

Name: EXTRACT POLICY INFO
Origin:
☐ Dataflow ☐ File
☑ Process 4.0 ☐ Element

Description:
RECORD POLICY-DATA
CALCULATE PREMIUMS
CALCULATE CASH-VALUES
ASSEMBLE CLAUSE-SPECIFIER
DERIVE POLICY-LICN
AFFIX CLASSIFICATIONS

Controls: PROCESS 7.0 Modification: PROCESS 7.0 (IMPY PROCEDURE) Destruction: Disclosure:

Name: GENERATE POLICY PAGES
Origin: PROCESS 5.0
☐ Dataflow ☐ File
☑ Process 5.0 ☐ Element

Description:
MERGE POLICY-DATA
SELECTED-POLICY-CLAUSES
PREMIUMS
NUMBERED-APPLICATION
BUYERS GUIDE
VALUE TABLES
AFFIX CLASSIFICATION NOTICES

Controls: PROCESS 6.0 Modification: PROCESS 7.0 (IMPY PROCEDURE) Destruction: Disclosure:

Name: ISSUED-POLICY
Origin: PROCESS 6.0
☐ Dataflow ☑ File
☐ Process ☐ Element

Description:
{ POLICY-PAGES }

Controls: PROCESS 6.0 Modification: PROCESS 3.0 Destruction: Disclosure: PROCESS 4.0

FIGURE A.6.3 Data dictionary (continued)

FIGURE A.6.4 Data dictionary (continued)

Name: VERIFIED-POLICY
Origin: PROCESS 6.0
☑ Dataflow ☐ File
☐ Process ☐ Element
Description:

{ COVER + POLICY-PAGES }

Modification: Destruction: —SINK—   Disclosure:
Controls:

Name: VERIFY APPLICATION
Origin:
☐ Dataflow ☐ File
☑ Process 1.0 ☐ Element
Description:

IF APPLICATION IS INCOMPLETE THEN RETURN TO AGENT

AFIX "CONFIDENTIAL" NOTICE TO APPLICATION-FORM AND MEDICAL-RECORD AND CONTROLS

DERIVE LICN FROM NAME, INSURANCE AMOUNT, AND BIRTHDATE

ENTER LICN ON APPLICATION-FORM AND APPLICATION-CONTROLS

Modification: PROCESS 7.0   Destruction: PROCESS 1.0   Disclosure: (GREY PROCEDURE)
Controls: PROCESS 7.0

Name: POLICY-PAGES
Origin: PROCESS 5.0
☑ Dataflow ☐ File
☐ Process ☐ Element
Description:

{ SELECTED-POLICY-CLAUSES + POLICY-DATA + POLICY-LICN + PREMIUMS + NUMBERED-APPLICATION + APPLICATION-LICN }

Modification: PROCESS 6.0   Destruction: PROCESS 5.0   Disclosure: PROCESS 5.0
Controls:

Name: VERIFIED-APPLICATION
Origin: PROCESS 1.0
☑ Dataflow ☐ File
☐ Process ☐ Element
Description:

{ APPLICATION-FORM + APPLICATION-LICN + MEDICAL-RECORD }

Modification: PROCESS 7.0   Destruction: PROCESS 1.0   Disclosure: PROCESS 1.0
Controls:

FIGURE A.6.5 Data dictionary (continued)

Name: VERIFY CONTROLS
Origin:

☐ Dataflow ☐ File
☑ Process 7.0 ☐ Element

Description:

IF TOTAL-APPLICATION-LICN IS NOT EQUAL TO
TOTAL-POLICY-LICN THEN
COMPARE EACH POLICY-LICN TO
EACH APPLICATION-LICN
ADD ALL UNMATCHED LICNs TO
CONTROL-ERROR
AFIX CLASSIFICATION NOTICE TO CONTROL-ERROR

Controls: Modification: PROCESS 6.0 Destruction: PROCESS 7.0 Disclosure: (VARY PROCEDURE)

Name: VERIFY POLICY
Origin:

☐ Dataflow ☐ File
☑ Process 6.0 ☐ Element

Description:

IF POLICY IS INCOMPLETE THEN ROUTE TO RECREATE
IF CONTROL-ERROR EXISTS THEN
COMPARE EACH APPLICATION AND POLICY LICN
OTHERWISE
'SPOT' COMPARE APPLICATION AND POLICY LICN
IF LICN MISMATCH THEN
COMPARE APPLICATION AND POLICY-DATA
IF POLICY-DATA MISMATCH THEN
ROUTE TO RE-CREATE

Controls: Modification: PROCESS 7.0 Destruction: PROCESS 5.0 Disclosure: (VARY PROCEDURE)

FIGURE A.6.6 Data dictionary (continued)

Process 7.0. The only new process (VERIFY CONTROLS) receives the two sets of LICNs and the batch totals of each set. Since these numbers are arithmetically related to the critical data elements, an error related to these critical elements will produce a mismatch in the totals. A mismatched total condition would precipitate a search through both sets of LICNs for mismatches. Thus, erroneous applications or policies can be identified by their LICNs. The existence of an error condition is signaled by the CONTROL-ERROR dataflow passed to process 6.0. Protection against the loss of the system processing state is enhanced by the retention of LICNs in a temporary control log file. This control log asserts the application's completion in processes 1.0 or 4.0. Processes 3.0, 5.0 and 6.0 can use their outgoing file dataflows as restart logs.

Process 6.0. This process (VERIFY POLICY) was a "toothless" control previously, only able to ascertain the proper number of pages in a policy. The availability of an error signal (CONTROL-ERROR) will now allow the process to become aware of an error in logical policy content. The suspect policy can be identified by its LICNs and examined for disagreement between the LICN from process 1.0 (on the application image) and the LICN from process 4.0 (on the data page) and the policy details (name, face amount, and birth date). Thus, the corruption of the critical data fields could be identified and corrected (as well as control errors introduced by errors in LICN processing). An additional data-element is presently available for state restoration in this process. The ISSUED-POLICY file provides such log information for the completion of process 6.0. Thus, this file, in concert with the CONTROL LOG of process 7.0, provides a final state verification for the system.

New Physical Model

During the final stage of structured analysis, the design is subjected to additional iterations during which the costs and benefits of various man–machine boundaries are explored. In a normal redesign project, such experiments would be of interest in control design (such as the introduction of source data capture in process 1.0). However, this particular case mandated security for an existing system, and the operational physical design was not to be modified unless required for controls.

In fact, the controls design above has carefully avoided any logical changes in the original specification which might normally be dictated by a general system redesign. (For example, the return of the figure A.2 current physical dataflow APPROVED-APPLICATION-WITH-MEDICAL-RECORDS to the NEW BUSINESS ASSISTANT, instead of directly to the scanning operation as dictated by the current logical data flow diagram.)

Consequently, many physical characteristics of the eventual system must be accepted as defined: new logical diagram processes 1.0 and 6.0 (see figure A.5) are manual, and process 4.0 includes transcription and automation. It follows that the data-flows connected with processes 1.0 and 6.0 must be in manual form (APPLICATION-CONTROLS and CONTROL-ERROR), and POLICY-CONTROLS will issue from an automated system. Thus, the new process is likely to require a man-machine boundary, but the selection of a manual or automation basis is a subject for benefits analysis in the present study.

As a control function, process 7.0 (figure A.5) should be carefully guarded against major risks, but what are the major risks? Consider this function from the view of figure 5.5 (*Internal–External Risks*). External risks such as sabotage and espionage would not be major considerations in this process. Sabotage would interrupt controls, but leave the system and its data operational. Espionage would seem to offer little threat, since control numbers do not contain enough information for privacy problems, and the total face value of issued insurance is considered to be public information by the organization. Internal risks, however, such as fraud or integrity might be a problem. Integrity loss is particularly critical, since potential errors in the control values could slow processing or discredit the controls. The internal–external risk model would therefore promote the automation of this process, minimizing the internal risks.

Intuitively, this would agree with the often-made and sensible observation that calculation of totals or comparison of numerical lists is something at which a computer would be much more adept. It must be remembered, however, that the selection of automation for this process would expose the dataflows and files to primarily internal risks, and controls should be considered for reducing this risk.

Identifying the Effective Controls

DeMarco assigns benefits analysis to the new physical modeling stage of structured specification. It would be appropriate to consider the implementation of the logical controls according to the security model and heuristics presented in chapter five. Physical controls would also be considered during these iterations, both as design additions required by environmental risks, and as subjects of benefits analysis. However, most general physical controls, such as fire control and system access pre-existed the project, and were not included in the task. Therefore, for the purposes of this case study, the logical controls will remain as focal points for the selection process.

A Prolog rules database can be constructed which reflects the logical security dynamics in a manner similar to the example in chapter 5. Figure A.7 through A.9 illustrate the construction of the database. A.7 reflects the controls and targets in rule form, A.8 lists the threats from the database, and A.9 is an extract of the various other rules which comprised the general population of the database.

control("Backup Application File")
control("Classification")
control("Logging")
control("Varying Procedures")
control("Logical Process Division")
control("Verification")
target("Verify Application")
target("Approve Application")
target("Assign Image Number")
target("Extract Policy Info")
target("Generate Policy Pages")
target("Verify Policy")
target("Verify Controls")
target("Verified Application")
target("Approved Application")
target("Numbered Application")
target("Numbered Approved Application")
target("Policy Information")
target("Policy Pages")
target("Issued Policy")
target("Application Controls")
target("Policy Controls")
target("Control Error")
target("Application In Progress")

FIGURE A.7 Controls and targets database

The database was submitted to the heuristics as discussed in chapter 5. A few additional features were added for interaction, and some efficiency modifications were necessary for the microcomputer implementation, but these did not alter the underlying logic from chapter 5.[3] A full listing of the program will be found at the end of the appendix.

The result of the first execution "pass" of the program asserted the Classification control to be the most important of all control elements. The heuristics were applied a second time (with Classification "assumed") in order to obtain a second-level appraisal. Verification and the Backup Application File received equally strong recommendations.

The report (including an abstract of the exposure analysis) is found in figure A.10. Not surprisingly, the set of controls was found to be significant

---

3   The Prolog program segment titled "Assume predefined controls" implements this layering capability as described in the discussion of exposure analysis in chapter 5.

```
threat("Air conditioning loss")
threat("Arson")
threat("Blackmail")
threat("Bomb threats")
threat("Browsing")
threat("Building collapse")
threat("Copyright violations")
threat("Data corruption")
threat("Equipment failure")
threat("Error")
threat("Espionage")
threat("Explosion")
threat("Fire")
threat("Flood")
threat("Fraud")
threat("Heat loss")
threat("Illness")
threat("Industrial action")
threat("Industrial sabotage")
threat("Misplacement")
threat("Misrouting")
threat("Personnel turnover")
threat("Power loss")
threat("Riot")
threat("Supplies shortage")
threat("Telephone degradation")
threat("Telephone loss")
threat("Terrorism")
threat("Theft of Trade Secret")
threat("Theft of Computer Service")
threat("Theft of Software")
threat("Theft of Equipment")
threat("Vandalism")
threat("Water supply loss")
threat("Wiretapping")
```

FIGURE A.8 Threats database

avoidance
(sheath("Classification","Espionage"),
liner("Classification","Application In Progress"))
accidental("Air conditioning loss")
accidental("Building collapse")
automated("Numbered Application")
automated("Policy Information")
confidence(mitigation(
sheath("Verification","Error"),
liner("Verification","Issued Policy")),0.8)
data("Verified Application")
data("Approved Application")
destruction("Vandalism")
destruction("Personnel turnover")
disclosure("Blackmail")
disclosure("Browsing")
intentional("Vandalism")
intentional("Wiretapping")
liner("Backup Application File","Verify Application")
logical("Backup Application File")
logical("Classification")
manual("Control Error")
manual("Application In Progress")
modification("Air conditioning loss")
modification("Blackmail")
process("Verify Application")
process("Approve Application")
sheath("Backup Application File","Misplacement")

FIGURE A.9 Extract of the Classification database

according to the model. The model tends to be more selective with physical controls (as in the example in Chapter 5). However, when the program is run with only the plurality rule (RULE 7), the controls Varying Procedures and Logical Process Division cease to be found significant. These two controls, while significant in the inversion model, are less significant across the population.

At the risk of belaboring the point, it might be useful to consider each of the controls from the logical design in relation to the recommendation. This would be particularly useful to those who would be defining the effective controls *without* the benefit of the expert system.

The following controls are significant:

Backup Application File
Classification
Logging
Vary Procedures
Logical Process Division
Verification

The following controls are recommended:

["Backup Application File","Verification","Classification"]

Exposure remains of Verify Application to Copyright violations
Recommendation: No known controls CNF 0

Exposure remains of Approve Application to Theft of Equipment
Recommendation: Logging CNF 0.6

Exposure remains of Assign Image Number to Telephone degradation
Recommendation: No known controls CNF 0

Exposure remains of Extract Policy Info to Illness
Recommendation: Logging CNF 0.6

Exposure remains of Extract Policy Info to Personnel turnover
Recommendation: Logging CNF 0.6

FIGURE A.10 Program output with Classification assumed

Data element controls. These controls include the Backup Application File, Document Classification, and the Life Issuance Control Number. Each is considered below.

Application backup copy. This control is primarily included as a protection against destruction of the application materials (these are *manual data*). Such destructive threats could be derived from integrity loss, environmental risks, or sabotage risks. The rules database indicated this control was significant because it protected this manual data from external risks, and it had a high plurality effect. This control appeared with a high confidence factor as a mitigating assurance for three processes and three data-elements against a large number of destructive threats. This file also supported restart procedures by implicitly recording the processing status.

Classification. This control applies to both manual and automated data, since the image containing the classification crosses the man–machine boundary twice. It is offered as a protection against disclosure (although it also provides insulation against fraud). Disclosure is primarily an external risk, and is modeled chiefly as a manual data risk. From a practical viewpoint, damage resulting from such disclosure would regard violations of client privacy, and involves moral and legal obligations of the organization in protecting against this risk. This control, by virtue of its model significance and its high population in the mitigation relations, was suggested as a candidate for implementation.

Life Issuance Control Number. The LICN appeared in the controls database only as a component of the verification control. This control, like the preceding one, guards both manual and automatic data. The LICN chiefly protects against modification. Such modification might result from integrity loss or fraud risks. This is particularly important in controlling automated data. Several such elements exist without logical controls in the present system. This control, as an underlying part of verification, is suggested by the heuristics.

Process element controls. Three logical controls are considered for protecting processes: logging, varying procedures, and verification. Each of these is discussed below.

Logging. This control would chiefly reduce the risk of process destruction. Such destruction might logically develop from sabotage or from the physical environment. Such destruction is generally an external risk, and as such is primarily a risk to automated processes. Logging was found to be significant by the program on the basis of its high population in mitigating relations. However, since it did little in the protection of any data elements, and was overlapped by the application backup, it did not see support in the first two rounds of processing. Also, since the present recovery controls in the computer-based elements of the subject system are considered strong enough to meet this threat, the logging function is not a likely candidate for implementation.

Varying procedures. These controls were given only the briefest consideration at the logical level, owing to the strong suggestion that these were insignificant. As a control protecting against the external threat of disclosure of relatively public processes (primarily an automated system risk), it offers little logical value. The program did not discover any plurality significance in the control, and the rules only related it to one process element (Approve Application). It is possible to conceive of such threats: for example, a competitor might wish to steal a copy of the computer program to avoid incurring development costs of a duplicate system. However, physical access controls in the computer-based system are likely to provide adequate control in preventing this risk. The logical disclosure controls are very unlikely candidates for implementation in this system.

Logical process division. Like the preceding logging control, the logical division of processes is likely to be justifiable only when "strengthened" security is required to protect against process destruction. Failure of one process in the New Life Issuance system, and the resulting system stoppage, is unlikely to be permitted to extend to a lengthy degree. The temporary loss of the system is one that could be endured without great cost, and such fail-safe controls as logical process division would be unjustifiable in these circumstances. The program found no plurality significance in the control, and its functions were often overlapped by other controls. While no additional such controls may be worthwhile, the existing divisions (e.g., application verification and approval) could be retained.

Verification. This control is offered as a mitigating control against process modification. This is primarily an internal risk; i.e., fraud or integrity loss. These are primarily process risks in manual systems. Present controls in this area were described above as weak and "toothless". This control was evaluated by the heuristics in concert with the Life Issuance Control Number, was found significant and frequently useful. It is therefore a strong candidate for implementation.

New Physical Data Flow Diagram

The translation of the New Logical Model into a physical data flow diagram is illustrated in figure A.11. Ineffective controls have been removed, and the inclusion of new logical process 7.0 in the IBM mainframe system (new physical process 5.0) documents its position on the machine side of the man-machine boundary.

As discussed above, the incorporation of most of the control number process into the automated function is desirable. For example, the APPLICATION-CONTROLS dataflow might be physically machine-readable (e.g., optical mark or bar recognition), enabling direct entry into the automated system. The previous existence of such devices in the data processing inventory of the organization should dictate the exact physical nature of this dataflow.

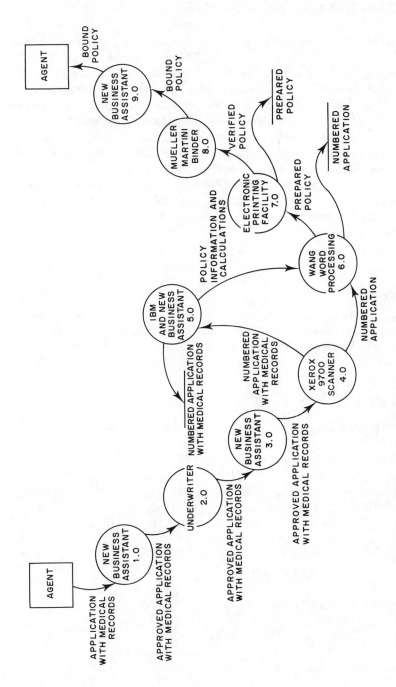

FIGURE A.11 New physical data flow diagram

TECHNICAL NOTES ON COMPUTER USAGE

The examples were run using Borland Turbo Prolog, running under MS-DOS 3.2 on a UNISYS IT (512k bytes memory). This version of Prolog is prone to stack overflows, and recursion avoidance was often required (meaning frequent use of the "fail" predicate), along with a plethora of cuts ("!") to eliminate backtracking. This, together with the interactive predicates, makes the working listing below a bit more cluttered than the tidy presentation in chapter 5.

The rules database could be constructed with a text editor, but this may create integrity problems. A small example such as this case had over 10,500 words in the database. There were actually two other Prolog programs: a database editor which aided in effectively creating the shield relations, and a report generator which provides more interesting listings than the relations illustrated here.

These source programs and compiled programs are available on diskette from the address given in the flyleaf.

REFERENCES

Bass, R. "A study in information systems security." M.Sc. working paper, Department of Computer Science, University of Tennessee at Chattanooga, 1985.
DeMarco, *Structured Analysis and System Specification*. New York: Yourdon, 1979.

FULL PROGRAM LISTING

```
/*—(CH5SPEC.PRO)—————————————————— */
/*                                                    */
/* CONTROLS SELECTION "TINY" EXPERT SYSTEM            */
/*                                                    */
/*    (from chapter 5, DESIGNING INFORMATION          */
/*    SYSTEM SECURITY, London: J.Wiley, 1987)         */
/*                                                    */
/*    Environment: IBM PC/AT 512K                     */
/*             MS DOS 3.2                              */
/*             Borland Turbo Prolog                   */
/*                                                    */
/*    Author: Richard Baskerville                     */
/*          POB 666                                   */
/*          Chattanooga, Tn 37401 USA                 */
/*                                                    */
/*———————————                                         */
```

```
/*      Some improvements have been made to         */
/*   elementary program for use in the case         */
/*   study. The ability to assume controls          */
/*   is added to the analysis program.              */
/*   Cuts have been added to certain                */
/*   predicates to increase determinism and         */
/*   improve execution time. The significant        */
/*   controls have also been asserted to            */
/*   reduce execution time. Exposure analysis       */
/*   is made optional.                              */
```

```
domains

  risk = avoidance(shield,shield) ;
      tolerance(shield,shield) ;
      mitigation(shield,shield)
  shield = sheath(symbol,symbol) ;
      liner(symbol,symbol)
  symbolist = symbol*

database

  accidental(symbol)
  assumed(symbol)
  automated(symbol)
  avoidance(shield,shield)
  confidence(risk,real)
  control(symbol)
  data(symbol)
  destruction(symbol)
  disclosure(symbol)
  intentional(symbol)
  liner(symbol,symbol)
  logical(symbol)
  manual(symbol)
  mitigation(shield,shield)
  modification(symbol)
  possible_controls(symbolist)
  process(symbol)
  recommend_ctl_list(symbolist)
  sheath(symbol,symbol)
  sig(symbol)
```

    target(symbol)
    threat(symbol)
    tolerance(shield,shield)

predicates

    a_shield_exists(symbol,symbol,symbol,real)
    add_rec(symbol)
    add_to_list(symbol)
    analyze
    append(symbolist,symbolist,symbolist)
    assume_ctls
    assume_ctls1(symbol)
    assume_ctls3
    build_des
    build_des2
    build_dis
    build_dis2
    build_mod
    build_mod2
    check_coverage
    confirm
    confirm1(symbol)
    count(symbol,symbol,integer,integer)
    count1(integer,integer,symbol,symbolist)
    covered(symbol,symbol)
    ctlthtpop(symbol,integer)
    exposed(symbol,symbol)
    external(symbol)
    high_freq(symbol,integer)
    highest(symbol,integer,symbol,integer,symbol,integer)
    internal(symbol)
    make_rec
    member(symbol,symbolist)
    number_of_lists(symbol,integer)
    physical(symbol)
    print_recommends
    recommend_ctls
    remove_list(symbol)
    sig_ctl(symbol)
    spec_recommend(symbol,symbol,symbol,real)
    start_list

```prolog
goal

    consult("controls.dbf"),
    analyze.

clauses

/*—(PHYSICAL/INTERNAL)——————————————— */

physical(C) :- control(C),                      /*RULE 1*/
    not(logical(C)).
internal(T) :- modification(T).                 /*RULE 2*/
internal(T) :- disclosure(T),                   /*RULE 3*/
    accidental(T).
 external(T) :- threat(T),
    not(internal(T)                             /*RULE 4*/
member(E,[E|_]).
member(E,[_|Ts]) :- member(E,Ts)

/*—(SIGNIFICANT CONTROLS)——————————————— */

sig_ctl(C) :- external(Th),                     /*RULE 5*/
    target(Tg),
    manual(Tg),
    data(Tg),
    a_shield_exists(Th,C,Tg,Cnf),
    Cnf > 0.5,!.
sig_ctl(C) :- external(Th),                     /*RULE 5*/
    target(Tg),
    automated(Tg),
    process(Tg),
    a_shield_exists(Th,C,Tg,Cnf),
    Cnf > 0.5,!.
sig_ctl(C) :- internal(Th),                     /*RULE 5*/
    target(Tg),
    manual(Tg),
    process(Tg),
    a_shield_exists(Th,C,Tg,Cnf),
    Cnf > 0.5,!.
sig_ctl(C) :- internal(Th),                     /*RULE 5*/
    target(Tg),
    automated(Tg),
```

```
            data(Tg),
            a_shield_exists(Th,C,Tg,Cnf),
            Cnf > 0.5,!.
sig_ctl(C) :- ctlthtpop(_,T),                      /*RULE 7*/
            ctlthtpop(C,Tc),
            Tc / T > 0.3,!.
a_shield_exists(Th,C,Tg,Cnf) :-                    /*RULE 6*/
    confidence(avoidance(sheath(C,Th),liner(_,Tg)),Cnf).
a_shield_exists(Th,C,Tg,Cnf) :-
    confidence(tolerance(sheath(C,Th),liner(_,Tg)),Cnf).
a_shield_exists(Th,C,Tg,Cnf) :-
    confidence(mitigation(sheath(C,Th),liner(_,Tg)),Cnf).
ctlthtpop(C,Cnt2) :- retract(threat(Tht)),
        ctlthtpop(C,Cnt1),
        asserta(threat(Tht)),
        count(C,Tht,Cnt1,Cnt2),!.
ctlthtpop(_,0) :- !.


count(C,Tht,Cnt1,Cnt2) :- sheath(C,Tht),
        Cnt2 = Cnt1 + 1,!.
count(_,_,Cnt,Cnt) :- !.


/*—(POSSIBLE CONTROL LIST CONSTRUCTION)————*/


build_mod :- target(Tg),                           /*RULE 8*/
        start_list,
        modification(Tht),
        a_shield_exists(Tht,Ctl,Tg,Cnf),
        Cnf > 0.5,
        add_to_list(Ctl),fail.
build_mod.
build_des :- target(Tg),                           /*RULE 8*/
        start_list,
        destruction(Tht),
        a_shield_exists(Tht,Ctl,Tg,Cnf),
        Cnf > 0.5,
        add_to_list(Ctl),fail.
build_des.
build_dis :- target(Tg), /*RULE 8*/
        start_list,
        disclosure(Tht),
```

```
            a_shield_exists(Tht,Ctl,Tg,Cnf),
            Cnf > 0.5,
            add_to_list(Ctl),fail.
build_dis.
build_mod2 :- target(Tg),                          /*RULE 8A*/
        start_list,
        modification(Tht),
        a_shield_exists(Tht,Ctl,Tg,Cnf),
        Cnf > 0.5,
        sig(Ctl),
        add_to_list(Ctl),fail.
build_mod2.
build_des2 :- target(Tg),                          /*RULE 8A*/
        start_list,
        destruction(Tht),
        a_shield_exists(Tht,Ctl,Tg,Cnf),
        Cnf > 0.5,
        sig(Ctl),
        add_to_list(Ctl),fail.
build_des2.
build_dis2 :- target(Tg),                          /*RULE 8A*/
        start_list,
        disclosure(Tht),
        a_shield_exists(Tht,Ctl,Tg,Cnf),
        Cnf > 0.5,
        sig(Ctl),
        add_to_list(Ctl),fail.
build_dis2.


start_list :- asserta(possible_controls([])),!.
add_to_list(Ctl) :- possible_controls(Ctlist),
        not(member(Ctl,Ctlist)),
        not(assumed(Ctl)),
        retract(possible_controls(Ctlist)),
        append(Ctlist,[Ctl],Newctlist)
        asserta(possible_controls(Newctlist)),!.
add_to_list(_) :- !.


append([],Ls,Ls).
append([H|Ts1],Ls2,[H|Ts3]) :- append(Ts1,Ls2,Ts3).
```

```
/*—(CONTROL SELECTION)————————————————— */


make_rec :- high_freq(C,_),                      /*RULE 10*/
     add_rec(C),
     remove_list(C),
make_rec,!                                        /*RULE 13*/
make_rec.


remove_list(C) :- possible_controls(Cs),
     member(C,Cs),
     retract(possible_controls(Cs)),
     remove_list(C),!.
remove_list(_).
add_rec(_) :- not(recommend_ctl_list(_)),         /*RULE 11*/
     asserta(recommend_ctl_list([])),fail.
add_rec(C) :- recommend_ctl_list(Cs),
     not(member(C,Cs)),
     retract(recommend_ctl_list(Cs)),
     append(Cs,[C],Newcs),
     asserta(recommend_ctl_list(Newcs)),!.
add_rec(_):-!.


/*—(FREQUENCY COUNTING)————————————————— */


high_freq(_,_) :- retract(possible_controls([])),fail.
high_freq(_,_) :- not(possible_controls(_)),!,fail.
high_freq(C2,N2) :- retract(control(C)),
     high_freq(C1,N1),
     asserta(control(C)),
     number_of_lists(C,N),
     highest(C,N,C1,N1,C2,N2),!.
high_freq(_,0).            N1 N,!.
highest(C,N,_,_,C,N).
number_of_lists(C,Cnt1) :- retract(possible_controls(Ps)),
     number_of_lists(C,Cnt2),
     count1(Cnt1,Cnt2,C,Ps),
     asserta(possible_controls(Ps)),!.
number_of_lists(_,0).
count1(Cnt,Cnt2,C,Cs) :- member(C,Cs),
     Cnt = Cnt2 + 1,!.
count1(Cnt,Cnt,_,_).
```

```
/*—(LOGICAL RECOMMEND CONTROLS)——————— */

recommend_ctls :- build_mod2,      /* Recommend Significant */
          build_des2,              /* and effective controls */
          build_dis2,              /* of all three types */
        make_rec, ,
          build_mod,               /* Recomme additional */
          build_des,               /* effective controls */
          build_dis,               /* all types if required */
        make_rec. ,

/*—(EXPOSURE/COVERED)——————————*/
covered(Th,Tg) :- recommend_ctl_list(Cs),     /*RULE 14*/
      control(C),
      member(C,Cs),
      a_shield_exists(Th,C,Tg,Cnf),
      Cnf 0.5.
exposed(Th,Tg) :- not(covered(Th,Tg)).        /*RULE 15*/

/*—(SPECIFIC CONTROL)—————————————— */

spec_recommend(Tht,C,Tgt,Cnf) :-
    exposed(Tht,Tgt), ,                       /*RULE 16*/
    a_shield_exists(Tht,C,Tgt,Cnf),
    recommend_ctl_list(Cs),
    not(member(C,Cs)),
    Cnf 0.5,
    sig(C),!.
spec_recommend(Tht,C,Tgt,Cnf) :-
    exposed(Tht,Tgt),                         /*RULE 17*/
    a_shield_exists(Tht,C,Tgt,Cnf),
    recommend_ctl_list(Cs),
    not(member(C,Cs)),
    Cnf 0.5,!.
spec_recommend(Tht,C,Tgt,Cnf) :- exposed(Tht,Tgt),
    a_shield_exists(Tht,C,Tgt,Cnf),           /*RULE 17A*/
    recommend_ctl_list(Cs),
    not(member(C,Cs)),!.
spec_recommend(Tht,C,Tgt,0) :- exposed(Tht,Tgt),
    C = "No known controls",!                 /*RULE 17B*/

/*—(ANALYSIS)—————————————————— */
```

```
        analyze :- control(C),
            sig_ctl(C),                        /* speed up list building */
            assert(sig(C)),fail.
    analyze :- write("\The following controls are significant:"),
            sig(C),nl,write(C),fail.
    analyze :- assume_ctls,
            recommend_ctls,
            print_recommends,
            check_coverage.
    print_recommends :- assume_ctls3,nl,
            write("The following controls are recommended:"),
            recommend_ctl_list(Clist),
            nl,write(Clist).
    check_coverage :- write("\Exposure analysis "),confirm,
            target(Tgt),
            threat(Tht),
            spec_recommend(Tht,C,Tgt,Cnf),nl,nl,
            write("Exposure remains of ",Tgt," to ",Tht),nl,
            write("Recommendation: ",C," CNF ",Cnf),fail.
    check_coverage.


    /*-(ASSUME PREDEFINED CONTROLS)——————— */
assume_ctls :- nl,write("Assume controls "),
        confirm,
        control(C),
        assume_ctls1(C),
        fail.
    assume_ctls.
    assume_ctls1(C) :- nl,write(C),confirm,
        retract(control(C)),
        assertz(assumed(C)).
    assume_ctls1(_).
    assume_ctls3 :- retract(assumed(C)),
        retract(recommend_ctl_list(Cs)),
        append(Cs,[C],Ns),
        asserta(recommend_ctl_list(Ns)),
        assume_ctls3,!.
    assume_ctls3.


    confirm :- write("(y/n)?"),            /*Interactive Keyboard*/
        readchar(Keyin),                   /*Confirmation     */
        str_char(Letter,Keyin),
```

```
    upper_lower(Letter,Answer),
    confirm1(Answer),!.
confirm1("y").
confirm1("n") :- !,fail.
confirm1(_) :- confirm.
```

Appendix B

Review of
STRUCTURED INFORMATION SYSTEMS ANALYSIS AND SPECIFICATION

Information system specifications have traditionally been a product of "style." The "style" of the analyst or the organization dictated the approach and level of detail required. The division of work between the analyst, designer and programmer was often decided within the context of each project. Structured approaches to systems analysis attempt to provide a uniform system specification. Dictates for the division of work and level of detail are fixed by the rigorous nature of the tools applied.

Structured analysis literature is dominated by the approaches of two authorities: Tom DeMarco [1979] and the work by Chris Gane and Trish Sarson [1979]. Both works provide similar techniques and benefits. The form presented in this paper is chiefly the technique presented by DeMarco.

Structured Analysis

The product of systems analysis is a system specification or target document. This document should delineate the optimal target system, and provide a vehicle for later evaluation of the success of the project. The specification should provide enough details to accurately predict the economic feasibility (cost–benefit), project schedules and performance characteristics of the proposed system. Thus, the specification must provide an effective model of the system being designed.

Structured specifications carefully remove physical elements from the target document. Logical specifications detail *what* must be accomplished, and physical specifications detail *how* this must be done. By eliminating the physical aspects from the model, the model may be logically manipulated for performance predictions *without* physically creating the target system.

The goals of structured analysis include the provision of a "maintainable" specification. This means that the document can be corrected without extensive re-analysis or re-design of the specification. The specification should also maximize the effective use of graphics in providing system details ("one picture is worth a thousand words"). The logical model of the system must be complete before the system implementation begins.

Structured analysts employ a set of "tools" to achieve this modeling. These tools include data flow diagrams, a data dictionary, and transform descriptions (composed of structured English, decision tables, hierarchy charts, etc.).

Structured specifications are removed from the managerial issues: cost–benefit, project management, politics, equipment selection, personnel considerations, and performance analysis. These problems are left to be resolved in the organizational climate of which the analysis in a part.

The structured approach resolves many problems which have plagued the specification of information systems. Last-minute changes wrecked those specifications on which system implementation had begun, thus changes were not permitted after this point (known as "freezing" the specification). Such changes can be easily incorporated in the "maintainable" structured specification. Redundancy is avoided and wordy descriptions eliminated by the reliance on graphics to convey the details of the design. Removal of the physical elements eliminated implementation dependencies from the design. The specification ceased to be "tedious", both to its creator and its user.

Structured Analysis Project

The use of the rigorous structured design approach has the effect of moving a considerable amount of the "codification" work out of the program-design stage, and into the analysis stage of system development. The improved use of graphics causes both narrative and redundancy to be dramatically reduced. The physical nature of the system is also carefully removed from the specification.

The steps involved in creating a new system through the use of structured analysis are generally similar to the traditional system life cycle:

1. Survey the existing system.
2. Conduct Structured Systems Analysis
3. Conduct hardware study and specification.
4. Create structured design.
5. Implement the design.

The one step that is dramatically different from traditional systems design approaches is step two (2), "conduct structured systems analysis and design." This step is the creation of the structured specification that will be described below. The steps in structured analysis are:

(1) STUDY CURRENT ENVIRONMENT — This entails modeling the current system from the viewpoint of the data. It is important that the model be verifiable. During this step the analyst must determine the context of the system;

identify the users; interview the users; create a physical data flow diagram of the current system; and collect sample data, forms and files.

(2) DERIVE LOGICAL EQUIVALENT — The data flow diagram created in the first step usually contains physical references to the components of the present system. These are rigorously replaced in the documentation with their logical equivalents. For example, the physical data flow diagram may refer to the transmission of the payroll report from the payroll clerk to the accounting manager — these physical references would be replaced by a logical description (such as transmission of the payroll report from the "preparation of checks" function to the "approve payroll" function). (See figure B.1.)

(3) MODEL NEW LOGICAL SYSTEM — The logical model is "remanufactured" to meet the current demands of the users. This process will be discussed below. Several "options" or variations of the new logical system may be specified for consideration by the users.

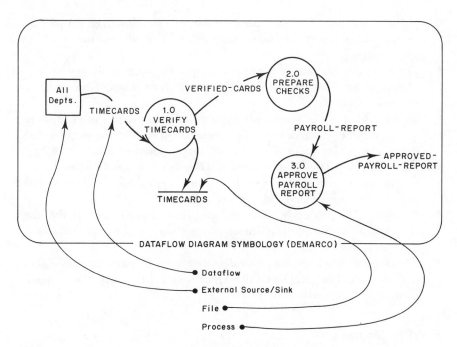

FIGURE B.1 DeMarco's data flow diagram conventions
(Tom DeMarco, Structured Analysis and System Specification, © 1979, p.47. Adapted by permission of Prentice-Hall, Inc., Englewood Cliffs, New Jersey.)

(4) ESTABLISH MAN–MACHINE INTERFACE — This step designates the scope of automation within the new logical model.

(5) QUANTIFY EACH OPTION — financial parameters such as plant costs, operating, conversion, training and risk are estimated for each feasible logical option. The structured specification "toolbox" currently has no tools with which to accomplish this step.

(6) SELECT OPTION — Management chooses the optimum solution for the best fit with the organizations needs, objectives and goals.

(7) PACKAGE SPECIFICATION — The selected logical system specification is completed: data dictionary, data flow diagram and transform descriptions are checked for consistency and completeness.
   The final, selected, packaged specification will be composed of data flow diagrams, data dictionary and transform descriptions. It will be characterized by:

- *Reliance on graphics* — details presented in the data flow diagram are not described in the text. This eliminates tedious wordiness in the specification.
- *Partitioning of the model* — the major component parts of the system are identified, i.e., "partitioned". Each part is then partitioned into *its* component parts.
- *Rigorous detail* — The partitioning process continues until an exquisitely fine level of detail is reached. The specification will be unambiguous in describing the logical performance of the proposed system.
- *Maintainable* — The completeness and the lack of redundancy in the specification permits changes to be made to the specification without easy oversight of unexpected "side-effects".
- *Iterative* — The process by which the specification is created (partitioning) is comparatively simple, but this simple process is repeated in cycles of finer and finer detail.
- *The use of logical, rather than physical components* — Descriptions of the data and processes in logical terms prevents implementation problems from confusing the specification phase.

Data Flow Diagrams

The diagramming conventions are rewarding in their simplicity. There are four basic elements (see figure B.1).

DATAFLOW — This details the communication or transportation of data. It should be thought of as a "pipeline" through which a single type of composite data may flow. Its name must be distinct and meaningful, e.g., VERIFIED-TIME-CARDS would be the only dataflow in the specification with this distinct name. The name is omitted for dataflows going to or emanating from files.

PROCESS — A process converts the incoming dataflows into the outgoing dataflows. It should be given a brief, meaningful label; e.g., APPROVE PAYROLL-REPORT. The use of a strong verb and singular noun will usually suffice.

FILE — These are temporary repositories of data, and are used for discrete files or database systems. These should also be given meaningful names. Dataflows connected to files should identify *net* flows of information, e.g., updating a record would represent a net flow of data *into* the file.

SOURCE/SINK — This represents the net originator or receiver of system data. A source/sink is a person or organization outside of the context of the system being considered.

Gane and Sarson [1979] use the same elements as DeMarco (illustrated in figure B.1), but vary in the symbols used, e.g., the process is a rounded rectangle. Other procedural annotation is added by some designers. DeMarco strongly suggests that initialization, trivial error paths and control flow be carefully omitted from these diagrams.

"Leveled" data flow diagrams refer to the partitioned, top-down nature of data flow diagram usage. The three elements of leveled data flow diagrams are:

CONTEXT DIAGRAM — this diagram will illustrate the system as a single "bubble" (process), with all dataflows representing the inputs and outputs of the system as a whole. This is the "black box" view of the entire system.

MIDDLE LEVELS — these begin with Level 0 (diagram 0). Level 0 represents the partitioning of the context diagram into the major processes and dataflows of the system. The top data flow diagram in figure B.2 is an example. The processes in Level 0 may require further partitioning. The data flow diagrams detailing this partitioning would be known as the Level 1 data flow diagrams. The middle dataflows in figure B.2 represent Level 1 dataflows. The front data flow diagram specifies the partitioning of Process 0.2 of the Level 0 data flow diagram. Further partitioning may still be necessary, e.g., Process 2.3 on the Level 1 data flow diagram might be partitioned on a Level 2 data flow diagram.

TRANSFORM DESCRIPTIONS — If a process defies further partitioning, it is known as a functional primitive. These processes can usually be described in detail by less than a single page of text. The bottom diagram of figure B.2 represents a Transform Description for the Level 1 Process 2.2 (Print PAY-CHECKS).

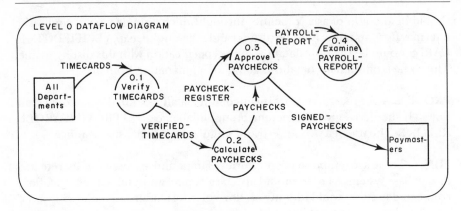

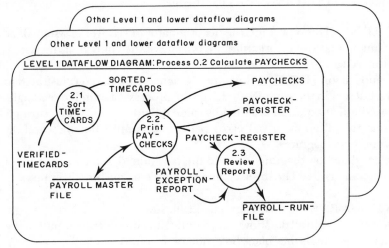

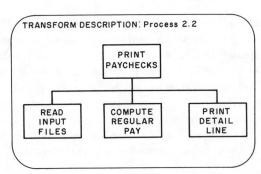

FIGURE B.2 Levelled data flow diagram conventions
(Tom DeMarco, Structured Analysis and System Specification, © 1979, p 71.
Adapted by permission of Prentice-Hall, Inc., Englewood Cliffs, New Jersey.)

Some conventions in creating these diagrams should be noted. For example, the numbering convention dictates that Process 0.2 is partitioned into Process 2.1, Process 2.2, Process 2.3, etc. Further partitioning of Process 2.2 would yield Process 2.2.1, Process 2.2.2, etc.

Input and output symmetry must be preserved between partitioned processes and their lower level data flow diagrams. For example, the input and output dataflows of Process 0.2 of the top data flow diagram of figure B.2 match the input and output dataflows of the Level 1 data flow diagram shown in the center of figure B.2.

Partitioning must be kept to a comprehensible level of detail for any data flow diagram. As a rule-of-thumb, a diagram with more than seven processes should be further partitioned into lower level data flow diagrams

When new logical systems are specified using structured analysis, an interesting technique is used to provide an integrated top-level approach to automation. The man–machine interface can be minimized by forcing interaction to the highest possible level. If the automation boundary can be established at a single "bubble", then descendants (partitions) of the processes detailed at this top level will be *all* automated or *all* manual.

Data Dictionary

This document contains the details of the logical model which cannot be easily diagrammed in the data flow graphics. Entries are detailed for every dataflow and file found in the data flow diagrams.

The data dictionary, like the data flow diagram, is a partitioned structure. Dataflows and files are partitioned into data-elements, and these data-elements may require further partitioning.

Figure B.3 illustrates data dictionary entries which specify the VERIFIED-TIMECARDS dataflow of figure B.2. The top entry details the composition of the dataflow as: a TIMECARD-HEADER-RECORD; multiple repetitions of TIMECARD-RECORD; and a TIMECARD-HASH-RECORD. (The braces around TIMECARD-RECORD are a repetition notation.)

The middle entry of figure B.3 details the data element TIMECARD-HASH-RECORD referenced by the VERIFIED-TIMECARDS dataflow entry. This entry is, in turn, detailed by other entries. The bottom entry of figure B.3 illustrates one of the lowest form of data dictionary entries. This is a data-element from TIMECARD- HASH-RECORD named TIME-EMPL-HASH, and is an 8 digit number defined as a total of employee numbers from the timecard dataflow. Further details of the conventions, constructs and language of these documents can be found in DeMarco [1979].

Redundancy is eliminated from the documentation by careful adherence to the "duties" of each element of the specification. The data flow diagram details

---

DATAFLOW NAME : VERIFIED-TIMECARDS

COMPOSITION:

    TIMECARD-HEADER-RECORD
  + { TIMECARD-RECORD }
  + TIMECARD-HASH-RECORD

ALIASES : None   CREATED BY : Process 1.3 (Transcribe TIMECDS)

DATA ELEMENT NAME : TIMECARD-HASH-RECORD

COMPOSITION:

    CURRENT-DATE
  + TIME-EMPL≠-HASH
  + HOURS-HASH

ALIASES : None   CREATED BY : Process 1.3 (Transcribe TIMECDS)

DATA ELEMENT NAME : TIME-EMPL≠-HASH

COMPOSITION:

    1 { digit } 8

Possible values : 0 to 99999999
         (total of all TIME-EMPL≠ in SORTED-TIMECARDS)

ALIASES : None   CREATED BY : Process 1.3 (Transcribe TIMECDS)

FIGURE B.3 Data dictionary conventions
(Tom DeMarco, Structured Analysis and System Specification, © 1979,
p 144. Adapted by permission of Prenctice-Hall, Inc., Englewood Cliffs,
New Jersey.)

rules about processing of data, while the data dictionary defines the composition of data. The use of self-defining terms and labels aids in the further elimination of redundant material.

Transform Descriptions

Descriptions of functional primitives may also be included in the data dictionary. These describe the rules for transforming arriving-dataflows into departing-dataflows. The transformation *policy* must be described, not its implementation method. These descriptions could take several forms, but are most commonly in structured English or hierarchy charts.

A hierarchy chart represents the partitioning of a process into computer programming modules. Hierarchy charts can also be useful in designing manual procedures [Wallenius, 1985]. The bottom diagram of figure B.2 represents a hierarchy chart for the Level 1 process 2.2 (Print PAY-CHECKS). IPO (Input–Process–Output) Diagrams are often used to specify each module in the hierarchy chart.

Structured English is a pidgin language, i.e., uses the vocabulary of one language (English), and the syntax of another language (a structured programming language). A functional primitive is specified in a series of imperative statements which use English verbs, names from the data dictionary, and a few "reserved words." For example, a structured English transform description of Process 2.3 might begin:

```
Do until there are no more EXCEPTION-DETAILS
    Read EXCEPTION-DETAIL
    If EXCEPTION is "Over 60 Hours"
      Then
        Telephone Department Manager
        Verify EXCEPTION
        If Verify is "no"
          Then
            Place PAYCHECK in HOLD-PAYCHECK
            Write EMPLOYEE-NAME in ERROR-NAME-LIST
```

Transform descriptions can also make use of decision trees or decision tables in detailing the functional primitive specification.

System Modeling

The first step in specifying a new information system is an examination of the existing system. If the tools above are used to document the existing system, several steps can be followed to convert these documents into a new system specification.

The first step is to remove any physical references or control flows. Thus individual and department names, job titles, program names or model numbers are removed. These are replaced with an imperative statement describing *what* the physical reference did to the data. Any control flows must also be replaced with a dataflow, e.g., "accounting instructs payroll" becomes the PAYCHECK-HELD-REPORT dataflow.

The second step is to derive the logical file equivalents of the present physical files. This involves "normalizing" the census of all stored-data references, e.g., identify access keys, eliminate repeating groups, etc.

The product of these two steps, when packaged, forms a logical model of the *current* system. The first step in converting this into a logical model of a *new* system is to establish the "domain of change" or context diagram of that portion of the current system requiring alteration.

This context diagram is partitioned for minimized interfaces using the conventions discussed above for data flow diagrams. The data dictionary is modified as needed. The result is a logical model of the new system.

Package Specification

Some additional details may be needed prior to completion of the specification. Usually conversion and start-up processes must be carefully specified. Shutdown processes and error messages are often neglected details which must be added to the document. Performance specifications are sometimes required by the users.

Finally, some explanations of the specification documents may be needed; for example, a discussion of data flow diagram and data dictionary conventions is usually necessary.

Structured analysis represents an attempt to bring order to a place where chaos once dwelt. Traditional systems analysis involves complex interpersonal relationships, compromised goals, diplomacy and the nebulous, untrained art of estimating. The process becomes so convoluted that the project's goals often degenerate away from the lofty "achievement of success" to a base and depraved "avoidance of failure" [DeMarco, 1979].

Structured analysis limits chaos in those elements of the design process which permit logical description. In this respect, the approach does bring a certain order to the chaotic ... by some estimates.

REFERENCES

Gane, C. and Sarson, T. *Structured Systems Analysis: Tools and Techniques.* Englewood Cliffs: Prentice-Hall, 1979.

DeMarco, T. *Structured Systems Analysis and Specification.* New York: Yourdon, 1979.

Wallenius, M.-E. D. "Applying the data processing tools of structured systems analysis to an office automation systems study." *1985 Office Automation Conference Digest.* Reston: AFIPS, 1985.

Appendix C

Review of
TWO FORMULATED SECURITY DESIGN METHODOLOGIES

FISHER'S APPROACH

Royal Fisher's *Information Systems Security* [1984] offers the first strong presentation of a systems engineering approach to the design of data security. Fisher specifically avoids implementation details of the controls which dominates all other literature on the subject. Fisher, a member of the Information Systems Management Institute of IBM, has documented both a "detailed" methodology and a *"Quik"* approach.

Fisher's detailed methodology is noticeably similar to the SPAN project work, and the two methodologies have doubtlessly benefited from IBM experience in the area.

Figure 4.5 depicts the organization of Fisher's approach. Fisher stresses the need for management to set appropriate policy, plans, and programs for data security. The data security plan constitutes part of an asset protection program which should be related to a disaster/recovery plan.

Fisher envisions a comprehensive data security plan which would be comprised of a number of individual plans and programs. A *Vital Records Plan* should detail the identity, protection, update cycles, and reconstruction means of records essential to the business's survival. An *Access Control Plan* limits access to any specific location to those people who work at that location, particularly during disaster recovery. An *Emergency Response Plan, Interim Processing Plan* and *Restoration Plan* delineate disaster preparedness and recovery. A *Data Classification Program* is recommended to assign levels of protection needed by the various data

Fisher also believes the role of the organization's Security Administrator is critical in the success of a security design. This will establish an organizational point at which the security of the data resource can be directed.

The above elements constitute the necessary organizational "climate" for implementation of a healthy security program. This idea is represented in figure 4.5 as SECURITY/ASSET PROTECTION ORGANIZATIONAL POLICY. After this climate is effected, the following steps comprise Fisher's methodology:

Define the data inventory. Fisher's first step is likely to be unnecessary in well-designed information systems. Database definition is considered to be a "remedial" step when required.

231

Identify exposures. Fisher's second step applies the scheme proposed by Courtney [1977]. This scheme narrows the scope of exposure classification by concentrating on the *effects* resulting from adverse actions or events rather than the threats precipitating such actions. The approach defines six groups of exposures representing six basic effects of adverse actions:

- accidental disclosure
- intentional disclosure
- accidental modification
- intentional modification
- accidental destruction
- intentional destruction

Fisher structures the exposure identification process by applying a "data control life cycle". Fisher proposes this model as a representative data flow structure through which all information travels from its creation to its elimination. The phases of this life cycle are derived from an IBM research project titled "SAFE" (Secure Automated Facilities Environment) [IBM, 1972]. This project attempted to define eleven basic information processing steps that enumerate all basic steps found in any information system. These steps are defined in Fisher's work as *Data Exposure Control Points (CPs)*. These control points are:

(CP1) Data gathering. This is the point of the manual creation and transportation of data; i.e., the point of inception of data into the information system. An example would be an employee filling out a timesheet.

(CP2) Data input movement. This considers manual movement of source documents to the work area where these are converted to machine-readable form (primarily a batch control point). An example would be collection of the timesheets by clerks and delivery to the accounting payroll administrator.

(CP3) Data conversion. The source documents are converted to machine-readable form. An example would be the keypunching of the timesheets into a computer terminal by the payroll data processing assistant.

(CP4) Data communication (input). The transmission of the machine-readable data is considered here. This could, for instance, mean electronic transmission or carriage to the data processing center by hand. An example would be the dumping of the payroll computer terminal's stored timesheet data onto an open communication line to the data processing facility.

(CP5) Data receipt. This is the receipt and storage of data, either by electronic communications or manual facilities. In our payroll example, the timesheet

data from the communications line is dated, time-stamped and logged from future processing.

(CP6) Data processing. This is the execution of application programs to perform the intended computations. Fisher points out that this is the most common control point considered by most installations. During this step, the data would be validated and any files would be updated. In our example, the payroll programs would be executed and the payroll would be calculated.

(CP7) Data preparation (output). This covers the preparation of data output media such as tapes, disks, diskettes or microforms. An example could include the payroll results being placed on both printed forms and magnetic tape.

(CP8) Data output movement. This is the manual movement of computer-produced output, on various media to a user pickup point. This covers systems which might delay the delivery of output to the receiving user. In the payroll example, the computer-printed paychecks might be locked in a secure cabinet until called for.

(CP9) Data communication (output). This is the actual transmission (electronic or manual) and delivery of output to the user. This point covers the task of moving the information from either CP7 or CP8 (when used). This point would include the electronic transmission of a response in a real-time system. For our example, this might mean the collection of the printed checks and subsequent delivery to the payroll manager.

(CP10) Data usage. This is the use of the data by the user, including storage of the data while in use. It is emphasized that the entire timeframe during which the user retains the data is under discussion at this point. In the example discussed, this point covers the storage of the checks in the payroll department, and any processing such as review, auditing, signing or crossfooting.

(CP11) Data disposition. This covers the disposition of data after the usage period. Included would be the methods, location and periods for storage. Final disposition is also considered. In our example, the checks would be distributed to the employees; the check register might be stored for three years in an archive, after which time the register might be shredded.

The exposures are more clearly defined by a detailed delineation of the control points of the system under investigation. Each type of data in the data inventory is examined at each control point for exposure to each class of risk. For example, at Control Point One in the payroll system described above, every data element would be considered. Exposure of the timesheet to various classes of risk would include:

Accidental Data Modification — an employee might transpose digits on an employee number or job number.

Intentional Data Modification — an employee might enter more hours for a job in order to increase pay.

Accidental Data Destruction — an employee might lose the timesheet during the week.

Intentional Data Destruction — an employee might destroy another employee's timesheet out of malice.

The identification process would continue for the remaining exposure classes, and the remaining control points. After this exhaustive list is completed, the exposures are "mapped" across the control points. This involves listing the exposures in a tabular form for control points and exposure classes. Patterns and similarities are sought in the table; e.g., the accidental destruction of the timesheets might be an exposure at every control point.

The usefulness of the mapping process is attenuated by the lack of evidence as to the "critical" nature of a potential loss. An exposure of the timesheets at CP1 to accidental destruction might cost the organization very little upon occurrence. A similar exposure at CP4 may result in a major financial loss.

Assess risk. This is the third step in Fisher's approach. This step is performed in exactly the same manner as the "Risk Analysis" approach described above.

Design controls. In his fourth step, Fisher follows the IBM classification of controls as *Preventative, Detective* and *Corrective.*.This popular scheme is discussed in the section on "Traditional Control Classes" found in chapter two above.

Analyze cost effectiveness. Fisher's final step is a straight-forward capital investment comparison of risk and control. The risk figure is treated as the "return on investment" and the control figure is treated as the "investment." Management is then free to make decisions regarding which controls are to be implemented. The decisions may be based on both a maximum acceptable level of risk, and a minimum acceptable return on investment.

For example, management may choose to accept individual control point risks at a level of $500,000 or below. Management may also choose to implement controls which promise a return of 40% or better.

As a heuristic aid to complete this analysis, Fisher provides a cost-effectiveness table consisting of

1. Class Rank.
2. Exposure Identification.

3. Risk.
4. Controls Success.
5. Cost Avoidance.
6. Controls Cost.
7. Net Cost.
8. Return on Investment.
9. Cost-Effectiveness Ranking.
10. Adequacy.

PARKER'S COMPUTER SECURITY PROGRAM

Parker precedes his methodology by dictating that a task force or permanent organizational function be established to conduct the security review. This body then delineates the scope of the review and plans the project. The remainder of the methodology is divided into six phases:

Identification and valuation of assets. This is a process which must carefully identify **all** EDP assets. A model is provided to help identify these assets. This model is based on type of asset (people, supplies, hardware, data, etc.), form of asset (moveable property, magnetic patterns, printed paper, etc.), location of asset (remote, internal environment, computer, etc.) and accountability (EDP Dept, vendors, etc.).

Several possible valuation techniques are briefly considered. These include Courtney's Risk Analysis as above, and application of the Delphi technique in a vein similar to Fisher.

Identification of threats. This step is aided by the application of a threat model to ensure a complete and orderly inventory. This model identifies threats by source, motive, act, result, and loss:

Source	DP employees, employees, vendors, outsiders, natural forces.
Motives	Incompetence, human failure, irrational behavior, personal problems, personal gain, professional crime, business gain, economic advocacy, political advocacy, social advocacy, religious advocacy.
Acts	Overt, covert, descriptive, single event, multiple events, continuous, physical, logical, local/remote, real-time, nonreal-time, collusion, testing, other.

Results   Disclosure, modification, destruction, use
                   of services.

Losses   None, monetary, denial of use/possession,
                   denial of exclusive use/possession, denial
                   of access, personal values, health/life,
                   privacy, other.

It is suggested that the model listed here be specifically adopted for the use of the system under study by carefully identifying the exact threats in the classes listed above. This comprehensive model is then to be broken down into submodels which clearly identify the threats in each part of the organization.

Risk assessment. This can be performed using the Courtney Risk Analysis method described above. However, Parker offers a less costly alternative which eliminates both guesswork and consensus determination: "Exposure Analysis."

Exposure analysis bases its loss projections on the numbers of people who could accidentally or intentionally cause losses. Parker identifies four basic sources of exposure to loss from people:

1. People with physical access to assets who have the capability to perform physical acts.
2. People with access who have operational capabilities.
3. People with access who have programming capabilities.
4. People with access who have electronic engineering capabilities.

Exposure analysis begins with the detailing of occupations with one or more of the access capabilities listed above. A matrix is generated listing these positions and the vulnerable assets (e.g., internal data, internal applications programs, computer equipment, etc.). Vulnerability of the assets is broken down by acts (modification, destruction, taking, disclosure, denial of use). The matrix is completed by plotting occupations to acts against assets using an ordinal scale. The scale represents exposure levels from none to 100% (See table C1).

After completion of the matrix, a monetary value is assigned to each vulnerable asset. The risk exposure of all assets can be computed by occupation, and an ordered list is created which details the risk level of each occupation based on the range of assets exposed to that occupation.

The list can then be used as a guide to any great exposures demanding immediate attention. One can see that little guesswork was involved in the determination of risk exposures in this procedure.

Parker also discusses other tools for risk assessment as companions for either risk analysis or exposure analysis. "Questionnaire Methods" can be used to obtain comprehensive exposure data in large organizations. "Scenario Analysis" involves the highly subjective invention of scenarios which describe how losses might occur. These are circulated to the pertinent managers for opinions as to the practicality of such events. Credible scenarios are compared with controls to identify deficiencies. (A similar method utilizing the Delphi technique was suggested by Jerry FitzGerald and Associates [FitzGerald, 1978].)

Safeguards identification. This last step includes selection and implementation of the identified safeguards. The use of checklists available in other literature is suggested as a source of potential safeguards. Selection of the appropriate control is considered the most thorny issue. Parker details twenty safeguard selection principles:

1. COST-EFFECTIVENESS — determined by the "prudent person criterion;" i.e., a panel of experts would agree that sufficient safeguards were in place.

2. MINIMUM RELIANCE ON REAL—TIME HUMAN INTERVENTION - manual functions are considered the weakest safeguard.

3. OVERRIDE AND FAILSAFE DEFAULTS — basically, this means that there should be safeguards on the safeguards.

4. ABSENCE OF DESIGN SECRECY— reliance on the secrecy of a safeguard mechanism is dangerous.

5. LEAST PRIVILEGE — the "need to know" principle of data access.

6. ENTRAPMENT — creation of an attractive vulnerability which is heavily safeguarded.

7. INDEPENDENCE OF CONTROL AND SUBJECT — those concerned with the safeguards are distinctly remote from those constrained by the safeguards.

8. UNIVERSAL APPLICATION - no exceptions to the rules.

9. COMPARTMENTALIZATION AND DEFENSIVE DEPTH — the configuration of safeguards to require multiple violations before a severe loss is incurred.

10. ISOLATION, ECONOMY, AND LEAST COMMON MECHANISM — the safeguards should be independent and simple.

11. COMPLETENESS AND CONSISTENCY — safeguard specifications should be tested prior to use.

Occupational Vulnerability Analysis
VULNERABLE ASSETS

OCCUPATIONS	Data			Application Programs			Systems Programs			Computer Equipment			System Service	
	M	DE	DI	M	DE	DI	M	DE	DI	M	DE	T	T	DN
Tape Librarian		4	4		3	3		3	3		1	1		
Data Entry Clerk	2	2	2											
Operator	1	5	5		5	5		5	5		1	1	5	5
Operation Manager	1	5	5		5	5		5	5		5	5		5
DB Administrator	3	3	3								1	1		
Systems Programmer		5	5		5	5	5	5	5		1	1	5	5
Applic. Programmer	1	1	1	2	2	2					1	1		
EDP Auditor	5	5	5	5	5	5	5	5	5	5	5	5	5	5
Systems Engineer							5	5	5	5	5	5	5	5
Security Officer		5	5		5	5		5	5	5	5	5	5	5
EDP Auditor	5	5	5	5	5	5	5	5	5	5	5	5	5	5

Acts Codes
M – Modification
DE – Destruction
DI – Disclosure
T – Talking
DN – Denial of Use

Exposure Scale
blank – no effect
1 – up to 20%
2 –up to 40%
3 – up to 60%
4 – up to 80%
5 – up to 100%

TABLE C.1   Parker's Exposure Analysis Matrix. (Donn B. Parker, Computer Security Management, © 1981, pp. 148–9. Reprinted by permission of Prentice-Hall, Inc., Englewood Cliffs, New Jersey.)

12. INSTRUMENTATION — safeguards must be monitored for failures and attacks.

13. ACCEPTANCE AND TOLERANCE BY PERSONNEL — unacceptable safeguards will always be circumvented.

14. SUSTAINABILITY— a safeguard must work fully over the life of its usage. Manual safeguards decline in effectiveness.

15. AUDITABILITY— safeguards must be testable.

16. ACCOUNTABILITY — a single individual chiefly responsible for the operation of the safeguard is designated.

17. REACTION AND RECOVERY— safeguards must not impede recovery from attack.

18. RESIDUALS AND RESET — assets should remain secure after activation of safeguard.

19. MANUFACTURER, SUPPLIER, AND SERVICER TRUSTWORTHINESS - a control which cannot be fully proven must rely on trust in the source of the control for reliability.

20. MULTIPLE FUNCTIONS - select safeguards with useful secondary functions where available.

Selection of appropriate safeguards should result in the continuance of existing or presently planned safeguards which have been proven appropriate, the elimination of existing or presently planned safeguards which have been proven inappropriate, and the phased implementation of new safeguards which have been proven appropriate.

The new safeguards can be ordered in various ways, but organization by both cost and urgency is suggested:
1. Lowest cost, greatest urgency.
2. Greatest cost, greatest urgency.
3. Lowest cost, lesser urgency.
4. Greatest cost, lesser urgency.

The methodology ends with the recommendation that the valuable information collected during the review be maintained and updated as an ongoing process of system adaptation.

REFERENCES

Courtney, R. "Security risk assessment in electronic data processing." *AFIPS Conference Proceedings NCC* 46, 1977, pp. 97–104.

Fisher, R. *Information Systems Security.* Englewood Cliffs: Prentice-Hall, 1984.

FitzGerald, J. "EDP risk analysis for contingency planning.". EDP Audit Control and Security Newsletter I (Aug, 1978): pp. 6–8.

IBM. *"Secure Automated Facilities Environment" Study* 3. Part 2 (May, 1972).

Parker, D. *Computer Security Management.* Reston: Reston, 1981.

Index